DIVERSE BY DESIGN

DIVERSE BY DESIGN

Literacy Education within Multicultural Institutions

CHRISTOPHER SCHROEDER

UTAH STATE UNIVERSITY PRESS
Logan, Utah
2011

Utah State University Press
Logan, Utah 84322-3078

© 2011 Utah State University Press

Manufactured in the United States of America
Cover design by Barbara Yale-Read
ISBN: 978-0-87421-806-0 (paper)
ISBN: 978-0-87421-807-7 (e-book)

Library of Congress Cataloging-in-Publication Data

Schroeder, Christopher L., 1970-
  Diverse by design : literacy education within multicultural institutions / Christopher Schroeder.
    p. cm.
  ISBN 978-0-87421-806-0 (pbk.) – ISBN 978-0-87421-807-7 (e-book)
  1. Hispanic Americans–Education (Higher)–Case studies. 2. English language–Study and teaching-
-Spanish speakers–Case studies. 3. Literacy–Social aspects–United States–Case studies. 4. Hispanic
Americans–Ethnic identity–Case studies. I. Title.
  LC2672.4.S37 2011
  808'.0420711–dc22
                              2010042194

4rbs

CONTENTS

ACKNOWLEDGMENTS

Books are rarely solitary efforts, and this one is obviously no exception. I wish to acknowledge those who read drafts—Loretta Capeheart and Masahiro Kasai and Victor Villanueva and Michael Spooner and Suresh Canagarajah and Denise Cloonan and Priscilla Litorja—and helped with data—Loretta (again) and Masahiro (again) and Terry Schuepfer, as well as Maria and Matt from institutional studies and Bonnie and Mary from the library. I also wish to acknowledge Neida, Sophia, and Angela, as well as Victor (again) and Tim, whose contributions made this study a stronger story, my *mga anak*—Mahal and Mateo—who make this work more meaningful, and Fred, my "Mexican friend," who with a Filipina wife and *hijos mestizos* might be living the Spanglish future. As always, these and other contributions made a better book; its flaws are all mine.

PREFACE

Tim Libretti

Often discussions of "multiculturalism" or "diversity" recycle the same rhetorical platitudes that urge us (meaning the peoples of the U.S.) to "celebrate our differences," that assert vacuously that "our differences are our strengths," or that patriotically echo our currency in declaring wishfully "*e pluribus unum.*" While such rhetorical flourishes do arguably contain profound wisdom, with too much frequency these flourishes forego the complex explanations they deserve and desperately need, remaining empty statements that, when not elaborated or interrogated, do more to perpetuate cultural conflict, racial tensions and prejudices, material and political inequalities, and all other kinds of inhumanity in U.S. culture and society, than they do to provide meaningful platforms from which to inquire into and address such problems. As a result of such postulates about diversity relaxing into platitudes sloppily invoked to evade tough social problems rather than spurring complex formulations that require explanations and arguments, on the whole as a people and culture we remain, I believe it is fair to say our behavior as a nation suggests, decidedly unpersuaded by any kind of postulation that diversity in our nation is a source of strength. At a minimum, our collective failure to genuinely understand and appreciate diversity makes it difficult, well-nigh impossible, to comprehend our full collective humanity and complexity. This lack of comprehension prevents us from developing the best knowledge we can about our world and from taking advantage of all people's talents, skills, and understandings to produce the most humane and productive of all possible cultures—one which, intuitively speaking, gives priority to meeting the basic human needs of all.

Indeed, Chris Schroeder opens this work in the introduction, following the sociologist Robert Putnam, with the assertion that despite the rhetoric we often hear and repeat about diversity, as a people and culture we are pretty much disturbed by and uncomfortable with diversity. John Sayles succinctly captures these duplicitous attitudes toward diversity in his representation of this discomfort in his 1996 film *Lone Star* in a scene dramatizing a heated conversation among teachers and parents in a Texas high school about, in particular, the teaching of Texas history. In this scene, one parent asserts, "If we're talking about food and music and all, I have no problem with that, but when you start changing who did what to who. . . ." A teacher then responds, "We're not changing anything. We're trying to present a more complete picture." "And that has got to stop," the parent retorts. What Sayles illuminates in this familiar dialogue is that as a kind of decoration, we can appreciate other cultures, but when it comes to any fundamental rethinking of our world which might be forwarded by a different cultural perspective, any fundamental alteration in what constitutes knowledge and understanding, or any fundamental ideological challenge that might threaten to motivate a reorganization of our socioeconomic relationships and practices—well, then, the appreciation stops and the repression begins. The recent legislation in Arizona banning ethnic studies in public schools in Tucson evidences this disturbance with diversity which Schroeder cites. Don't mess with Texas—or Arizona, apparently!

Or, in the case of *Diverse by Design,* go ahead and mess with Texas and Arizona! Indeed, in this work Schroeder effectively, if at times implicitly, challenges the thinking and efficacy behind such strenuous efforts as we see in Arizona to marginalize, if not outright to fully repress, any engagement with diverse cultural frameworks and historical experiences. Schroeder's work not only endorses the formulation that "our diversity is our strength," but it explains and argues why this is so, taking on this serious task of cultural persuasion and exploring the social consequences, the transformations, that follow—or ought to—from really respecting diversity. Those who earnestly ask, "Why is our diversity our strength?" and do not treat it as a rhetorical question, as Schroeder doesn't, will find in this work some concrete and compelling answers to that question.

One of the major theses of this work, which constitutes such a compelling answer to this basic and too-often unanswered question, might at first glance seem somewhat simple or even intuitive but is deceptively complex. Schroeder articulates this answer in his introduction, identifying it as one of the hypotheses that drove the project: "people who use more than one language, and thus have more than one way to express experiences and examine environments, have more resources than those who had only one language at their disposal—a *creative multilingualism,* if you will." Far from treating "multilingualism and multiculturalism" as "obstacles to be overcome," as he demonstrates they usually are treated, Schroeder compellingly argues that we need to see them as "intellectual resources to exploit."

Rooted in detailed studies of human lives within the actual institutional structures of Northeastern Illinois University (NEIU), where Chris and I both teach in the English Department (discussed more below), this study forces us to grapple in concrete ways with the remaking of institutional structures, the transformation of pedagogy into a practice that really does unleash the power of the oppressed, and really, if the arguments are genuinely followed to their logical ends, the remaking of the socioeconomic system, culture, and polity of the currently divided United States. While the focus of this book is not on formulating a plan to remake our socioeconomic and political structures, Schroeder does repeatedly remind readers that these conflictual discussions over the role of diversity in literacy and education "are more than academic debates over language standards that ultimately involve the distribution of social resources and the acquisition of social capital, including norms for reciprocity and trust that . . . produce more effective democracies and economies and longer and happier lives" (5). Schroeder's project of rethinking the role of diversity in education has as its aim, in part, to encourage institutions of higher learning, particularly public ones, to optimize their social function and responsibility to cultivate the talents, abilities, and democratic acumen of the citizenry so we can collectively address social challenges and improve the commonweal. In this sense, this project vigorously forwards a new social ethos that extends beyond the educational sphere to that of public policy, showing us how to create institutional structures that humanely house us all and recognize us all by aiming no longer to weed out or exploit people by reproducing and maintaining racial hierarchies that underwrite exploitation but rather to engage and develop people's talents to serve the public good, which implies a very different kind of world and which would entail a radical challenge to our current socioeconomic order and its driving priorities.

Indeed, the personal stories which appear in this study of Neida Hernandez-Santamaria, Sophia López, and Angela Vidal-Rodriguez as they experience their lives through the institutional structures of Northeastern Illinois University, an institution that purports to be hospitable to a diverse student body, highlight the way the university creates an environment that often does not encourage or in a genuine way recognize diversity, particularly linguistic diversity, but instead requires students, if they are to hold on to their integrity and to the strengths and resources with which their diverse backgrounds and cultures equip them, to constantly negotiate and resist the academic environment at NEIU. As the current Chair of the English Department in which Chris and I teach, reading these personal/institutional narratives was a sobering exercise, particularly as I am the "white guy" teaching Chicano Literature whom Sophia López mentions in her narrative. The English Department has a long way to go to become a truly Hispanic-serving department and to remake ourselves into a department more relevant to the diversity of our world with all the opportunities and challenges it presents. I will discuss these challenges and opportunities in more detail below. The point I want to stress now is that these stories highlight how ineffective we have been as an institution in supporting and cultivating these students' talents and learning and also in learning from them. The institution, myself included, seems to have been more effective in repressing diversity and the intellectual resources it contains, even if these narratives to some extent recount stories of overcoming repression. Schroeder writes in his introduction, "While ethnic diversity might challenge social solidarity and restrict social capital, these challenges can be overcome . . . by establishing more expansive identities" (6). Schroeder gives us some concrete footholds to participate in establishing these expansive identities which will aid us as an institution in recognizing our students' merits, in validating knowledge and creativity they already possess, and in encouraging them to participate more actively in their own learning and production of knowledge—and, to invoke a German philosopher, in educating the educators. The virtue of this book is that it makes us aware of how often in unwitting ways, simply by going through the academic routines in which we've been trained and adhering to rigid and uncreative standards that perhaps no longer comprehend our world and its evolving literacy and communication practices, we repress diversity and lose opportunities to gain and develop new knowledge and to create innovative new modes of being and praxis. Putting personal stories before us, Schroeder challenges us to confront the impacts of our institutional and academic practices on real human lives and to live up to our humanitarian values by attempting to realize them in innovative and creative practices that more effectively cultivate them.

Schroeder specifically explores the pedagogical benefits, as well as longer term social and broadly human benefits, of acknowledging and leveraging linguistic and cultural diversity, especially that of students, in the classroom to optimize teaching, learning, and the process of knowl-edge production generally. The recent legislation in Arizona banning ethnic studies in the public schools in Tucson underscores and exem-plifies the basic ignorance and racist backwardness which form just part of the context in which Schroeder's straightforward and intuitive claims accrue controversial status. The more serious obstacles, however, at least in terms of their insidious unspokenness, are basic and often unarticu-lated sets of assumptions and policies informing writing pedagogy and literacy standards at the university in addition to the implicit premium placed on—and insistence on, even enforcement of—English fluency and mastery as an index of one's intelligence, ability to learn, and poten-tial to contribute meaningfully to the social good—indeed, as an index of one's human worth. Because of this dense and highly charged context involving both overt racist ideologies, which are often attended by pres-sures to endorse and even legislate assimilation to a dominant culture, and deeply entrenched assumptions about what constitutes academic credibility, which also often contain assimilationist pressures as we see in the case studies here, Schroeder's thesis takes on a controversial aspect by virtue of the cultural arsenal he must take on.

The source of controversy for Schroeder's argument and approach might be that he offers these arguments in deeply embattled educational and social contexts, as other scholarship provides strong and perhaps undeniable support for his argument that not just multiculturalism, but more specifically multilingualism, enables more effective production of knowledge about and understanding of our world and thus, it would seem to follow, greater prospects for developing a more humane culture that promotes the good life for all. Daniel Nettle and Suzanne Romaine (2000), for example, in their vital and cautionary study *Vanishing Voices: The Extinction of the World's Languages*, detail the grave stakes and devas-tating effects to our knowledge of our world involved in the elimination of languages around the globe. In particular, they point out the inherent violence and danger that inhere in the often well-meaning cultural poli-cies aiming to create a monolingual world premised in, in my view, a mis-begotten view that monolingualism would somehow diminish and help us manage social conflict and heighten understanding among diverse peoples. Against this snowballing belief, Nettle and Romaine write,

> Some of those who have dismissed indigenous languages and cultures as primitive and backward-looking and seen their replacement by western

languages and cultures as prerequisites to modernization and progress envision a future ideal in which everyone speaks only one language. Such views are misguided for many reasons. . . . We wish to stress that an elimination of linguistic diversity on such a massive scale would do the evolution of the human mind a great disservice. Thousands of languages have arrived at quite different, but equally valid, analyses of the world; there is much to learn from these languages, if we only knew about them and understood them. The most important revisions to current ways of thinking may lie in the investigations of the very languages most remote in type from our own, but it is these languages which are most in danger of disappearing before our very eyes. (70)

In addition to highlighting the forms of thought contained in other languages, forms of thought which provide us potentially with other ways of approaching our world, other means of problem solving, and other means of developing our culture and organizing social relationships, Nettle and Romaine also provide compelling examples of specifically how languages (again, not just cultures!) currently threatened with extinction contain, organize, and comprehend knowledge about our environment vital to a sustainable existence. Giving one such example, they write,

> Today scientists have much to learn from the Inuit people about the Arctic climate, and from Pacific Islanders about the management of marine resources. Much of this indigenous knowledge has been passed down orally for thousands of years in their languages. Now it is being forgotten as their languages disappear. Unfortunately, much of what is culturally distinctive in language—for example vocabulary for flora, fauna—is lost when language shift takes place. The typical youngster in Koror, Palau's capital, cannot identify most of Palau's native fish; nor can his father. The forgetting of this knowledge has gone hand in hand with over-fishing and degradation of the marine environment. (16)

Indeed, these findings underpin in compelling ways Schroeder's point that "people who use more than one language, and thus have more than one way to express experiences and examine environments, have more resources than those who had only one language at their disposal" (7). We see in these examples how linguistic diversity serves the interests of all, which is important to recognize as often so-called diversity programs are seen as being developed to serve only targeted "ethnic" or "racial" populations exclusively and as being of little use to those who identify with or are counted as part of the dominant culture. Indeed, the recent Arizona legislation (HB2281) in part rationalizes banning ethnic studies because it understands these classes to be designed for students of particular ethnic groups. Hopefully Nettle's and Romaine's argument—and the arguments in this book—persuade audiences of the crucial fact that the knowledge diversity offers us is necessary, if not for our survival, certainly to create the best possible culture and social system to enhance the lives of all.

If we accept Nettle and Romaine's arguments, though, Schroeder still pushes us farther, making us think about how we will actually go about transforming institutional structures, disciplinary models, and curriculum so they accommodate, support, and cultivate diversity and optimize the production of knowledge in the service of the public good. Schroeder's study, if taken seriously at NEIU, would really push us as an institution to treat ethnic diversity not simply as a kind of commodity used to market the university ("The Most Ethnically Diverse University in the Midwest" streams across the Web site home page) but as a source of innovative knowledge that might be the basis of an alternative way to structure and develop social relationships and productive forces to, say, eliminate poverty; or to engender new ways of seeing and understanding that put an end to the criminalization of people of color so that we could redirect all the energy we extravagantly squander in the service of repression into positive acts of creation that actually honor and cultivate people's humanity. Who knows? If these cultural reservoirs are harnessed, the possibilities are endless.

Moreover, if Schroeder's study were taken seriously at NEIU, instead of emphasizing our role in creating wage earners ("Preparing the 21st Century Workforce" also streams on the home page) we might be pushed to emphasize the role public universities can and ought to play in producing a democratic, imaginative, and creative citizenry that is not content to simply get a job or a career but to link work in innovative ways to a larger social mission. As an institution whose moniker reads "Learn in the City, Lead in the World," Schroeder's study would push us to challenge the resistance to efforts to institute a "foreign" language requirement. If other languages embody different kinds of knowledge, then we must cultivate people's acquisition of these intellectual resources. All of our populations, whether considered "ethnic" or "racial" minorities or members of a dominant culture, need to acquire the ability to engage and understand the world from diverse perspectives.

Northeastern is, in fact, an environment that wants to be hospitable to diversity and in many ways is; the diversity of its student populations makes these conditions almost inevitable. And, of course, NEIU is a place where people work to create new knowledge and new ways of being and praxis. Still, Schroeder's study pushes us to understand that the educators must be educated to learn from students, and to create an environment responsive to the students' needs and attentive to the knowledge they bring to us and the processes through which they creatively produce knowledge. The English Department here, in particular, has much to learn and many steps it can continue taking in these directions. For starters, the disciplinary identification of "English," Schroeder's study suggests, may be woefully obsolete. It is no longer clear what "English" means. Does it mean that we teach "Anglophone" literature as well as the teaching of writing in the English language? Does it mean we teach the literature and culture of England and its colonial derivatives, which was how the literature of the United States had long been understood? Neither of these rationales makes much sense anymore. It would be hard to argue that many components of U.S. literature, such as Native American or Chicano literatures among many others, are derivations of the English literary tradition. Additionally, we find writers in the U.S. literary tradition who write in languages other than English.

It is certainly time to overcome these imperializing traditions. And while we are in the process of decolonizing our department, the stubborn obsolescence of "English" as a disciplinary identifier presents something of an obstacle to the evolution of literary, literacy, and cultural studies at NEIU. A former English Department Chair used to trumpet the fact that he prevented the English Department from being merged with the Department of Foreign Languages and Literatures (a department that is changing its name to "World Languages and Literatures"). Schroeder's study suggests, however, that such a merger is exactly what makes most academic sense, especially if we believe academic and social relevance must coalesce. Indeed, the population at Northeastern speaks dozens of languages. It makes little sense to speak of many languages as "foreign," except as a powerful rhetorical gesture designed to sustain narrow and racist conceptions of national identity and culture to undergird the repressive racial, class, and indeed colonial hierarchies currently structuring (and unequally stratifying) the U.S. socioeconomic racial patriarchal capitalist order. Indeed, we certainly cannot speak of a monolithic undifferentiated "American" culture. We can find evidence of many significantly different and substantial cultures in the United States that develop out of different class experiences, racial and ethnic cultural traditions and historical experiences, gender differences, regional conditions, political traditions, and so forth.

Back in 1991, Paul Lauter strenuously argued with great detail and sophistication, in *Canons and Context*, that, as the title suggests, the literature of the United States is not constitutive of a homogeneous tradition but is composed of a variety of cultures that might have been forged through complex interactions with one another but that are nonetheless decidedly independent and differentiated so as to necessitate comparative cultural analysis. Likewise, we need different aesthetic categories and different modes of valuing aesthetic practice that are sensitive to the fact that people write for different reasons, to different audiences, with different rhetorical and formal procedures, and in different social and historical contexts. Frederick Douglass's slave narratives, for example, are written for a far different purpose from, say, Longfellow's poetry. For Lauter, we cannot really evaluate a work of literature without understanding what it means, which often requires understanding the specific cultural conditions out of which a work is produced. This act of understanding also necessitates a willingness to understand that means overcoming the variety of race, class, and gender prejudices, among others, that condition how others are viewed, as well as often our own academic training. As Lauter notes elsewhere, "As we have come to learn with the overthrow of the doctrine of 'separate, but equal,' if people need not be dealt with physically, socially, seriously, their experiences are not likely to be seen as providing a basis for significant art"(36). In short, recognizing, appreciating, and learning from diversity so we can produce more effective knowledge means, as Schroeder's book demonstrates as well, taking people seriously and being able and willing to recognize our own boundedness in disciplinary traditions and routines. In Schroeder's case, he suggests we need to stop and look at different discursive modes our students and others use and work to understand them as opposed to immediately dismissing their writing as incorrect or, worse, stupid. In the sphere of literary study, I can think of many examples of important literary works produced by writers of nondominant cultures that have been dismissed or judged as lacking literary value because they have been judged and interpreted using standards and tools foreign to and ignorant of the cultures out of which those works were produced. We all lose when this happens, and when we do it to students, as we can see in the narratives in this book, we ourselves not only lose, but we risk leaving a casualty, or at least a trauma, in our wake.

For an English Department, or a Department of Literary, Cultural, and Literacy Studies, overcoming traditions and our own limitations of understanding and knowledge, which grow quickly in a rapidly chang-ing profession and discipline, is key. The trick seems to be to have knowl-edge of our own ignorance, to know what we don't know and need to know, and to make hires and develop curriculum to cure that igno-rance. Often, though, this is difficult given constraints of time, space, and money and given the reality of collegial interactions. Colleagues with different takes on disciplinary priorities (and on diversity) define key gaps in curriculum differently, which by extension means defining knowledge differently. One of my colleagues argues year after year that we need to hire a Joycean, that this constitutes the major gap in our cur-riculum, despite the fact that we do not offer classes or have experts to teach Native American literature, Asian American literature, indigenous literatures, and Puerto Rican literatures, among others. To me, these latter literatures offer important alternative narratives and bodies of knowledge that provide us different insights into aesthetic experiences, different ways of sensing and experiencing the world, different histori-cal understandings of our world, and perhaps even more effective ways of thinking about addressing social problems and developing a humane culture and society. In any case, *Diverse by Design* pushes us to rethink these gaps and to challenge traditional academic structures and institu-tional routines, interrogating their value in terms of the knowledge they offer and the creativity they foster for engaging our world productively and meaningfully.

That our world needs to be engaged with an eye toward substantial social change to create a more humane culture I hope is without ques-tion. Currently, our unemployment rate hovers officially at about 10 per-cent, and by some estimates it is unofficially closer to 16 percent. One might legitimately have cause here to question the meritocratic basis of capitalist society which deems, effectively, that people get what they deserve, rising and falling on their own merits. Do we really believe that one in ten or one in six of our citizens deserves to suffer and not have his or her basic human needs met? Even if we do, it nonetheless seems obvious to me that as a nation we are wasting a lot of talent and human resources when we have grave needs. In the state of Illinois, for example, we have been warned that many teachers will be laid off next year and

that class sizes will swell because of intense budget shortfalls. This situation hardly indicates that we do not have a serious need for teachers or
that those teachers who get the axe lack merit. It means we have a system that fails to take full advantage of the talents and resources of our
population. To repeat, what we see in the personal stories in this book
are that NEIU failed as an institution to really take advantage and optimize the talents of the likes of Angela Vidal-Rodriguez or Sophia López.
From their narratives, we can see they have plenty to offer and plenty in
the way of intelligence, but Northeastern seems to have not effectively
cultivated those gifts, as is our responsibility, so they can be offered to
the larger public.

In many ways, this is a key message of *Diverse by Design*: we can do
better as an educational system to identify, develop, and make use of
the strengths and talents of our students and our environment and
people generally. Learning how to approach, engage, and understand
diversity will help us unleash a great deal of creativity and knowledge
and improve our larger social system and world. To get there, though,
we must be willing to change a capitalist culture in which the dominant mentality is that of exploitation. Indeed, even when it comes to
ways of articulating multiculturalism and diversity, we can see they
can be deployed in the service of exploitation or liberation. As Avery
Gordon and Christopher Newfield (1997) argue in their work *Mapping
Multiculturalism*, "Multiculturalism rejected racial subordination but
seemed sometimes to support it" (3); and, "Multiculturalism sponsored
contacts among people of color that avoided white mediation and oversight by white opinion. And yet, it became a popular term in manage-
rial circles for controlling a multiracial and gendered workplace" (5).
David Palumbo-Liu (1995), in fact, sees the widespread and accelerated
development and institutionalization of multiculturalism in the 1980s
and 1990s as motivated by economic developments that made requisite
the recruitment of women and minorities into the skilled labor force in
order to sustain corporate profitability. Imagine, however, what could be
achieved if we followed Schroeder's approach to diversity, and instead of
trying to repress, control, or manage difference, we absolutely engaged
it as a resource.

Anzia Yezierska (1994), ahead of John Lennon, already did imagine.
In her 1923 autobiographical immigrant short narrative "America and
I," Yezierska recounts leaving Russia and coming to America with her
"heart and soul pregnant with the unlived lives of generations clamoring

for expression" (1865), hoping that "the hidden sap of centuries would find release": "I was to find my work that was denied me in the sterile village of my forefathers. . . . I'd be a creator, a giver, a human being! My work would be the living job of fullest self-expression" (1865). Opposed to immigrant stories we hear about people coming to the United States to achieve fame and fortune, Yezierska tells the story of wanting to come here in order to find work in which she realized her full creative potential and that was linked to a social mission, as being a creator means being a giver. She finds herself frustrated in finding only different varieties of sweatshop labor that pay little, involve horrible and unhealthy working conditions, and kill the soul.

Then, one day she hears a lecture at the Women's Association by the director of welfare at the United Mills Corporation. The lecture is about efficiency and the happy worker, and the director tells his audience, "Efficiency is the new religion of business. . . . In big business houses, even in up-to-date factories, they no longer take the first comer and give him any job that happens to stand empty. Efficiency begins at the employment office. Experts are hired for the one purpose, to find out how best to fit the worker to his work. It's economy for the boss to make the worker happy" (1870). She takes this lecture to heart and visits a vocational guidance counselor, expecting to find someone who will help her identify her talents and help her find work that makes full use of them in a socially meaningful way. Instead, she is told to learn English and that she needs to prove to America that she has something special to offer before America has need of her. Her response is quite meaningful and absolutely germane to this preface and to Schroeder's book: "But I never had a chance to find out what's in me, because I always had to work for a living. Only I feel it's efficiency for America to find out what's in me so different, so I could give it out by my work" (1871). By the end of the story, Yezierska has achieved success, but she does not look back and reflect on the suffering and ladder climbing as a meaningful and significant part of her journey but rather as needless suffering she endured when America could have been taking advantage of her talents. She ends the story imagining a day when America is ready to accept the gifts of those who come.

The idea of efficiency Yezierska offers is one that challenges the rationality of capitalist exploitation. It is efficient for us not to make people prove themselves and suffer in the process but to make every effort to identify people's talents and strengths. At Northeastern, we have many

students who have experienced the world as much more of an obstacle than a support structure and are so burdened with work that they
haven't been able to identify or even cultivate their gifts. *Diverse by Design*
helps us see not just how the university has not most effectively served
these students, but how it could do so much more effectively by working
with diversity more smartly and humanely. Moreover, such an approach
would be more efficient and productive for the world at large. Imagine
having every person working at his or her full creative potential in the
service of the public good! This book helps us do that.

DIFFERENT STANDARDS
Prologue

No one thinks they need Tagalog, so if they are going to learn it, I must teach them, which means that I must learn it first.

They hear Tagalog at their *tita's* house where their *lolo* and *lola* also live, but we are much more comfortable in English. Sometimes, their *tita* asks if I'll offer ESL classes at her clinic for her staff—Filipino, Mexican, Puerto Rican, Jamaican, and, she always adds, Bulgarian, Albanian, Italian, African American, and Jewish. I could be her token white employee, she says. My Spanish, says one of her Spanish-speaking employees, is cute, which, I laugh, is actually an insult.

Rani and I met as undergrads, and after I left for graduate school while she stayed for hers, we exchanged letters and calls until we met for ice cream one afternoon as I was visiting my mother between course work and comps. Soon, I decided I would return to St. Louis where I could study for comps, write the dissertation, and see her. At the time, I hadn't realized that although legislation prohibiting inter-racial marriages had been overturned before we were born, these relationships remained technically illegal in some places as a result of lingering language in state constitutions until after our kids were born.

Our first was born while we were living in a tiny apartment in St. Louis, and we named her Mahal, which means *love* and, she reminds me, *expensive*. After the dissertation, we left for a small island off the coast of north Florida where I started my first full-time position. A year later, we moved to Long Island, just outside of Queens, where our son was born. Even though we wanted to name him after his *lolo*, both his *lolo* and his *lola* urged us to choose a more American name, so we agreed, a few days after his birth, to Mateo.

I didn't recognize our difference until we came to Chicago, which is where their *lolo* came in 1972 with their *lola* and *tita* and *nanay* following two years later. When we arrived thirty years later, we lived three blocks from them for our first few years, and our *mga anak* still stay with them when we're working. There, TFC—the Filipino

Channel—plays all day and most of the night, and we eat *adobo* and, on birthdays, have *pizza* and *pancit* with its long noodles for long lives.

Filipinos, I'm told, lack a distinctive cuisine because they fuse foods from the countries that surround, and have occupied, their islands. This fusion is everywhere at their house, but it is more uneven in ours. Mahal is sometimes Mahal and sometimes Hali, but Mateo is Mateo at school and at home. Only my parents call him Matt, which always, just for a moment, confuses me.

Part One

THE PROBLEMS

INTRODUCTION

I admit I was surprised.

At the time, I acknowledged, if not agreed with, the complaints of colleagues who, when they looked from behind podiums, perceived problems. More than eight in ten of us, according to a survey in the *Chronicle of Higher Education,* believe that high-school graduates are unprepared or only somewhat prepared for college, and four in ten of us believe our first-year students are not well prepared for college writing (Sanoff 2006).

Although this perception is shared by only one in ten of our public high-school counterparts, these concerns seem more than merely professorial perceptions, as recent national reports suggest. After all, fewer than six in ten adults read books not required for school or work, and almost two in ten seventeen-year-olds never or hardly ever read for fun. At the same time, fewer than five in ten high-school seniors write three or more pages in their English classes maybe once or twice a month, and almost four in ten are never or hardly ever given such assignments while nearly all elementary students—those who will soon be in our classrooms—spend three or fewer hours on writing assignments each week, which is just a fraction of the time they spend watching television (National Commission 2003; National Endowment 2004).

These and other conditions lead some, such as the University of Delaware English professor Ben Yagoda (2006), to see, in problems of linguistic usage and style, signs of what he calls "unfortunate cultural trends." In an article for the *Chronicle,* he identifies, as characterized in the subtitle, the seven deadly sins of student writers: dangling modifiers, omitted or unnecessary commas, improper semicolons, wrong words, and plural pronouns with singular antecedents, as well as problems produced by spell check. These, he suggests, reflect not only a general neglect of grammar in secondary and primary classrooms but also "the shocking shoddiness" of student work, as well as a limited experience with reading good writing, which forces students to rely upon "the archive of conversations that are in their heads" that, he believes, are inadequate (B13).

College students, in other words, are generally unprepared, and specifically in writing. They don't read and write, and these and other conditions, such as their lack of concern and experience, produce writing that more resembles speaking. While I might not have presented the problem in the same "literacy and culture are falling" way, I certainly couldn't contest such accounts—even though I am more convinced by other explanations, such as the argument that the media and schools pose challenges to conventional intellectual traditions, particularly print-based ones (e.g., Aronowitz 2008, 15–50).

If, however, these accounts are accurate, then such explanations have to be all the more accurate, conventional wisdom suggests, for students with fewer educational and economic resources, such as those at Northeastern Illinois University (NEIU), the ostensibly most (ethnically) diverse university in the Midwest. In fact, new NEIU faculty are warned, in a session at faculty orientation, that NEIU students differ from their college counterparts in more than ethnicity:

Student Differences: NEIU and Average Four-Year Public Institutions	NEIU (%)	Average (%)
minorities	55	29
ESL	45 (2000)	09
first generation college	79 (2001)	34 (1995/96)
family income below $25,000	37 (2000)	17
first-year student living with family or relatives	96	30
last average high school grades	17 As 26 Cs	34 As 07 Cs

Source: Center for Teaching and Learning 2004[1]

At the same time, other differences, we are told, help predict their classroom performances:

---

1.   In preparing this presentation, the NEIU Center for Teaching and Learning (CTL) used multiple sources (the National Survey of Student Engagement, the National Center for Education Statistics, the Cooperative Institutional Research Program, the NEIU Office of Institutional Studies and Planning, and others), so the comparisons range from students at average four-year public colleges to all students across the country.

Performance Predictors

	NEIU	*National*
First-Year Students' Mean ACT Scores (2000)	17.3	21.0
Attendance (%)		
part-time students (1998)	44	41
part-time seniors (2000)	60	24.5
Family Lives		
provide 20 hours or more care for dependents	20 (first-year) 22 (seniors)	04 (first-year) 12 (seniors)
employed more than 20 hours per week	36 (first-year) 54 (senior)	08 (first-year) 23 (senior)

Source: Center for Teaching and Learning 2004

For these and other reasons, NEIU students, we are also told, are less likely to return and to graduate than their peers at comparable institutions:

Retention and Graduation

	NEIU (%)	*Comparable Institutions (%)*
first-year (2001 cohort)	69	71
year three (2000 cohort)	51	58
year five (1998 cohort)	31	40
six-year graduation (1996 cohort)	14	31

Source: Center for Teaching and Learning 2004

If, according to our colleagues across the country, college students are generally underprepared or unprepared, then surely NEIU students who face greater challenges, my NEIU colleagues and I are told, must be even more so.

Or so I thought.

Diversity, despite what we say, disturbs us. According to Robert Putnam (2007) of *Bowling Alone* fame, those of us who live in diverse communities participate less in community projects and contribute less to charities, are less confident of local leaders and in local news programs, and have fewer friends and more television time. These conditions, Putnam maintains, are not the result of poor race relations or ethnic hostility as much as a general withdrawal from social life, a distrust of our neighbors no matter their skin color or facial features. After testing every other possible explanation, Putnam concludes that U.S. Americans, in both attitude and behavior, are uncomfortable with diversity.

This condition seems a strange situation for a country so connected, even before its inception, to immigration—after all, human civilization did not originate here. And by all accounts, this condition seems to be increasing *and* expanding. Between 2000 and 2005, the number of immigrants in U.S. households increased by 16 percent, and these new immigrants are bypassing traditional entry points, such as New York and California, and are selecting locations, such as the upper Midwest, New England, and the Rocky Mountain states, that typically receive little new immigration (Lyman 2006). Perhaps nowhere are these conditions more clear than college classrooms. While the total enrollment in U.S. higher education increased by 1.6 million students (+11.2 percent) between 1991 and 2001, the minority enrollment increased by 1.5 million (+51.7 percent)—those categorized as race/ethnicity unknown doubled during the same period—while the white enrollment decreased by 500,000 (American Council 2005).

This strange situation—a discomfort with diversity and increasingly diverse society and schools—poses potential problems although for some the problem is less this cultural diversity and more mainstream approaches that privilege difference and identity over an inequality that exists as neither racism nor sexism but classism (e.g., Michaels 2006). While others (e.g., Delbanco 2007) criticize such dismissals of race and gender, most likely recognize the reverential role of cultural identity— the holy trinity of ethnicity, class, and gender—that constitutes identity politics in the United States.

Conflicts over identity politics often involve issues of group membership within nation- states, typically involving the relation of the self to other selves, self-identities and group identities, or these in relation to the distribution of social goods (Schmidt 2000). These conflicts often revolve around tensions between ethnic and national identities; in the United States they revolve around the tension between our English-colonial origins and the ethnicities brought to us by citizens immigrating from all countries of the world. In fact, part of the larger culture wars involves the relation between culture and identity across the country, a condition that cannot be separated from social inequality and racialized ethnicity (47–56, 83).

These conflicts over identity politics are particularly pressing for education and language. In part, these conflicts have always been a part of our history, in that the United States, since its declaration of independence from Great Britain, has promoted a belief in a distinct (U.S.) American identity although as early as 1782 Hector St. John Crèvecoeur questioned the relation of cultural and national identities in this diverse country. Such tensions repeatedly reappear throughout U.S. history, as seen, for example, in the bilingual education demands of German immigrants in the nineteenth century or the Americanization initiatives within schools in the early twentieth century.

Nonetheless, many believe that a good (U.S.) American speaks English, and public schools should provide instruction in both thinking and patriotism, both of which are necessary for democracies (D. Baron 1990, 154–163). In contrast, ethnolinguistic experiences are much more complicated. Although English is the language of power, the United States is one of the most multilingual countries in the world, and despite the perceived threat of Spanish, German was, at least until 1950, the most dominant non-English language.

Perhaps as a result of these and other conditions, social perceptions are conflicting. For some, the dominance of English is threatened by those who use a language other than English in public places, and for others the status of English reflects unequal competition among ethnolinguistic groups within a multilingual country. Both support their positions with data: the use of English is highly correlated with income, wealth, and occupational standing, and yet a second language is not correlated with low income as long as English fluency exists (Schmidt 2000, 83–95). In the United States, these conflicts often surface as debates over the designation of an official language, linguistic civil and political rights, and educational policies for language minority students, all of which can be found throughout the professional and personal lives of those concerned with education and literacy. On the one hand, we believe in the rights of individuals to their own languages. On the other, we sponsor a single common language—monolingual and standard—for participation and communication.

When I started at NEIU, I expected differences even before attending orientation: NEIU regularly announces that it is the most diverse university in the Midwest. Soon, I suspected that these ethnolinguistically diverse students could help me continue the work I had started that, though useful, seemed somewhat limited (e.g., Bauer 2003; Lucas 2001). For instance, the collection of essays I proposed to and coedited with Helen Fox and Patricia Bizzell (2002) had been reprinted twice and was cited as an example of the "most progressive" composition theories even as it was criticized, and fairly I should add for, in failing to address syntactic and grammatical differences, not being progressive enough (Canagarajah 2006b, 595).

This work was also limited, I thought, by its speculative theorizing, so I hoped to test these theories by juxtaposing central arguments and assumptions—literacy as negotiation (Schroeder 2001) and discursive differences as intellectual resources (Schroeder, Fox, and Bizzell 2002)—with empirical evidence.[2] What better place, I thought, than this university where more than fifty languages are used? Here, students and faculty often negotiate among distinctly different discourses. If, I speculated, I could find instances of alternative forms of intellectual work in such obvious situations, perhaps I could proceed to less-obvious ones, which might then form the basis for a more large-scale investigation.

To conduct this study, I turned to students who had been admitted to NEIU through the Proyecto Pa'Lante (PP) program, a special admissions program for Latino students who otherwise didn't qualify for general admission.[3] Such a decision seemed obvious. As an official Hispanic-Serving Institution (HSI), NEIU admitted more Latinos (38.4 percent) between fall 2003 and fall 2006 than African Americans (11.1 percent), Asian Americans (13.4 percent), and even Caucasians (32.8 percent). At the same time, the metro Chicago area, where almost two in ten are Hispanic, is home to the second largest populations of Mexicans and Puerto Ricans in the country (Guzmán 2001; U.S. Census 2006). In addition, Chicagoland Latinos, and Chicago neighborhoods, have been the focus of much recent research (e.g., Cintron 1997; De Genova and Ramos-Zayas 2003; Del Valle 2002; Farr 2005a, 2005b; Guerra 1998).

All I needed was a place to start, which I found while reading the call from the National Commission on Writing (2003) for a writing revolution. In its report, the Commission relied extensively data from the National Association of Educational Progress (NAEP), a federally

---

2.   This hope is not, I realize, a novel idea. At the same time, I also realize that sociocultural phenomena cannot easily be manipulated as independent data with experimental methods, and the very features that fascinate many of us—the divergences and discrepancies—are often dismissed in traditional statistical analyses as error variances. For more, see Bialystok and Hakuta (1994, 189–190).
3.   Throughout this project, I report the terms used by institutions, such as the university (e.g., *Latino*) or the government (e.g., *Hispanic*). These designations, I realize, are problematic (e.g., Kells, Balester, and Villanueva 2004 or Guerra 2004) and often elide significant differences (e.g., J. Gonzalez 2000). Nonetheless, my goal is greater description even as I acknowledge that these descriptions sidestep significant issues of ethnolinguistic identity.

mandated national assessment—otherwise known as the Nation's Report Card—that compiles data from students at various grade levels across the country. Once I discovered that these data could establish a baseline, I culled questions about reading and writing both inside and outside schools, as well as expectations for and attitudes about literacy, from the 2002 NAEP survey of 18,500 seniors in 700 high schools across the country to survey these PP students who, as high-school seniors in 2003, had been admitted in fall 2004 (n=124). At that time, I expected, after establishing a baseline, to analyze performances—written and spoken—for evidence of linguistic contact and cultural negotiation, and I thought their special admission status might actually enhance these efforts.

Along the way, I would need to find more multilinguals for assistance and to confront questions of awareness and intention, but I was comfortably confident about this project and my prediction, which although perhaps naïve seemed relatively straightforward: people who use more than one language, and thus have more than one way to express experiences and examine environments, have more resources than those who have only one language at their disposal—a *creative multilingualism*, if you will (e.g., Kachru 1987). From here, I could reframe this multilingualism and multiculturalism, often seen as educational obstacles to overcome, as intellectual resources to exploit, which could then be situated within larger debates over educational equity that is the goal of multicultural education (e.g., Banks and Banks 1995).

Given the circumstances, the differences in languages in their homes and the education of their parents were not unexpected:

Languages and Ethnicities at Home

	NEIU PP % *(n = 124)*	*U.S. Hispanic %*	*National Peers %* *(n = 18,500)*
use a language other than English half the time	25	24	6
use a language other than English most or all the time	58	37	10

Source: National Assessment of Educational Progress (NAEP), 2002 Writing Assessment

At home, more than eight in ten of the PP students used languages other than English half the time or more as contrasted with only slightly more than six in ten of their national Hispanic peers and between one and two in ten of their national peers. Also, the proportion of those who identified as Mexican or Puerto Rican, given the demographics of the metro Chicago area, was predictable:

Hispanic Background

	NEIU PP (%)	U.S. Hispanic (%)	National Peers (%)
Mexican	69	60	n/a
Puerto Rican	16	10	n/a
Cuban	03	05	n/a
Other Hispanic	11	24	n/a
Not Hispanic	00	01	n/a

Source: National Assessment of Educational Progress (NAEP), 2002 Writing Assessment

Almost seven in ten identified as Mexican, and between one and two in ten identified as Puerto Rican in contrast to their national Hispanic peers, of whom six in ten identify as Mexican while one in ten as Puerto Rican.

As suggested by these results, the fall 2004 PP students were more likely to use a language other than English at home and to self-identify as Mexican or Puerto Rican than even their national Hispanic peers. At the same time, these students were more likely to come from homes where their parents had less education than their national peers:

Education Levels of Parents

	NEIU PP (%)	U.S. Hispanic (%)	National Peers (%)
fathers who didn't finish high school	36	29	12
fathers who graduated from college	08	20	35
mothers who didn't finish high school	34	31	11
mothers who graduated from college	11	20	35

Source: National Assessment of Educational Progress (NAEP), 2002 Writing Assessment

Between six and seven in ten of their parents had finished high school in contrast to more than seven in ten of their national Hispanic peers and almost nine in ten of their national peers. At the same time, only one in ten or less of their parents had graduated from college in contrast to two in ten of their national Hispanic peers and between three and four in ten of their national peers.

Given these conditions, perhaps the presence of literacy materials might not be surprising. In general, these PP students encountered less print at home than their peers although in terms of electronic texts these differences largely disappeared:

Literacy Materials at Home

	NEIU PP (%)	U.S. Hispanic (%)	National Peers (%)
have 26 or more books	53	58	77
receive magazines regu-larly	53	62	75
receive newspaper at least 4 times a week	37	42	55
have a computer to use	89	81	90

Source: National Assessment of Educational Progress (NAEP), 2002 Writing Assessment

While slightly more than five in ten had more than twenty-five books and received magazines regularly, between seven and eight of their national peers have similar exposure to books and magazines in their homes. Although fewer students came from homes that received magazines, even fewer of these PP students—not quite four in ten—had newspapers in their homes as opposed to between five and six in ten of their national peers. However, like their national peers, almost nine in ten of these PP students had access to computers in their homes.

In general terms, these PP students had parents with less education and homes with less print although they had similar access to computers. Aside from these differences, the fall 2004 PP students reported similar experiences in other areas:

Television and Videos

Television and Videos Outside of School on School Days

	NEIU PP (%)	U.S. Hispanic (%)	National Peers (%)
6 or more hours	02	08	08
4–5 hours	12	15	12
2–3 hours	43	42	39
1 hour or less	36	29	35
none	07	06	06

Parental Rules for Amount of Television on School Days (%)

	NEIU PP	U.S. Hispanic	National Peers
strict rules	08	05	04
moderate rules	36	43	36
no rules	56	52	61

Source: National Assessment of Educational Progress (NAEP), 2002 Writing Assessment

Nearly six in ten of these PP students, like their national peers, watched at least two or more hours of television or movies on school days, and, also like their peers, more than nine in ten of these students had parents who imposed limited or no rules about the amount of television they could watch. However, these PP students were more likely to have parents who *monitored* their viewing habits:

Parental Knowledge of Time Spent Watching Television on School Days

	NEIU PP (%)	U.S. Hispanic (%)	National Peers (%)
usually	39	08	07
sometimes	27	11	09
hardly ever	18	68	70
not sure	15	13	14

Source: National Assessment of Educational Progress (NAEP), 2002 Writing Assessment

Between six and seven in ten of these PP students reported that their parents at least sometimes knew how much television they watched on school days as opposed to between one and two in ten of their national peers.

In much the same way, these PP students reported similar expectations for and different awarenesses of homework:

Parents and Homework

Parental Rules for Finishing Homework

	NEIU PP (%)	U.S. Hispanic (%)	National Peers (%)
strict rules	25	16	13
expectations	54	65	64
no rules	21	13	14
no homework	00	06	09

Parental Knowledge of Whether Homework Was Finished Each Day

	NEIU PP (%)	U.S. Hispanic (%)	National Peers (%)
usually	29	22	26
sometimes	36	23	22
hardly ever	25	39	35
not sure	08	09	08
never had home-work	02	07	10

Source: National Assessment of Educational Progress (NAEP), 2002 Writing Assessment

Nearly eight in ten of these PP students, like their national peers, reported that their parents had at least expectations, if not strict rules, for finishing homework, yet between six and seven in ten of these students reported that their parents at least sometimes knew whether they finished their homework each day as opposed to fewer than five in ten of their national peers.

At the same time, these PP students had similar or better experiences with reading and writing both in school and for themselves:

Reading In School and Out Of School

Amount of Reading Each Day in School and for Homework

	NEIU PP (%)	U.S. Hispanic (%)	National Peers (%)
more than 20 pages	22	17	18
16–20 pages	16	10	10
11–15 pages	19	14	13
6–10 pages	23	24	23
5 or fewer pages	21	35	36

Amount of Reading for Enjoyment on Own Time

	NEIU PP (%)	U.S. Hispanic (%)	National Peers (%)
almost every day	12	14	19
1–2 times per week	25	24	22
once or twice a month	42	30	26
never or hardly ever	20	32	33

Source: National Assessment of Educational Progress (NAEP), 2002 Writing Assessment

Almost six in ten of these PP students reported reading more than ten pages for school as opposed to slightly more than four in ten of their national peers, and while similar numbers—around four in ten of these students and their national peers—reported reading for themselves once or more a week, more of these PP students talked about their school and reading with their family and friends than their national peers:

Talking about School

Discuss Studies in School with Family

	NEIU PP (%)	U.S. Hispanic (%)	National Peers (%)
every day	34	19	18
2–3 times a week	18	21	23
1 time a week	20	21	21
1 or 2 times per month	18	19	19
never or hardly ever	11	20	20

Discuss Reading with Family or Friends

	NEIU PP (%)	U.S. Hispanic (%)	National Peers (%)
almost every day	16	09	09
1–2 times a week	38	26	26
once or twice a month	28	35	33
never or hardly ever	18	29	31

Source: National Assessment of Educational Progress (NAEP), 2002 Writing Assessment

Slightly more than seven in ten of these PP students talked to their families about their studies once a week or more in contrast to slightly more than six in ten of their national peers, and between five and six in ten of them talked to family and friends about something they read at least once a week as opposed to between three and four in ten of their peers.

Despite these differences between talking and reading, their self-motivated writing seemed similar:

Self-Motivated Writing

Write in a Private Journal or Diary on Own Time

	NEIU PP (%)	U.S. Hispanic (%)	National Peers (%)
almost every day	07	12	11
1–2 times a week	12	11	11
once or twice a month	19	14	14
never or hardly ever	61	63	65

Write Stories and Poems for Fun on Own Time

	NEIU PP (%)	U.S. Hispanic (%)	National Peers (%)
almost every day	07	10	08
1–2 times a week	08	12	11
once or twice a month	27	23	21
never or hardly ever	58	56	60

Email Family and Friends

	NEIU PP (%)	U.S. Hispanic (%)	National Peers (%)
almost every day	18	23	26
1–2 times a week	39	26	27
once or twice a month	23	21	22
never or hardly ever	20	30	25

Source: National Assessment of Educational Progress (NAEP), 2002 Writing Assessment

On their own time, nearly two in ten of these PP students, like their national peers, kept a journal or wrote stories and poems at least once a week, and between five and six in ten of them emailed family and friends as often.

Nevertheless, these PP students had the same or stronger beliefs in and attitudes about reading:

Reading Attitudes

Respond: *When I read books, I learn a lot.*

	NEIU PP (%)	U.S. Hispanic (%)	National Peers (%)
strongly agree	23	18	18
agree	63	63	62
disagree	11	14	17
strongly disagree	02	04	04

Respond: *Reading is one of my favorite activities.*

	NEIU PP (%)	U.S. Hispanic (%)	National Peers (%)
strongly agree	10	10	13
agree	40	27	26
disagree	11	14	17
strongly disagree	10	20	22

Source: National Assessment of Educational Progress (NAEP), 2002 Writing Assessment

While eight in ten or more of these PP students, like their national peers, agreed or strongly agreed that reading helps them learn much, five in ten of these PP students agreed or strongly agreed that reading is one of their favorite activities in contrast to not quite four in ten of their national peers.

At the same time, their perspectives on writing were even more positive:

Writing Attitudes

Respond: *Writing helps me share ideas.*

	NEIU PP (%)	U.S. Hispanic (%)	National Peers (%)
strongly agree	31	22	19
agree	62	49	48
disagree	07	20	22
strongly disagree	00	09	11

Respond: *Writing (e.g., stories and letters) is one of my favorite activities.*

	NEIU PP (%)	*U.S. Hispanic (%)*	*National Peers (%)*
strongly agree	07	11	10
agree	43	29	25
disagree	45	42	42
strongly disagree	06	18	23

Source: National Assessment of Educational Progress (NAEP), 2002 Writing Assessment

More than nine in ten of these PP students agreed or strongly agreed that writing helps them share ideas, in contrast to fewer than seven in ten of their national peers, and five in ten of these PP students agreed or strongly agreed that everyday writing, such as stories and letters, was one of their favorite activities, again in contrast to between three and four in ten of their national peers who share similar sentiments.

In other words, most of these PP students, like their national peers, believed that reading helps them learn much, and yet these PP students

NEIU PP Juxtaposed with National Peers

Less than Nat'l Peers	*Equivalent*	*More than Nat'l Peers*
exposure to English		exposure to other languages[4]
education of parents		
number of print texts		
	computers at home	
	amount of time spent watching television and movies	
	parental expectations for watching television and doing homework	
		parental awareness of watching television and doing homework
		reading for school
	reading for themselves	
		talking about school and reading
	writing for themselves	
	belief in reading	
		enjoyment of reading
		belief in writing
		enjoyment of writing

Source: Author survey of fall 2004 Proyecto Pa'Lante students

4.   Again, this argument is one I expected to make.

were more likely to have similar beliefs about writing and to enjoy both reading and writing more. As I reviewed these and other results, I was surprised by the composite (represented in table "NEIU PP Juxtaposed with National Peers").

If ethnicity and education could somehow be ignored, these PP students could reasonably be expected to have similar, if not better, experiences at the university as their *national* peers. At the same time, these PP students bring significant histories with and attitudes about reading and writing that could challenge conventional conclusions about educational experiences.

As a result, the more pressing question, I realized, was bigger than linguistic contact and cultural negotiation and included educational institutions and larger social conditions.[5] What happens, in other words, when these PP students enter an official Hispanic-Serving Institution with an institutional identity as the most (ethnically) diverse university in the Midwest?

From this survey, I had some sense of who PP students are, which I could add to my sense of where they came from. For example, I knew that people in the metro Chicago area are more likely to use a language other than English at home and to be less confident of their English than others across the country:

Languages in U.S. Homes (percent of those 5 and older)				
	Total Population (n = 279,012,712)	*Latino* (n = 39,540,935)	*Metro Chicago* (n = 8,816,524)	*Chicago Latinos* (n = 1,625,774)
only English	80.3	21.6	71.8	15.7
a language other than English	19.7	78.4	28.2	84.3
English less than "very well"	8.7	39.1	12.8	43.1

Source: 2005 American Community Survey, U.S. Census Bureau (2006)

I also had some sense of local communities. For instance, I knew that some in the local Mexican American community creatively refashion disrespect into self-respect, and I also knew that others rely extensively on extended social networks and use oral and literate practices to manage

---

5.   For more, see Schroeder (2006).

their literacy needs within schools and throughout societies, both here in Chicago and in Mexico (Cintron 1997; Guerra 1998).

At the same time, I knew these experiences were often quite different in significant ways. On the one hand, the ethnolinguistic experiences of those who come from Mexico are different from those who are educated or born here, such as the use of language to continue cultural traditions—*ranchero* speech or Mexican proverbs or religious interactions—or to forge new identities—particularly in classrooms—as well as their relations to Spanish as a native or heritage language and its impact on thinking (Farr 2005b). On the other, these experiences are different from those of Puerto Ricans whose presence in the metro Chicago area was established later and reflects the historical and economic relationship between Puerto Rico and the United States (Del Valle 2002). Throughout the metro Chicago area, these groups tend to have different ideas about the role of language in social assimilation and cultural authenticity (DeGenova and Ramos-Zayas 2003). At the same time, these distinctions do not eliminate the difficulty of generalizations about even these local experiences, particularly in terms of language and literacy within homes and at schools (Del Valle 2005).[6]

What I needed to know is what these PP students experience within the institution. Within composition studies, the experiences of ethnolinguistic minorities have been widely recounted (e.g., Gilyard 1991; Rose 1989; Roth and Harama 2000; Shen 1989; Villanueva 1993) and reported (e.g., Casanave 2002; Chiseri-Strater 1991; DiPardo 1993; Sternglass 1997), but with a few notable exceptions (e.g., Villanueva 1993), many of these accounts neglect Latinos, especially in a large-scale way. Composition studies, as Carol Severino (2009) explains, is limited by an "embarrassing paucity" of research about Latinos, including a "scarcity of publications" from those working at Hispanic-Serving Institutions. While this problem, in part, is addressed, she suggests, by a recent collection of essays on teaching writing at HSIs, both the collection editors and Severino note the particular need for more from those who work in the

---

6.   In addition to this research of the metro Chicago area, other research depicts ethnolinguistic experiences of Spanish speakers in other parts of the United States. For example, Zentella (1997a) examines Spanish and English among Puerto Ricans in a New York neighborhood, and Silva-Corvalán (1994) explores the impact of English contact upon Spanish in Los Angeles county. Still other research focuses more generally upon Spanish in the United States as both a primary and a heritage language (e.g., Roca and Colombi 2003; Roca and Lipski 1993).

Midwest and with Puerto Ricans (Kirklighter, Cárdenas, and Murphy 2007, 8; Severino 2009, 143–144).

Even as these needs—Severino cites NEIU and Chicago—are obviously addressed by this study, it also addresses another problem. Often, education and literacy research, including accounts by Latinos (e.g., Garrod, Kilkenny, and Gómez 2007), emphasizes individuals in specific situations and produces cultural explanations—unprepared or misprepared students who struggle in classrooms—and specific recommendations while ignoring larger systemic issues (Valdés 1996, 15–24). In doing so, this research often overlooks the ways these experiences and explanations are shaped by particular institutions and other social structures. For example, Michelle Hall Kells (2002, 2006) uses the results of her randomized language attitude survey of first-year Mexican American college students in south Texas to critique educational and linguistic obstacles faced by ethnolinguistic minorities and to defend the Tex Mex of these student writers as participants in a creoloid continuum. On the one hand, Kells usefully suggests the need both to understand the impact of these attitudes on their identity and to analyze these attitudes to shift their perceptions of these language practices. On the other, she limits her focus to the writing classroom and, in so doing, separates these spaces from the institution that shapes their educational experiences, especially over time.

As Severino indicates and Kells illustrates, composition studies clearly must develop its understanding of Latinos and HSIs and must "restructure and reform" through "alliances with related disciplines" to understand "the linguistics, sociolinguistics, pedagogies, and politics of diversity" (Severino 2009, 145). At the same time, it must also recognize that experiences involve individuals within institutions where meaning is made and where the future of education and literacy within secular societies will be determined (Miller 2005).[7] Both limitations are addressed by this project.

In *Literacy in American Lives*, Deborah Brandt (2001) complicates conventional literacy narratives in the United States, even using a relatively limited sample, through an analytic approach she calls *sponsors of literacy*. As Brandt defines these, literacy sponsors are "agents, local or distant, concrete or abstract" that "enable, support, teach, and model, as well as recruit, regulate, suppress, or withhold literacy—and gain advantage

---

7.   For more, see Horner and Lu (1999, 203–205).

by it in some way," the "delivery systems for economies of literacy" that serve as "a tangible reminder that literacy learning throughout history has always required permission, sanction, assistance, coercion, or at minimum, contact with existing trade routes" (19). From interviews with eighty people from south central Wisconsin born between the 1890s and the 1980s, she convincingly argues that literacy sponsors have shifted over time from education, religion, or local businesses to more distributed and different sites and sources; that literacy sponsors of adults, including teachers, are distinctly different from those of children and students; and that economic forces shaping literacy learning and literacy instruction elicit "crucial ethical and policy questions" for education that U.S. schools have ignored (197–207).

While Brandt in this study moves well beyond schools to challenge popular perceptions of literacy learning and literacy standards, she nonetheless turns, near the end, to an exploration of literacy and stratification at the end of the twentieth century, and she suggests that despite increasingly democratic educational opportunities, access to and rewards for literacy are still clustered with "material and political privilege," which, while always existing, have become more significant as literacy becomes "so central to economic and political viability" (169). In the past, literacy, she explains, would have signaled social status, yet today it is increasingly a means to social advantages, which only aggravates social inequalities (169). While this problem, she maintains, is often analyzed in terms of the relation of schools to students or homes, the larger problem, she believes, is the way that these correlations of literacy with socioeconomic conditions both reflect and mask the ways that literacy learning, both inside and outside schools, occurs in "systems of unequal subsidy and unequal reward—systems that range beyond the influence of any individual family's assets, beyond any one pile of cultural capital that a student or a home might accumulate" (169–170). A better approach, she argues, will clarify the relation of literacy to economic inequality and political discrimination, and it can suggest alternative roles for schools within society in order to increase their "democratizing influence in literacy and learning" (170).

These suggestions are consistent with the current interest in the educational success of college students, particularly underrepresented minorities, within the United States. For example, William G. Bowen, Matthew M. Chingos, and Michael S. McPherson (2009) tracked students who, in 1999, entered twenty-five flagship and statewide institutions across the United States through their withdrawal, transfer, and/or graduation, particularly in terms of the impact of parental education, income, gender, ethnicity, high-school grades, test scores, financial aid, and institutional selectivity. These researchers concluded that even when considering these other factors, ethnic and economic minorities consistently have lower graduation rates and need longer to complete their degrees. At the same time, other research considers educational results in relation to college culture. For example, Rebecca D. Cox (2009) concludes, after five years of interviews, that both students and professors, despite good intentions, misunderstand and fail each other, and she demonstrates ways that conventional college culture, including conventional notions of academic literacy, can function as obstacles to students' educational success.

While these and other studies are beginning to document, in quantitative and qualitative terms, the impact of institutions upon individuals, this research has only begun to establish the role of institutions in educational success and literacy learning, particularly in the ways that they, as sponsors of social norms and specific literacies, shape the experiences of individuals. To better understand this role, I conducted an *institutional case study*, which approaches institutions as discursive systems that authorize some practices, policies, and philosophies while prohibiting others. This method, as explained and illustrated by Jeffrey T. Grabill (2001), maintains the advantages of case studies, including the focus on the local and the particular, to explore complex issues and everyday experiences while expanding the scope beyond either individuals or situations to highlight their interrelation, particularly in the ways that they, together, provide meaning and value for literacy. Grabill is more concerned in his institutional case study about the ways that communities are, and can be, organized around issues, whether ideas or ethnicity, in order to theorize the construction of communities, yet he seems to lose sight of the experiences of individuals within institutions and the impact of social contexts upon institutions and individuals, or the way these experiences, as existing within institutions, reflect larger historical and social conditions (87–117).

In contrast, everyday experiences are central to my institutional case study of the most (ethnically) diverse university in the Midwest, a university also officially designated as an Hispanic-Serving Institution. After examining, in the next chapter, historical and social context for this institution, this project turns, in the following chapter, to the experiences of the Proyecto Pa'Lante students over four academic years within this institution (fall 2004–spring 2008). Throughout this time, I collected quantitative and qualitative data as I monitored their efforts throughout this institution, which are presented in chapter two. In this project, I used multivocal ethnographic methods—first established by anthropologist Joseph Tobin and his colleagues (see Li 1996, 4)— to document the progress of students from the largest incoming ethnic group at the ostensibly most (ethnically) diverse university in the Midwest. In doing so, I was influenced, in part, by the issues suggested by Guadalupe Valdés (1992) as central to understanding the experiences of multilingual minorities in the United States, including their differences in the use of linguistic resources, the impact of their histories of reading and writing, the literacy instruction they receive, and the responses to their writing. In establishing this account, I often relied upon data I had collected. Along with, for example, the survey data already presented, I conducted classroom observations of some PP students; surveyed faculty primarily responsible for literacy instruction; interviewed faculty, staff, and administrators; and collected artifacts, such as newspaper columns, teaching bulletins, and university memos.

In addition to the data I collected, I included data collected and reported by the university. Although I cannot always attest to the methodological rigor of the results from the institution, I am less concerned with the accuracy of these numbers and more interested in the ways these data, and the reports of them, provide insight into institutional perceptions and perspectives. A good example is the report from the NEIU General Education Committee on the impact of general education courses upon students' oral and written proficiencies and other areas. In preparing this report, the Committee used standardized tests and local instruments, such as a collaboratively designed critical thinking rubric, and it asked faculty, for example, to evaluate the clarity, support, style, and conventions of prewriting and postwriting from NEIU students who were admitted in 2004–2005, students who had completed or nearly completed their gen ed requirements, and students who graduated the previous year. From these and other sources, the Committee concluded that the writing of students had significantly improved after these introductory courses and that it exhibited no significant differences from the writing of students at peer institutions. While other evaluations of these data might produce different conclusions, the relevant issue for this project is the official position that these introductory courses improve students' communication proficiencies and that NEIU students' abilities resemble those at other similar institutions.

Sifting through these data, I searched for repetitive and systematic experiences, which I placed into patterns. All the while, I juxtaposed old and new data, looking for contradictions and inconsistencies, as I began to assemble an account of the experiences of the PP students within this institution. In doing so, I drafted reflections to document initial suspicions, and I triangulated these concerns with other minority multilinguals both on and off campus.

Soon after starting, I realized this study had more to the story. Certainly, all studies have stories (Carroll 1997), and telling these is complicated and contested (Clifford and Marcus 1986). At the same time, I started to suspect the limits of the PP data I was collecting as I attempted to account for the intersections of these individuals and this institution, and the potential contributions of other accounts. For instance, I began interviewing a PP instructor whose seminar course I was observing in order to better understand the observations I was collecting, and throughout these debriefings, I discovered, more and more, how much her experiences as both a child in Chicago and a student at NEIU had significantly shaped her perspectives as a PP instructor.

As a result, I asked her and two others to provide first-hand accounts—*institutional autobiographies*—of their experiences at NEIU to thicken the description of this project. In his advocacy and illustration of institutional autobiographies, Richard Miller (2005) argues that by considering personal development within institutional contexts, conventional autobiographical narrators, who are perceived as independent and free, are situated within social institutions, which are shaped by their histories and practices. While negotiating complicated and sometimes arbitrary systems, these narrators document their efforts, within and through these institutions, to both make meaningful lives and acquire social legitimacy (138–140).

In addition to a coauthored chapter with the PP instructor, another chapter was authored by an undergraduate who, having taken an incomplete in an introductory writing course with me, delivered a manuscript of several hundred pages, more than a year later, that she hoped would satisfy course requirements. Although her parents had immigrated to the United States before she was born, she struggled to find her identity throughout her college career. Another chapter was authored by a graduate student who, having heard my presentation at a graduate student workshop, later offered to help me with this project, and even took a graduate writing course with me. In contrast, she came to the United States after earning an undergraduate degree from a prestigious Mexican university although she too was forced, as a result of her experiences with education and language in Chicago and at NEIU, to reconsider her notions of identity.

Given their extensive contributions to the story I am trying to tell, I asked them to introduce themselves:

Neida Hernandez-Santamaria (contributor to chapter three)

My name is Neida Hernandez-Santamaria. Mother of a daughter, Miranda. Wife of a noble and honorable man, Harold. Daughter to Cuban and Costa Rican immigrant selfless loving parents. Sister to two united, loyal, supportive unique sisters, Ivonne and Maggie. Mentor and friend to any who seek my help. I was born and raised in Chicago, having grown up in the Albany Park neighborhood and currently residing in the far northwest side of the city. I attended public schools from kindergarten through college. I earned my BA with a major in Spanish and minor in Psychology, MA in Educational Leadership and Development: Higher Education Leadership from Northeastern Illinois University. Currently, I am pursuing an EdD in adult education from National-Louis University.

Sophia López (chapter four)

Sophia López is a working-class queer woman of color. Born in Chicago, she is the daughter of Mexican immigrants and has a large extended family in Pilsen. Spanish is her first language. When her family moved to the northern suburbs, she was placed in the English as a Second Language program. She attended schools that were mostly Anglo and middle class and felt torn between the language and culture of home and her new American identity. English became her dominant language and, to survive, she grew distant from her Mexican roots. The first in her family to attend university, she transferred into Northeastern in fall 2002. A required English 101 course with Professor Christopher Schroeder initiated a radical process of self-discovery and transformation. She began exploring the strong interplay between race, class, and power. Reconciling the Mexican and American, working class and middle class, Spanish and English, was a shattering experience. Seeking community on campus, she began participating in a wide range of student clubs and activities, including student government and the Latino Advisory Committee at NEIU. She joined political Latino organizations and became a writer for *Que Ondee Sola*, a campus-based Latino student magazine. Together with other Latino students, she pushed for the creation of a Latino cultural and resource center at Northeastern. As a staff writer and columnist for the campus newspaper, she became a fierce advocate for the Latino community on campus. Wanting Northeastern to live up to its federal designation as a Hispanic-Serving Institution, she helped bring attention to the unique challenges Latino students continue to face. She is currently working toward a career as an English and bilingual education teacher.

Angela Vidal-Rodriguez (chapter five)

Angela Vidal-Rodriguez is a Mexican immigrant who came to the United States in 2002. Unlike many Mexican immigrants, Angela comes from a low-end high-class family characterized by her parents' academic devotion. Her father is a prestigious cardiologist and former researcher. He still writes for important national cardiology journals and magazines. Her mother, a former intensive care unit specialist and present residency professor, also writes for national journals. With this background, Angela was educated in the best private schools of her hometown. Later on, Angela finished her economics bachelor's degree in one of the most recognized private universities in Mexico City, where she was a tutor for math and statistics since her second semester, research assistant for two years, and the president and vice president of the student economics council for two years consecutively. After she finished her thesis titled "Education as Household Income Determinant: Mexico Case for 2000," Angela decided to leave behind a part-time teacher position in a private community college and part-time advisory position with the Mexican Department of Education for complete economic independence and, more importantly, a long-awaited dream of an international experience. After one year of living in Chicago working as a waitress and taking ESL classes, Angela was admitted to the masters in business administration program at Northeastern Illinois University with a graduate assistantship that again allowed her to work in a university. Angela graduated in May 2005 and is now working as a full-time academic advisor for the McNair Scholars Program at Northeastern Illinois University.

Since completing their contributions, each has experienced significant changes—Neida completed her EdD; Sophia graduated and is now teaching ESL classes; and Angela has enrolled in a PhD program.

As much as is useful and possible, these contributors and others speak for themselves. In instances where anonymity was requested or otherwise important, I employed a protocol for pseudonyms and anonyms that was negotiated with the publisher. For example, those who published articles or were interviewed in local or national publications are cited by name while those who gave background interviews or offered survey responses are given pseudonyms or contribute, in a limited number of instances, to composite characters. In addition, some interviews have been edited for hesitation syllables or other inadvertent utterances while attempting to preserve their conversational flavor.

Besides preserving these voices, I also tried to preserve the experience of this project. When it expanded from study to story, I attempted to attest to this shift through the use of the alternatives outlined by Patricia Bizzell (1999)—variant Englishes, nontraditional cultural referents, personal experience as persuasion and empathy, casual refutation, appropriative history by including the self, ironic humor, indirect conclusions, a presumption of shared contexts, and respectful reproduction of original work (11–17). In particular, I hoped to experiment with the syntactical styles of Spanish and Tagalog—the accumulation, at least as I understand these, rather than the adumbration, of meaning—that also fill my work and home as a means to different forms of intellectual work.[8] When, however, some readers struggled—maybe I am too indulgent or indolent—with structure and sense, I reverted to more conventional structures and forms to increase comprehension and enhance conclusions, particularly about the language policies and literacy philosophies in multicultural societies.

Together, these histories, experiences, and efforts attempt to account for the intersection of ethnolinguistic minorities at the most ethnically diverse university in the Midwest. The result, I hope, is a credible and (at least semi-) coherent account of an institution that finds its identity in its ethnic diversity as it is experienced by the very ethnolinguistically diverse individuals it serves. In its account of places and people, this study-as-story-as-study offers an examination of individual experiences and institutional practices and, from these, some conclusions about

---

8.   For more, see Schroeder, Fox, and Bizzell (2002).

language policies and literacy philosophies not only at NEIU but also, in the last chapter, within NCTE for those whom we profess to respect. At the same time, these interpretations and conclusions seem relevant to other minority multilinguals in other institutions, and as such, this study adds to our understanding, I hope, of ethnolinguistic diversity within multicultural communities, including the ones where my kids and I live.

As such, these debates must go beyond academic discussions about education, literacy, and language to include the distribution of social resources and the acquisition of social capital—including norms for reciprocity and trust that, Robert Putnam (2007) maintains, both produce better democracies and economies and lead to longer and happier lives. While ethnic diversity might challenge social solidarity and restrict social capital, these challenges can be overcome, he explains, by establishing more expansive social identities (137–139). Such recommendations mean that language policies and literacy philosophies are central to the future of multicultural communities, especially in this increasingly globalized world.

Appendix

2002 WRITING ASSESSMENT (NAEP) SURVEY QUESTIONS (CLUSTERED)

Personal Information

- What is your gender?
- Which [race/ethnicity] best describes you?
- If you are Hispanic, what is your Hispanic background?

Homes

Parental Education

- How far in school did your father go?
- How far in school did your mother go?

Language

- How often do people in your home talk to each other in a language other than English?

Presence/Absence of Literacy Materials

- Is there a world atlas in your home? It could be a book of maps of the world, or it could be on the computer.
- About how many books are there in your home?
- Is there a computer at home that you use?
- Is there an encyclopedia in your home? It could be a set of books, or it could be on the computer.
- Does your family get any magazines regularly?
- Does your family get a newspaper at least four times a week?

Parental Involvement

- On a school day, about how many hours do you usually watch TV or videotapes outside of school?

- Did your parents know whether you finished your homework each day?

- Did your parents know the amount of time you spent watching TV on a school day?

- Which statement best describes the rules that your parents have about getting your homework done?

- Which statement best describes the rules that your parents have about the amount of TV you can watch on school days?

Experiences with and Uses for Writing and Reading

- About how many pages a day did you have to read in school and for homework?

- How often do you read for fun on your own time?

- How often do you talk about things you studied in school with someone in your family?

- How often do you talk with your friends or family about something you have read?

- How often do you write e-mails to your friends or family?

- How often do you write in a private journal or diary on your own time?

- How often do you write stories or poems for fun on your own time?

Beliefs in and Attitudes about Literacy

- Please indicate how much you disagree or agree with the following statement: When I read books, I learn a lot.

- Please indicate how much you disagree or agree with the following statement: Reading is one of my favorite activities.

- Please indicate how much you disagree or agree with the following statement: Writing helps me share my ideas.

- Please indicate how much you disagree or agree with the following statement: Writing things like stories and letters is one of my favorite activities.

Different Standards
PART I

I unlocked my office to find a copy of the campus newspaper that someone had slid beneath the door. I stepped over it and around it as I unpacked my bag and gathered folders for class. With a few minutes before I had to leave, I picked up the newspaper and dropped into a chair. I soon guessed why it was there.

The headline—"Blowing the Whistle on the English Department"—promised a scandal. "A significant number of influential tenure track faculty in the English Department," announced our colleague in the opening sentence, "are defrauding students of the appropriate education which they had paid for and wrongfully depriving them of the grades and degrees they might otherwise deserve" (White 2007b). His coworkers, who, he asserted, "cannot put together grammatically correct, intelligible phrases and sentences," had recently refused at a department meeting to ratify his motion in support of "grammatically correct" comprehensive exam questions. (One voted for it, and one voted against it, while the others and I abstained.) Then he criticized the theoretical focus of the MA program and critiqued several comprehensive exam questions before offering his credentials—a full professor at NEIU for forty years and published in leading journals.

While the entire article was unexpected, the next part I read was especially so:

> When I noted that students also regularly report they cannot understand what some of their English professors say and write, here is how one professor responded by email to me:
>
> *Prof. X.* In your remarks at the meeting today, you referenced colleagues who cannot write grammatically . . . were you referencing [me]? If so, what do you find objectionable?
>
> *Prof. White:* Honestly [name deleted], do you not know that it [your published essay] is filled with misplaced modifiers, vague antecedent references, unidiomatic phrases, malapropisms?

> *Prof. X.* So which do you find objectionable?
>
> Every grammatical error anyone makes is objectionable, and when English professors year after year carelessly pile up one error after another, it is especially objectionable, shameful and professionally irresponsible when they, along with their colleagues, seem not to care. (White 2007b, deletions in original)

I tried to concentrate on the rest—he reported that he had informed campus administrators of "these unsound, unreasonable, and unfair practices," which "need to be promptly addressed" before more students "are cheated out of their education and tuition money"—but while I was waiting for class, I wondered whether those emails he quoted were messages I had sent.

After a long day on campus, I returned home and, after turning on the computer, juxtaposed the messages in the newspaper with the ones on the screen. The first, I discovered, was similar:

> In your remarks at the meeting today, you referenced colleagues who cannot write grammatically in newspaper articles—were you referring to one of mine recently published in the *Independent?* If so, what did you find objectionable?

The second—his response—was essentially the same, but the third seemed different. In the article, the unnamed professor reportedly responds in this way:

> *Prof. X:* So which do you find objectionable?

Rather, I had written this response:

> So which did you find most objectionable?

The differences—the omission of particulars and the revision of *did* and *do* and the deletion of *most*—seemed small, but these amount to the difference between a request for specific examples and a dismissal of his objections.

When he initially complained at a department meeting, I was interested because I suspected he was referring to an article I had written in the campus newspaper. As the PP students started their third year, the university had been criticized in a *New York Times* article for its retention and graduation rates, especially those for underrepresented minorities (Finder 2006). In my article, I acknowledged this problem but suggested a shift from how long these students need to earn their degrees to how much they are learning, which would involve a different set of questions, including how long students should take and what they should be learning (Schroeder 2007).

When he didn't respond to my request for more information, I gave a list of his complaints and a copy of my *Independent* article to a colleague who teaches a graduate stylistics course. She returned both later that morning, saying she could neither identify his objections nor find significant others. At that point, I decided to ignore his criticisms, especially given that they seemed more like stylistic preferences than syntactic violations. After reading his article, I was unsure what to do—evidently, my private email had been redacted and published without my consent or even knowledge in an article accusing my colleagues and me of educational fraud.

Even as I was confronted with this situation, I had received a copy of the HSI grant proposal for a campuswide writing program. I had long heard much about this initiative and had been promised, but not provided, details until I was sent, as the PP sutdents started a fouth year, a copy of the submitted proposal. At the time, I was instructed to concentrate instead on the search for a composition colleague who would support this effort and strengthen our program. Five days later, I was told, even before I had read the proposal, that the university had been awarded millions of dollars to implement this program.

1

THE MOST ETHNICALLY DIVERSE
UNIVERSITY IN THE MIDWEST

Although NEIU, according to the Carnegie Classification of Institutions of Higher Education, is considered a public four-year institution, no one—neither students nor faculty—can come to this institution without learning, often before arriving, that it is a diverse institution:

> Founded in 1867, Northeastern Illinois University continues to meet the demand for quality, affordable education, serving 12,000 students at the 67-acre main campus on Chicago's north side and three additional campuses in the metropolitan area. NEIU is the most diverse university in the Midwest (according to U.S. News and World Report) and a federally-designated Hispanic Serving Institution. (NEIU Homepage)

In fact, this invocation of diversity functions as an institutional appeal to prestige that is part of the basic appeals of U.S. universities today.[1]

The problem, however, is that such designations are difficult to define. If considered, for example, in relation to all institutions in the Midwest, NEIU (2007) had the same campus ethnic diversity index (.66 with 30 percent Hispanic) as the University of Illinois-Chicago (.66 with 24 percent Asians), which also has the same level of economic diversity (35 percent).[2] Nonetheless, anyone who, in reviewing the America's Best College rankings on which these designations are based, selects these

---

1. These efforts are successful, according to Frank Donoghue (2008), because the focus is the rankings and not the methodology (111–138). In this instance, researchers at *U.S. News and World Report* adopted a methodology from the *International Journal of Public Opinion Research* to establish the proportion of minority students—but not international students—and the combination of ethnic groups—non-Hispanic African Americans, American Indians and Native Alaskans, Asian Americans and Pacific Islanders, Hispanics, and non-Hispanic whites—while including those who did not identify with a particular ethnic group as non-Hispanic white. The result is an index of campus ethnic diversity that ranges from 0.0 to 1.0, which is reported, along with the percentage of the largest ethnic minority group, by the magazine (Methodology).

2. According to *U.S. News*, the campus ethnic diversity of NEIU (.66) was slightly higher in 2008 than that of UIC (Methodology 65).

two institutions for comparison—one a master's university and the other a national university—will notice that these institutions do have significant differences:

	NEIU	UIC
date of origins	1867	1965
undergraduate enrollment	9,257	15,006
tuition (in-state/out-of-state)	$5,549/$9,629	$9,902/$22,292
ranking within peer group[3]	tier four, or the lower 25% among master's universities (n = 574)	tier three, or 50%–70% among national universities (n = 262)

Source: America's Best Colleges, 2008 U.S. News and World Report

In other words, NEIU is considerably older, substantially cheaper, and somewhat smaller, and it serves a different social function, which together with its ethnic and economic diversity, does distinguish it from UIC and others throughout metro Chicago and the Midwest.

Diversity, despite how we talk, is difficult to define. In general, *diversity* can be used in at least four different ways—actual human cultural diversity in categorical terms; images of cultural diversity as a form of representation; specific expectations about social order; or a particular set of beliefs (Wood 2003, 88–89). For some, diversity became an educational issue in the 1950s after the *Brown v Board of Education* decision, while for others it became significant, at least in higher ed, in the late 1980s with the publication of Allan Bloom's *The Closing of the American Mind* (Prendergast 2003; Wood 2003). Both moments are significant in the institutional history of NEIU, which was initially established to serve as a normal school for teachers who wanted to work in the Chicago Public Schools (CPS). As CPS confronted cultural challenges, NEIU was transformed, over time, into a public university that adopted the ethnic diversity of its students as an institutional identity, a process that began in the 1960s and 1970s and continued through the 1980s with the acquisition of its status as a federally designated Hispanic-Serving Institution.

While definitions and designations are difficult, the bigger challenge is institutional responses to cultural diversity, which cannot be separated from larger social contexts. For example, the use of ethnic diversity as an institutional and even disciplinary identity is one way

3. After assigning institutions to peer groups on the basis of Carnegie Foundation categories, researchers at *U.S. News* gather as many as fifteen types of data, or what they call "indicators of academic quality," to generate a total weighted score.

that educational politics reflected larger national politics at a time when minority identities became a means of legitimacy for education and social activists not only at NEIU but also in NCTE and other organizations (e.g., Parks 2000, 22). Over the years, cultural diversity shaped NEIU and afforded an institutional identity, and yet it has also created conflicts that have largely been framed as educational obstacles to overcome, if not in policy and philosophy then certainly in practice. While this endorsement of cultural diversity has shaped institutional and disciplinary identities, these institutions and disciplines have also been shaped by larger social contexts.

EDUCATION AND LITERACY: AN INSTITUTIONAL HISTORY

Although education and literacy have been linked since the fifth century BCE in Athens, contemporary understandings emerged in the Enlightenment, which has been characterized by some as an educational movement (Graff 1987). In part, these understandings presumed a link between schooling and moral and social improvement, as well as a concern with citizenship training after the emergence of national states, that purportedly could integrate diverse societies without losing social and economic differences. Established by the end of the nineteenth century, these understandings, which dominated the twentieth century, consisted of creating a common culture rooted in the moral and later moral-political economies of literacy as a means to social homogeneity, and these approaches to education and literacy replaced local routines and rhythms with new social values, including punctuality, regularity, docility, and order (173–175).

Such efforts, in personal and political forms, are clearly evident throughout the history of the United States where the colonial (1780s) and early national (1780–1880s) periods were characterized by the relationship between citizenship and print, particularly newspapers. During these periods, reading and writing were considered to be essential features of self-government and civic responsibilities, which together constituted the ideal citizen. Although only one aspect of literate culture in the nineteenth century, this particular literacy and its relation to national identity, as embodied for example in Benjamin Franklin, reflect Enlightenment beliefs that humans are reasoning creatures and that writing is a means to and a representation of reason (Collins and Blot 2003, 74–76). At the same time, literacy was often identified by religious leaders as a means to spiritual salvation, as a way of imposing religious and social values upon individuals (Soltow and Stevens 1981, 11). Throughout this period, the purpose and meaning of literacy were defined not only by this tradition of evangelical Protestantism but also a literacy ideology within "a Victorian commitment to modernization" throughout U.S. culture that eventually produced the common school in the United States (25).

Along with expanded voting rights in the United States at the end of the nineteenth century came increasing concerns about the values of the working class and the poor, which were addressed by a proposal for public education for both the wealthy and the poor (Collins and Blot 2003, 78–79). To ensure social unity, certain prohibitions, such as discussions about politics and religion, were institutionalized within schools where competing literacies—an upper- and middle-class literacy often associated with lyceums and acquired at private schools, in families, and within churches, and a working-class literacy often learned at work, in families, and within emerging labor institutions—were reconfigured in complicated combinations of Enlightenment beliefs about personal growth, education, and social justice, as well as control of the working class and the poor. As a result, the symbolic form of national identity shifted from direct participation and civic ideals to the consumption and production of a distinctly U.S. American literature (76–78).

In this way, institutionalized literacy instruction reinforced social stratification throughout the United States. By 1870, this socialization was primary the responsibility of common schools, and the combination of passionate nationalism, Protestant morality, and capitalist ethics, driven by newspaper publishers and editors and educational reformers targeting both homes and schools, had established literacy as a "cultural imperative" throughout the United States (Soltow and Stevens 1981, 91). Although literacy rates were strongly correlated with nativity, ethnicity, and occupation until 1850, the differences between native and foreign-born men had largely been eliminated by 1870 while women and ethnic minorities still significantly lagged at least until the end of the nineteenth century (193–201). In general, women were permitted to read, listen to others read, or be lectured to but were restricted to the private sphere and prohibited from participating in public speech or print, and ethnic minorities were denied access to education and literacy altogether although some, despite the criminalization of literacy instruction, taught themselves to read and write (e.g., Frederick Douglass).

Throughout the modern national period (1880s–1960s), significant social shifts—from a more democratic to a more hierarchical society with the emergence of debates about social mobility and meritocracies—are accompanied by shifts in education and literacy—from common schooling to individualized, tracked education based upon sorting and ranking (education) and from a civic-moral necessity to an economic, autonomous skills with a standard language (literacy), in part the result of the legislation of monolingual English in education and government in response to massive labor migrations (1880s–1920s), the organization of English studies in response to the expansion of secondary education (1890s), and an attention to language education in response to internal migrations from rural to urban settings (1910s–1950s). While women were increasingly permitted access to public education and public literacies throughout this period, ethnic minorities continued to be systematically excluded well into the twentieth century (e.g., Richard Wright).

In addition to serving social stratification, education and literacy in the United States have also confronted issues of cultural identity. Since its declaration of independence from Great Britain, the United States has promoted a belief in a distinct (U.S.) American identity, yet as early as 1782, Hector St. John Crèvecoeur, in his *Letters from an American Farmer*, questioned the relation of national and cultural identities in this diverse state, and these tensions reappear in debates over education and language throughout U.S. history, as seen, for example, in the bilingual education demands of German immigrants in the nineteenth century or the Americanization initiatives within schools in the early twentieth century (D. Baron 1990, 154–163). After World War I, the educational goal of Americanization initiatives was expanded to include patriotism and cognition—good English made good Americans and good thinkers—and both native and nonnative English-speaking students were ignored in the development of curricula and the training of teachers, who were largely monolingual English users with no exposure to English instruction to nonnative English-speaking students (150–162).[4] As forms of cultural colonialism, U.S. schools promoted English proficiencies both at home and abroad: English was required in schools throughout the U.S. Southwest and in Puerto Rico and the Philippines where English Only educational requirements were eventually rejected, at least officially while these expectations remain highly

---

4. Others have criticized similar assumptions about the native monolingual in composition studies (e.g., Matsuda 2006;Trimbur 2008).

politicized issues for both schools and communities in the United
States (164–170).

This account of the social and cultural function of education, literacy,
and language provides a relevant historical context for NEIU, one that
is acknowledged by NEIU's President Sharon K. Hahs (2007b) in her
inaugural address. Although lengthy, this excerpt illustrates her sense
of the institutional history and mission, particularly as these are situated
within larger social contexts:

> Today in this lovely, modern setting it takes some imagination to appreciate
> the rich history of Northeastern. One hundred and forty years ago, in 1867, a
> group of visionary civic leaders in Chicago—people whose names are largely
> lost to us today—decided that Chicago needed a teachers college—or to use
> the 19th century term—a normal school. It was a time of uncertainty and
> great opportunity. The nation had just survived what remains even today the
> most deadly war in history—a war where its very existence was at issue. Illinois
> had given much to the war—thousands of soldiers, the general who led the
> Union to victory, and the president who defined the nation for succeeding
> generations. Chicago was then, as now, one of the most dynamic cities in
> America. It had been barely two years since the war ended; the president who
> inspired the nation was dead. The nation, though wounded, was in the pro-
> cess of a great transformation—the Industrial Revolution. Chicago attracted
> entrepreneurs and immigrants. Then, as now, people of vision realized that
> education was essential to the nation's progress. Education required teach-
> ers. What we know today at Northeastern began as an experimental teachers
> college, Cook County Normal School, in Blue Island, Illinois.
>
> Over the years the name would change, the location would change, the
> mission would change, but the commitment to learning and teaching would
> continue from generation to generation. In 1961 what was, by then, called
> Chicago Teachers College North moved from the Sabin School to this beau-
> tiful site. We achieved university status a decade later, in 1971, and became
> what we are called today, Northeastern Illinois University. The University has
> not only changed and grown, but it has expanded to address specific urban
> needs. In 1966, we established our Carruthers Center for Inner City Studies
> as an important expression of our commitment to inner city communities
> and especially our African American community; just three years later, in
> 1969, we established El Centro campus with a special focus on service to
> the large, diverse, and growing Latino community; in 1978 we founded the
> Chicago Teachers' Center, offering professional development programs for
> urban teachers and administrators; and in 1996 we joined the University
> Center of Lake County as a founding member of a consortium of public
> and private universities offering college-level coursework in Lake County. To
> complete the picture, this mix of essentially urban locations and partnerships

also includes the acres of unspoiled Illinois prairie land, it is located just south of Chicago—a beautiful preserve for future generations to learn from and enjoy.

This rich history tracks the dynamic growth of the city and the region. While keeping faith with its original mission—to provide an important resource for students from Illinois—today Northeastern attracts students from all over the world and is poised to become a model of regional public education with a truly global mission. (2007b)

This account of NEIU provides a chronological outline that highlights three periods—the origins of the institution in relation to Chicago Public Schools (CPS); its transformation into a state university; and its acquisition of its current institutional identity—that are central moments in its evolution from a teachers college after the U.S. Civil War into the most ethnically diverse university in the Midwest. Each of these moments acknowledges the impact of historical and social contexts upon the institution as it exists today.

THE ORIGINS OF THE INSTITUTION

Since its inception in the nineteenth century, this institution has been connected, officially and unofficially, to the Chicago Public Schools (CPS) system, which is widely known for its problems and possibilities (e.g., Kozol 1991, 40–82; Rose 1995, 135–192). Throughout the nineteenth century, the CPS system was a place where educational reformers worked to improve educational conditions throughout Chicago, and by the time this institution (the one that would become NEIU) was established, as the Cook County Normal School, in 1867, Chicago had a public school system that resembled other large cities across the country (Rury 2005a). As a result of state legislation in 1872, public education in Chicago, with an enrollment that was increasing faster than the population of the city, was to be supervised by a board of education with members appointed by the mayor.

Over the next thirty years as this institution emerged, the CPS system faced numerous cultural challenges, including demands from German immigrants for German education, competition from private, mostly Catholic, schools, and objections from citizens, again mostly Catholic, to reading the Protestant Bible in classes. Although some classes were taught in German as a result of the largest non-English speaking ethnic group in the city, the CPS system was charged, as the *Chicago Tribune*

explained in 1886, the same year of the Haymarket affair, with the
obligation "to teach loyalty, love of country, and devotion to American
principles and institutions" through U.S. American history and civics
courses. While Jane Addams helped to educate thousands of immigrants
at Hull House as did others at other settlement houses that typically
included classes for adults, these efforts were officially linked to CPS in
1918 when Frances Wetmore relocated her classes from the University of
Chicago settlement to the CPS system where she had been appointed to
administer "Americanization" education for the public schools, an effort
that continued in Chicago throughout the Depression as a result of the
Works Progress Administration (Rury 2005a).

At this point, the connection between CPS and this institution was
clearly established. Through the 1940s, those who wanted to work in
CPS were expected to have graduated from this institution—Cook
County Normal School—where tenure for its faculty was obtained in the
same way as it was in CPS: after a probationary period, applicants had
to complete a written exam created and administered by the Chicago
Board of Education, and those who passed the written exam then had to
complete an oral exam before a committee chosen by the Board, which
if successful would result in the title of *certified teacher*, tantamount to tenure in the CPS system (Frederick 1978, 7–8).

In these and other ways, education in Chicago reflected larger tensions across the country (e.g., Aronowitz 2008, 23–24). On the one
hand, CPS was governed by a state school code that explicitly connected
English instruction and national identity, and the Americanization
efforts of CPS spanned the first two of three significant English-Only
movements—the 1880s - 1890s and World War I (D. Baron 1990, 113).
On the other hand, Chicago had acquired a national reputation by the
twentieth century as a center for progressive education reform, not only
with Francis Parker, a leader in progressive education who believed in
educating the whole child and having a strong language background,
as principal of the Cook County Normal School, and John Dewey at the
University of Chicago Laboratory School but also others in the city and
suburbs who created experimental curricula, linked schools to communities, and established teachers' councils for professional development
(Rury 2005a).

In addition to reflecting national trends in education, Chicago specifically and Illinois generally also reflected national debates over language
and identity. With its mix of industrial and rural, Illinois is, according

to Dennis Baron (1990), representative of language debates throughout the United States, and by privileging English but recognizing other languages, Illinois has been, he argues, more "tolerant" than other states (112–113, 117). At the same time, ethnolinguistic minorities have always posed challenges to the state (Judd 2004).

In particular, its long history of legal intervention in language policies only reinforces issues of identity politics. For example, Chicago decreed in 1867 that official notices must be published in other languages, but this requirement was overturned by the Illinois Supreme Court in 1891. As early as 1889, Illinois required English as the language of instruction in all public and parochial schools, which provoked "a nativist reaction" that fragmented the state (D. Baron 1990, 119). When the state, in 1923, passed one of the first language laws in the country, it designated its official language as *American*, and while legislators, in 1969, revised state law from the nationally and even internationally popular *American* to *English*, its message about sanctioned and authorized identities is nonetheless clear.

These messages become all the more meaningful in light of larger social and cultural conflicts throughout the metro Chicago area. At the end of the nineteenth and the beginning of the twentieth centuries, the Chicago Public School system was beset by controversies, from attacks by the mayor over anti-American textbooks to widespread graft and corruption, that led to an investigation in the 1940s by the National Education Association, which resulted in the threat of sanctions. In an attempt to address these problems, state legislators expanded the power of the CPS administrators, which signaled the beginning of a new era within CPS (Rury 2005a).

In the midst of these educational innovations and cultural conflicts, the social function of Chicago Normal School was also changing. When it officially changed its name in 1938 to Chicago Teachers Center, it was the only tuition-free four-year institution in the city, and it offered bachelor's degrees in education and received North Central Accreditation in 1940. As a result of overcrowding, the Chicago Board of Education opened two branches in 1949 on the north side of Chicago—Foreman and Sabin—that over time expanded its scope. For example, the day students at Sabin, according to a faculty member who taught there, were working-class Irish, Polish, Italian, German, Czech, Greek, and Jewish while the night students were mostly CPS teachers who wanted advanced degrees or additional credits for salary increases and promotions (Frederick 1978).

At the same time, the institution was being reformed by faculty who, for example, lobbied for a faculty ranking system, elected a faculty council, and opened a local chapter of American Association of University Professors (AAUP) even as some, particularly those who were products of the University of Chicago, collaborated on interdisciplinary projects and instruction (Frederick 1978, 16–19). These efforts were motivated in part by rumors that the institution would relocate to a new north-side location and become an independent college. Eventually, these rumors became reality, and in 1961, both sites were closed when a new facility, constructed at the site of the NEIU main campus, was opened. Renamed as Chicago Teachers College-North (CTC-North), this new institution had been established by the Chicago Board of Education, with support from the Ford Foundation, primarily to prepare CPS teachers (Sachs 1987; Sochen 2005).

As initially conceived, this new institution, as a "monument" to CPS Superintendent Ben Willis, was to be interdisciplinary and innovative, and Roy N. Jervis was selected to oversee the transformation from a teachers college to an independent institution. According to faculty who witnessed this transformation, this vision—both the plans for curricular interdisciplinarity and the promise of increased salaries—was initially innovative and inspiring even by standards today. For example, it would feature a four-course sequence in comparative world cultures, and it would have multilingual instructors who provided instruction not in scholarly languages, such as German and French, but in those more often used, including Spanish, Russian, and Chinese, as well as Portuguese, Hindi, and Swahili. In this new institution, communication instruction would be based upon structural linguistics and separate from literary study, in part because Jervis distrusted traditional English Departments (Frederick 1978, 21–24).

As redesigned, this new institution was organized around five divisions—the study of society and the institutions of man; the study of interpersonal communication of ideas; the study of human personality; the study of natural science; and the professional education of elementary school teachers—that, according to faculty who were involved in this transformation, reflected larger social and political issues, from *Brown v. Board of Education* to the post-Sputnik era. At the same time, the students were more diverse—increasingly from the north side of Chicago and the north and west suburbs, not exclusively female, and better prepared.

However, faculty and administrators suspected, even before the end of the initial year, that Jervis would resign as a result of health issues, which happened in the first summer after the reconfiguration, and this administrative position became a shared position consisting of three administrators although one—Jerome M. Sachs—assumed primary responsibilities. An organizer of a union of experimental institutions that included Antioch, Sarah Lawrence, and Goddard, Sachs insisted that CTC-North would continue its commitment to innovation and excellence even though he, unlike Jervis, encouraged the direct participation of faculty, who wrote the first of several faculty constitutions and eventually revised the promotion process. In these and other ways, Sachs and the faculty transformed this institution into a more traditional institution with departments and majors and with more and, according to some, better students (Frederick 1978).

THE SHIFT TO A STATE SCHOOL

From its inception, this institution had a distinct mission to serve the Chicago Public Schools system, and it was shaped by Chicago and Illinois in ways that were consistent with larger debates about education and literacy across the country.

These years—the early to middle 1960s—were the golden years of the institution, according to one faculty member who witnessed them, as it developed an identity as a small, comprehensive institution with excellent faculty, a growing library, and quality students (Frederick 1978, 42–44). At the same time, these were not particularly good years for CPS, which was experiencing conflicts, including civil unrest, over social inequalities throughout the system. For example, more and more criticized the use of portable buildings—called Willis Wagons after CPS Superintendent Ben Willis—for overcrowded African American schools, and many throughout Chicago organized sit-ins, marches, and boycotts to challenge these conditions. When external reports recommended drastic measures to resolve these and other educational inequalities, Willis dismissed their conclusions as unnecessary interference by professional educators (Rury 2005b).

In addition, these years were not particularly good for some at CTC-North. For example, Angelina Pedroso, a Cuban-born lawyer from the University of Havana who had earned two degrees in Chicago, was informed in 1965 that she had been selected to interview for a tenure-track position. However, she was told in her interview with the Chicago

Board of Education, according to Pedroso, that she was unqualified to be a professor at a U.S. university, and she was given a pencil and paper and told to take dictation. After she successfully transcribed the alphabet, one of her interviewers complained that someone had taught her to read and write, and then her application portfolio was tossed into the air, at which point she was told to gather the contents from the floor. As Pedroso explained, she resolved not to cry, and in the end, she obtained the position, becoming one of the first Latino faculty at the school, and she held it until 2010 (see also Cruz 2007, 175–176).

Throughout this time, the relationship between this institution and CPS system was increasingly strained. For example, faculty openly discussed their desires to shift from the Chicago Board Education, particularly a superintendent who opposed racial desegregation of CPS, to the State of Illinois, which was a part of the larger vision to transform from a teachers college to a traditional university. Although the Illinois Board of Higher Education (IBHE), in 1964, recommended the acquisition by the state, Willis resisted this recommendation because, he claimed, it would increase the costs for students who wanted to become teachers (Sachs 1987, 25). In spite of his resistance, the recommendation was approved by the Chicago Board of Education a year later, and negotiations among the Board, the Board of Governors of State Colleges, state legislators, and the governor changed CTC-North into Illinois Teachers College-Chicago North with Sachs selected, reportedly without consultation or even warning, as its first president (Frederick 1978, 45–46).[5]

As the new president, Sachs declared his intention to preserve the history of innovation, such as the student exchange programs in the 1960s with the University of Puerto Rico and an Israeli kibbutz (Sachs 1987, 81). At the same time, he intentionally chose not to imitate other institutions but to commit to solving problems of urban education and to providing access for students with "educational deficiencies" (82). With Sachs as the new president, the institution was shaped over the next decade by campus controversies, from protests over tenure decisions he made to even a personal attack on him by the Weathermen shortly after their Chicago riot and coordinated with their Chicago trial (63–76).[6]

---

5. For more, see Sachs (1987).
6. One of the students who was arrested as part of the attack on Sachs was later identified, in the trial of the Chicago Seven, as an undercover police officer who had

In addition to being shaped by these challenges, the institution expanded its campuses and curriculum in a concerted effort to establish socially relevant education. In 1966, it opened the Center for Inner City Studies to prepare teachers for minority and disadvantaged communities, and after adding degree programs for secondary teachers and in other disciplines, it was renamed in 1967 as Northeastern Illinois State College. Shortly thereafter, it opened El Centro, a satellite campus to serve Latino communities in Chicago, and it was renamed after gaining university status in 1971 to Northeastern Illinois University.

Together, this leadership and these expansions led to the addition of support programs, in part a response to complaints from ethnic minority students that the institution was failing to meet their needs. In response to these criticisms of the administration and the institution, Sachs offered to cancel classes in order to hold a series of discussions on a range of topics that, from his perspective, not only provided an alternative to violence on college campuses across the country but also "restored the college's experimental attitude" (Sachs 1987, 76). At that time, one faculty member who had been using Chomsky to teach students with limited English proficiencies was recruited by one of her students for this "weird world of student advocacy" in support of the institutionalization of support programs, including Project Success and Proyecto Pa'Lante and the English Language Program, which existed in a reciprocal relationship: the programs would recruit students, and these students, as this former faculty member explained, knew how to use the programs.

In many ways, these efforts, she maintained, reflected larger political issues across the country. For example, these students, energized by the Open Admissions movement, clamored for greater access, and as the United States became increasingly involved in Vietnam, more Vietnamese students appeared on campus. However, these efforts were not always embraced by the institution in spite of its commitment to access and innovation, as seen, for example, in the history of Proyecto Pa'Lante. When a group of Puerto Rican students advocated for both a Puerto Rican counselor and a special recruitment program, campus administrators responded by explaining that a minority recruitment program already existed. However, these students insisted upon their own program, which eventually led to the formation of Proyecto

applied for reinstatement as an NEIU student after the trial, but Sachs insisted that the student had to finish the year of suspension for occupying the president's office.

Pa'Lante with Maximino De Jesus Torres, whom the students selected, as its first director (Cruz 2007, 109).[7]

Despite these difficulties, the institution has provided opportunities for students, as this situation also illustrates. Although Torres initially intended to be a Catholic priest, he left the seminary and, in 1952, came to Chicago to work as a laborer. After being discharged from the Air Force, Torres attended NEIU when it still was a teachers college where, by his own estimation, he was one of three Latinos, and the first Puerto Rican, to graduate. At first, he taught in Catholic and public elementary schools, and then he returned to NEIU to assume responsibility for Proyecto Pa'Lante, as well as to advise the Union of Puerto Rican Students (UPRS). According to Torres, many of these students had been rejected by the institution and, as a result, had to attend a junior college. Motivated by these experiences and by larger political movements, the Puerto Rican students argued that the institution could better serve the needs of Latino students in the metro Chicago area with a special program that would admit approximately one hundred students each year and support them to graduation (Cruz 2007, 109).

As such, this proposal was a part of larger efforts of the UPRS, which, in addition to sponsoring cultural events on campus, also lobbied for more Latino faculty and more support programs in math, reading, and English, which shaped the institution in significant ways. For example, these efforts led to the hiring of Samuel Betances, a Harvard-educated sociologist, who joined Pedroso, Torres, and others. However, these efforts had mixed results. On the one hand, an increasingly politicized UPRS attacked these faculty throughout the 1970s—negative articles in the UPRS-published newspaper, boycotts of their classes, and confrontations on and off campus, and eventually several UPRS students were linked to the Armed Forces of National Liberation, a group advocating armed resistance to the presence of the United States in Puerto Rico, with one of them eventually testifying against the others. On the other, these faculty had long careers at NEIU—Torres retired from PP and NEIU after twenty years; Betances recently retired from active teaching and currently lives, as an emeritus professor, only a few blocks from campus, and Pedroso taught Spanish for more than forty years until she retired in 2010.

---

7. A similar situation exists today in the debate over a cultural center. Some students insist upon a Latino cultural center at this Hispanic-serving institution while administrators insist upon a multicultural center at this most ethnically diverse university in the Midwest.

Despite the different outcomes, these efforts contributed to the institutionalization of academic support programs, such as Proyecto Pa'Lante (PP) and the English Language Program (ELP). At least initially, PP and ELP had a close relationship, according to one faculty member who collaborated on the formation of both and other education and literacy initiatives on campus. In particular, PP wanted courses to prepare its students, and the English Department offered little support for students whose English was limited. At the same time, other factors, according to some, contributed to these conditions. For example, the first ELP Coordinator had previously been denied tenure in the English Department, and his successor served one or two terms before leaving this academic support program to become English Department Chair. While others were hired, at that point, to contribute to ELP, these tenure-track appointments were split between ELP, which remained an academic support program, and an academic department, either Linguistics or English, for evaluation of performance for tenure and promotion.

Even as administrators, faculty, and students were responding to social and political events in the 1960s and 1970s, the institution was also acting in response to its own needs, as illustrated for example by an anecdote from the inauguration of Sachs as the first president of the newly formed state institution. According to a faculty member who witnessed the institutional transformations, these inaugural events, filled with academic ceremonies, were attended by various dignitaries, including Paul Stone, a downstate legislator and Board of Governors Chair who helped negotiate the transfer of supervision from the Chicago Board of Education to the State of Illinois. During a reception, this faculty member mentioned his hopes for the future as a state institution, and as he explains, Stone responded that its current challenge was increasing the number of students it served, which would be central to its success. Although this faculty member, as he recounts the event, was troubled at the time, he only realized the implications over the next years as, in his words, the institution changed, "fundamentally and permanently" for the worse (Frederick 1978, 47).

At the very least, the institution had acquired an ongoing problem, in which, as one faculty member explained, first-generation students who graduated from NEIU often sent their children elsewhere for college. Around the same time as it became a state university, the institution opened satellite campuses—the Center for Inner City Studies and El Centro—and an available solution could be found in the metro

Chicago community, particularly the large pool of immigrants who came to the city. For example, the main campus is located in what were the leading port of entry neighborhoods throughout the 1980s, which had only shifted slightly to the south and east by 2000 (Paral and Norkewicz 2003, 14).

Unlike many metropolitan areas in the South and West, the metro Chicago area has largely been settled by the "foreign-born" (Paral and Norkewicz 2003).[8] By the 1850s, the metro area had 40,000 immigrants, which had increased to more than 500,000 in 1890. At first, these immigrants largely came from northern and western Europe, particularly Germany (161,000) and Ireland (70,000), but by the 1880s, they increasingly came from eastern and western Europe, including Russia (122,000) and Italy (45,000) by 1910. While immigration was nearly halted by federal restrictions in the 1920s for fourty years, it quickly resumed in 1965 after new national legislation ended quota systems for particular groups and extended visas without national preferences. On the one hand, these new conditions reinvigorated Polish immigration in the 1990s, which had been a characteristic of the area for 100 years. On the other, it encouraged immigration from other parts of the world, including Asia, the Pacific Islands, and Africa, as seen for example by the increase in Indian immigrants from 600 in 1960 to almost 77,000 in 2000 (4).

Although a diversity of immigration has been a defining feature, the metro Chicago area has also been shaped specifically by a long presence of Mexican and Puerto Rican populations. In the 1880s, the Mexican consulate was established in Chicago, and by the 1920s, this area was considered to have the largest Mexican population beyond the Southwest. Many Mexican immigrants came to Chicago to fill gaps created by those who left to fight in World War I, and unlike other immigrants, Mexicans were not subject to the same restrictions in the twentieth century. Over time, the number of Mexican immigrants increased from 24,000 in 1960 to 582,000 in 2000 (Paral and Norkewicz 2003, 4). At the same time, thousands of Puerto Ricans came to Chicago between the 1950s and the 1970s in ways that reflected the complicated economic and political relations between the United States and Puerto Rico (Paral, Ready, Chun, and Sun 2004, 23; Del Valle 2002). Today,

---

8.   Paral and Norkewicz (2003) use the U.S. Census Bureau definition of complete metro areas, which in this case includes the following counties: Cook, DeKalb, DuPage, Grundy, Kane, Kankakee, Kendal, Lake, McHenry, and Will in Illinois; Lake and Porter in Indiana; and Kenosha in Wisconsin (8).

the metro Chicago area is considered to have one of the largest populations of Mexicans and Puerto Ricans in the country that coexist though
not without tensions (De Genova and Ramos-Zayas 2003; Guzmán 2001;
Morales 2002, 222–223).

In these and other ways, immigration has shaped the metro Chicago
area throughout the twentieth century. Although the number of immigrants in the region had declined from one million in the 1930s, it
increased throughout the 1990s by 61 percent to a record total in 2000
of 1.4 million from more than 1,000 countries and all the major regions
of the world. By 2000, immigrants constituted nearly two in ten residents
throughout the region—more than two in ten in Chicago and between
one and two in ten in the suburbs—with the largest groups from Mexico
(582,000), Poland (138,000), and India (77,000). Of these 1.4 million
immigrants, nearly five in ten came from Latin America, which is nearly
the same as those from Europe and Asia combined. Altogether, these
trends and conditions made the metro Chicago area fifth in the nation
in terms of the number of foreign-born people and ninth in the percentage of foreign-born populations (Paral and Norkewicz 2003, 3,6, 8–9).

In many ways, the metro Chicago area reflects larger conditions
across the country:

A Juxtaposition of the United States and Metro Chicago (2006)

	United States (n=299,398,485)	Metro Chicago (n=9,506,859)	Latinos in the United States (n=44,254,278)	Latinos in Metro Chicago (n=1,828,296)
Sex and Age				
male (%)	49.2	49.2	51.7	52.6
female (%)	50.8	50.8	48.3	47.4
median age	36.4	35.3	27.3	26.6
18 to 61 (%)	75.4	73.9	66.2	65.1
62 years and over (%)	15.1	13.3	06.7	05.0
Immigration				
non US-born (%)	12.5	17.8	40.0	43.5
entered after 1990 (%)	55.8	56.5	60.1	58.3
Income				
median house-hold ($)	48,451	57,008	38,747	44,562
poverty rate (%)	9.8	9.0	19.3	15.9

Language				
only English (%)	80.3	71.8	21.6	15.7
other languages (%)	19.7	28.2	78.4	84.3
English < very well (%)	08.7	12.8	39.1	43.1
Education				
hi school grad (%)	84.1	84.6	60.2	58.5
college grad (%)	27.0	31.6	12.3	10.8

Source: American Community Survey, U.S. Census Bureau (2006)

Although, at first glance, the metro Chicago area seems to resemble the rest of the country, it does differ from other large metropolitan areas with significant Latino concentrations. Generalizations about Latinos are complicated (e.g., J. González 2000), but some, such as cultural critic Ed Morales (2002), have suggested a collective identity, or *Spanglish*, that is not only characteristic of Chicago, which, Morales suggests, brings together east coast and west coast Spanglish culture, but also can also lead the way to reconcile differences among distinctly different cultural identities across the United States (223).

While immigration has shaped the metro Chicago area, it is only part of a larger ethnic diversity across the region, including African Americans and others, that resembles the ethnic diversity across the country. Even though, for example, Cook County, which includes Chicago, lost more than 33,000 African Americans along with 200,000 non-Hispanic whites between 2000 and 2006, it still has the largest African American population in the country, and it reported a 12 percent increase in Latinos (130,000).[9] Across the country, ethnic minorities surpassed 100 million—nearly a third of the population—for the first time in 2006, primarily as a result of higher birth rates and immigration rates among African Americans and Latinos; in fact ethnic minorities are the majority in one in ten counties across the country[10]—and ethnic minorities, according the U.S. Census Bureau, will constitute half of all U.S. residents by 2050 (Little 2007; Ohlemacher 2007).

---

9.   In fact, every Illinois county except one reported an increase in Latinos since 2000 (Little 2007).

10.   The headline, however, is, "Whites Now Minority in 1 in 10 Counties" (Ohlemacher 2007).

THE ACQUISITION OF AN INSTITUTIONAL IDENTITY

In many ways, the longstanding relationship between this institution and the city persisted throughout its transformation from a teachers college to a state institution. Shaped by social and educational forces both nationally and locally, the institution needed numbers while the students demanded support. In part, collecting numbers aided ethnic minorities specifically, who could obtain access through special admission programs such as Project Success (primarily for African American students) or Proyecto Pa'Lante (primarily for Latino students). At the same time, these results also provided potential benefits for all NEIU students, who could receive support from the Reading Program or the English Language Program (ELP).

In other ways, the institutional history shaped, and continues to shape, the educational experiences of ethnic minorities and their institutional peers. For example, the institutional reconfiguration inaugurated by Jervis and continued by Sachs required no required introductory writing course through the 1980s, and only when the English Department started to lose the race for majors to education and business, according to a faculty member with a joint appointment in ELP and English, did it begin to address the topic of writing instruction. In 1991–1992, the English Department Chair, who had initially been hired as the ELP Coordinator, and the Arts and Sciences Dean proposed the first writing requirement.

At the time, ELP faculty, especially those who had participated in the transformations of the 1970s, were hesitant to endorse such a requirement because, according to one, they were unsure about the way that nonnative English-speaking students would be treated in the English Department. In the end, they decided to support a single-semester requirement and to reassess the situation later, at which point they would decide whether to support a second required semester.

As a result, the English Department Chair hired three full-time instructors to teach introductory writing courses in the English Department—such courses, though not required, had been assigned elsewhere by Jervis—and in the words of another colleague, the unofficial writing program expanded from ELP to include English. Over time, a second required semester was added by the Colleges of Business and Education but not by the College of Arts and Sciences, which remains the requirements today—those who major in business or education must complete two introductory writing courses while those who major in arts and sciences must only complete one.

At the same time, the impact of this institutional history is bigger than required courses. Between ELP and English exists, in the words of a former ELP Coordinator, a "comfortable gap," in which ELP, according to English, fails to prepare students for college writing, and English, according to ELP, is unclear about its expectations.[11] In part, these differences are disciplinary, which are similar to conditions elsewhere (e.g., Matsuda 1999; Phillips, Stewart, and Stewart 2006). Nonetheless, these distinctions, and the institutional history that produced them, can still be seen: ELP is a support program that, though perceived to be supportive of students, nonetheless lacks the institutional power of a degree-granting department. At the same time, these differences pose additional problems for the students, especially those who are placed into ELP, and for the institution, particularly in terms of coherent educational and literacy philosophies.

Even as ethnic diversity, in terms of concerns about treatment within English, shaped institutional requirements and educational experiences, it was also reshaping the institution generally. In addition to increasing its ethnic diversity generally, the institution acquired the official status as a Hispanic-Serving Institution (HSI), which, according to the first ELP Coordinator, was one of his most important contributions to the campus (Center 2007c).

In the 1980s, the HSI designation was established after discussions among educational leaders and policymakers discovered that nearly half of all Latinos were enrolled in approximately 6 percent of U.S. postsecondary institutions, and that HSI status, as originally defined in Title V of the Higher Education Act, is a designation awarded to accredited and nonprofit higher-educational institutions with 25 percent or more of their full-time undergraduate enrollment as Hispanic. In academic year 2005–2006, the number of HSI institutions had increased from 234 in 2003–2004 to 252 with an additional 67 that had Hispanic enrollments between 20.0 percent and 24.4 percent. In general, NEIU resembles other HSIs—most are urban, and many are part of the public education system—with the exception that unlike the majority that are community colleges, NEIU is a four-year institution—the only one, in fact, of the

11. This "gap" was one of the concerns identified in the recently funded proposal for a campuswide writing initiative, but based upon discussions and observations, little has been done, several years later, to address it.

nine HSIs, along with the five emerging HSIs, in Illinois, all of which are located in the metro Chicago area (Santiago 2008).

The definition of an HSI has been debated across the country, within composition studies, and on our campus (e.g., Allen 2006; Kirklighter, Cárdenas, and Murphy 2007; López 2007b). At NEIU, HSI status, according to the NEIU President (Hahs 2007a), is best understood as a "mosaic in progress" that remains to be assembled into "a coherent and beautiful design" that consists not only of the federal designation and enrollment percentages but also

- membership in the Hispanic Association of Colleges and Universities (HACU), including the reception of its 2007 Outstanding HACU Member Institution Award;

- academic support programs, such as *Proyecto Pa'Lante*, which was identified as a program of excellence by ¡Excelencia! in Education, and ENLACE, which supports Latinos who are study-ing educational leadership in graduate school;

- the El Centro campus that targets Latinos and offers a curricu-lum that includes a minor in Latino and Latin American studies;

- a faculty with almost one in 10 (9 percent) tenured or tenure track Hispanic; and

- a graduation rate for full-time Latinos who started at NEIU (18.6 percent) that is equivalent to that of the general student popula-tion at NEIU (18.5 percent).

However, this HSI designation, for some, is "misleading" because it sug-gests that the institution is invested in Latino students (López 2007b).

Although some can debate what the HSI designation means or should mean, none could disagree that it has been beneficial to the institution. For example, this designation has allowed the institution to compete for federal Title V funds, which are only available to HSIs, that were used in 2000 to establish the Center for Teaching and Learning that offers numerous faculty development workshops and programs and is respon-sible for the Blackboard technology provided for every course on cam-pus. Even as data were still being collected for this study, the institution was awarded $2.8 million in 2007 to revise its first-year writing program and to implement required writing-intensive courses, as well as to estab-lish a Center for Academic Literacy.

At the same time, this HSI designation is only part of a larger institutional identity of ethnic diversity, which was nationally recognized in 1997 when *U.S. News and World Report*, in the first year of including ethnic diversity in its America's Best Colleges survey, ranked NEIU as the most (ethnically) diverse (master's) university in the Midwest. In many ways, this condition has become part of an institutional identity, as seen, for example, in official statements:

> Northeastern Illinois University, as a public comprehensive university with locations throughout Chicago, provides an exceptional environment for learning, teaching, and scholarship. We prepare a *diverse* community of students for leadership and service in our region and in a dynamic multicultural world. (Mission Statement; italics mine)

> Northeastern Illinois University will be a leader among metropolitan universities, known for its dedication to its urban mission, for the quality of its programs, for the success of its graduates, and for the *diversity* of its learning environment. (Vision Statement; italics mine)

> *Diversity:* NEIU values the inclusion of a broad spectrum of students, staff, and faculty in the life of the University. We celebrate and foster global perspectives. We encourage the open and respectful expression of ideas and differences in thoughts, experiences, and opinions. (Statement of Values; italics mine)

In addition, *diversity* is cited as a part of the "curricular/pedagogical" dimension of the strategic goals of the institution (NEIU 2008).[12]

Beyond these official statements, *diversity* is recognized by faculty in ways that range from perspectives to practices, as seen for example in these responses to a campuswide survey conducted by the Center for Teaching and Learning (2006):

- I address learning style diversity by requiring different kinds of assignments—group work, oral presentation, written reflections, written observation papers.

- I use it [diversity] as a resource for other points of view, other ways of doing things. They often can flesh out with details concepts that I'm presenting in class.

- I always make sure that my readings include multiple perspectives—I don't consider them "special," they are part of my core

---

12. The mission, vision, and values statements, as well as the other elements of the strategic plan, were approved by the NEIU Board of Trustees on September 18, 2008.

curriculum. I think it is vitally important to include the writing
of and about women, lesbians and gays, African Americans,
Latinas, Asians, and others of all genders. In addition, my assignments address issues of diversity.

When asked how they respond to diversity in their curriculum and
classrooms, NEIU faculty indicated that they use group activities (34
percent) and specific reading (21 percent) and writing (19 percent)
assignments while less than one in ten indicated that their classes or disciplines were unsuited for issues relating to diversity.

Beyond describing the present, *diversity* also provides direction for
the future, as indicated by the NEIU President at the end of her 2007
inaugural address:

> Some of you have heard me say that NEIU is the University of the Future.
> Admittedly, it sounds like a catchy phrase. It is a catchy phrase. It is also
> our wonderful reality. This past February I attended a higher Education
> Legislative Briefing in Springfield. At the briefing an Illinois Status Report
> was presented which included a demographic projection of high school grad-
> uates in the year 2018. The projection for the state as a whole 11 years from
> now reads very much like the demographic profile of NEIU's student body
> today. Let me run down the numbers, using the categories from the Report:
>
> - In 2018, Illinois will have roughly 56% white students; today NEIU
>   has 48%;
> - Illinois will have 13% Black students, today NEIU has 11%;
> - Illinois will have 0.4% Native American students; NEIU has 0.3%;
> - Illinois will have 8% Asian Americans; NEIU has 9.5%;
> - and Illinois will have 23% Hispanic students; today NEIU has 25%.
>
> Literally, the future is now at NEIU; we are the University of the Future.
> This is an extraordinary learning environment. A gift.

Given the commitment of the institution to prepare students "for an
active role of leadership in a global community," she asked faculty to
consider an undergraduate global studies major with (ethnic) diversity
at its center:

> It might consist of an appropriate core with a variety of specializations such
> as Latino and Latin American Studies, African and African American Studies,

Asian Studies, languages, the arts, environmental science. The peoples of this world are bound more tightly together today than ever before. Diversity, which for years had a very domestic agenda, has broadened as a concept to include literally the whole world. Few institutions are as prepared to take up diversity as a central tenet of their mission as is Northeastern. In embracing diversity we're not just asserting a goal but proudly affirming a reality. Northeastern is poised to become a major player, by example, in the evolution of American higher education.

As a part of this consideration, she announced that the institution would be seeking private funds for an endowed professorship in global studies, and she explained that the institution had already received its first donation of more than $150,000, in support of this goal (Hahs 2007b).

This sense of potential is also shared by some faculty. For example, a survey of faculty who started at NEIU between 2002 and 2006 and were still working at the institution in 2007 found that the most satisfying experience was working with NEIU students (Center 2007a). When asked for additional comments, one offered the following observation:

> Access to a diverse student body provides an opportunity to develop methods that would be effective for educating this population. NEIU has an opportunity to inform the higher education community about educating a diverse population which is not being realized because we spend too much time counting CUs and not enough time working on creative pedagogies, reading literature about what works, what is known and building on it. Too many people ... do not spend enough time on campus. This is a comprehensive university with many graduate programs. We need to cultivate a culture that supports learning and professional development of students.

In part, this potential is the result of the educational challenges posed by ethnic diversity, which can be seen clearly in terms of language and literacy. For example, a report from the NEIU Language Skills Assessment Task Force (2005) acknowledges these challenges:

> The need is clear. Increasing student diversity, increasing numbers of students for whom English is a second language, decreasing levels of preparation of our entering students, ACT test scores, and extensive data from faculty all point to the need for an approach that does more to prepare for the writing competencies they need to be successful in college and beyond. (NEIU Language, 13, 5).

In a similar way, ethnic diversity generally and the Latino concentration specifically are central to the executive summary of the recent HSI grant:

"IMPROVING RETENTION THROUGH ACADEMIC LITERACY" is proposed for Title V funding at Northeastern Illinois University (NEIU) in Chicago, Illinois for 2007–2012. As a comprehensive, public university, NEIU serves a highly diverse student population that includes a large portion of non-traditional students. First-generation students comprise 80% of all incoming freshmen, 56% of undergraduates attend full-time, and the average age of undergraduates is 26. NEIU's Fall 2006 undergraduate enrollment by ethnicity is 43% Caucasian, 11% African American, 29% Hispanic, 10% Asian, and 0.3% Native American. NEIU is the only public four-year Hispanic Serving Institution (HSI) in the Midwest, with an enrollment of 12,056 students (9,257 undergraduates) in Fall 2006.

This theme continues in the introduction to the proposal, which cites the *U.S. News* ranking, the HSI status, and the metro Chicago area:

Because of its unique location in the Chicago metropolitan area, NEIU serves a population diverse in age, culture, language, and race. This diversity means that academic programs utilize a variety of perspectives to enrich the teaching and learning experiences and to prepare students for the multiculturalism that characterizes our society. The increasingly diverse administrative staff and faculty also demonstrate the commitment to diversity. (NEIU 2007, 1)

Despite this commitment, institutional efforts are limited, the authors of this application suggest, as illustrated by retention and graduation rates. In particular, the 2005 six-year graduation rate (17 percent) is, according to these authors, the lowest among comparable HSIs, the second-lowest among Illinois public institutions, and last among Illinois graduation rates for African Americans, Asians, Latinos, and whites, as well as for all underrepresented students, a condition that is only exacerbated by a transfer-out rate (42 percent) that is the highest among all Illinois public institutions.

These conditions, according to this proposal, are the result of numerous factors: academic underpreparedness generally; poor college preparation in CPS schools; a large population of nontraditional students; a lack of coordination among student-support services, particularly in terms of writing; and a poor performance on the English Competency Exam. Given these, the solution, as proposed in this application, is a campuswide writing initiative to revise the first-year writing program, integrate writing throughout the disciplines, and establish a Center for Academic Literacy. By revising the first-year writing program and providing writing-intensive faculty development, the proposed initiative promises to increase retention rates and improve graduate rates, and it will result in both the enrollment of Hispanic and other low-income students at levels consistent with the community demographic profile and the improvement of their six-year graduation rates (13 percent for Hispanic students in 2005). Finally, it promises to establish "best practice methods" in writing- intensive courses for nonnative English users, as well as students from homes where English is not used, and to implement better coordination with feeder high schools and community colleges for "overcoming basic skill deficiencies," as well as offer appropriate financial aid advising for the resources needed by these students (NEIU 2007, 4–10, 13).

THE MOST ETHNICALLY DIVERSE MASTER'S UNIVERSITY IN THE MIDWEST

While some might question the contribution of additional requirements to retention and graduation rates, most will likely recognize the significance of ethnic diversity to this institution, which emerged in the late nineteenth century as a teachers college for Chicago Public Schools. At the institution today, ethnic diversity not only provides national recognition and additional funds but also affords an explanation for its limited educational efficacy. In these and other ways, ethnic diversity functions as an identity politics that clearly benefits the institution, but what is the impact of identity politics upon its ethnically diverse students?

The answer seems mixed. On the one hand, the institution provides access to many students, primarily from the metro Chicago area, who otherwise might not attend a four-year university. For example, more than nine in ten first-year NEIU students at the start of this project (fall 2004) came from the metro Chicago area. On the other, these students often encounter obstacles to their efforts to earn degrees, as acknowledged by former Illinois State Senator Miguel Del Valle in his opening remarks at a 2006 hearing cosponsored by the Illinois Legislative Latino Caucus and NEIU:

> We all know how important the university is to the City of Chicago and the State of Illinois, but as a Latino and someone who attended this university, I have to tell you that this university holds a special place in my heart as a

Latino because of the contributions it has made over the years to the Latino community and helping individuals like myself develop and assume leadership roles in the community as a result of the skills I was able to attain while attending here, both during my undergraduate and graduate years, so I'm really pleased to be here today.

The reason for his return, and for the hearing, is clear in his conclusion:

> We need Northeastern. Latinos need Northeastern. Latinos have been served by Northeastern in the past. But at a time when we need Northeastern more than ever before, we have a Latino enrollment rate that is not growing, that is stagnant. And we have a completion rate that according to this report is low. And what is the university going to do about that? That's what we hope to hear today. (Illinois 2006)

The report to which Del Valle refers is one from the Consortium on Chicago School Research that documents a substantial gap between the college goals of Chicago Public School students and their actual enrollment and graduation, a gap that, according to this report, is greater for CPS Latino and African American students (Roderick, Nagaoka, and Allensworth 2006, 83, 35).

Although the primary purpose of this report is to document the differences between the goals and achievements of CPS students, it revealed challenges at NEIU where, for example, almost six in ten incoming first-year students at the start of this project (fall 2004) were CPS graduates. According to the authors of the report, nearly two-thirds of the 2002 and 2003 CPS graduates who attended four-year institutions went to one of seven schools—NEIU and UIC, as well as the University of Illinois at Urbana-Champaign (UIUC), Chicago State University (CSU), Northern Illinois University (NIU), Columbia College of Chicago (CC), and Southern Illinois University at Carbondale (SIUC). At these schools, CPS students, the authors argue, likely have different college experiences:

	Institutional Overall Six-Year Graduation Rate	Six-Year Graduation Rate for CPS Students (1998 and 1999)	Six-Year Graduation Rate for Underrepresented Minorities
UIUC (n = 684)	81.0	72	63.8
NIU (n = 508)	52.9	N/A	34.6
UIC (n = 1353)	46.0	48	35.3

SIUC (n = 409)	43.0	N/A	34.8
CC (n = 443)	27.3	21	17.0
NEIU (n = 884)	17.9	13	11.7
CSU (n = 560)	15.2	18	15.2

Source: Roderick, Nagaoka, and Allensworth 2006, 72–73, 19

Of these institutions, only one had a six-year graduation rate above the national average at the time (53 percent) with another at the level of the national average and the remainder below the national average. At the same time, only two institutions—UIC and CSU—had rates for CPS students that were higher than overall institutional rates (Roderick, Nagaoka, and Allensworth 2006, 72–73). Moreover, some institutions seem to struggle regardless of the students they admit:

	CPS Six-Year Graduation Rate for Students with Unweighted GPA of 4.0	CPS Six-Year Graduation Rate for Students with Unweighted GPA of 2.0
UIUC	88	44
UIC	72	14
CC	57	7
CSU	37	7
NEIU	29	5

Source: Allensworth 2006, 4

In other words, CPS students, regardless of their high-school experiences, struggle more at NEIU, and at its sister school (CSU), which together serve significant proportions of Latino and African American students,[13] than they do at other institutions popular among CPS students (Allensworth 2006, 4).[14]

While these results could reflect a number of factors, they nonetheless raise significant questions for an institution that is so connected to the community and that serves ethnic minorities. Unfortunately for NEIU, these questions were asked within a national forum: the graduation rates

13. According to Sachs (1987), NEIU and Chicago State were confronted with the challenge of new names and identities at the same time, but Chicago State had selected its name first. Nonetheless, the relationship between these two institutions, although often overlooked, is significant, insofar that together they serve the largest ethnic minority groups—Latino (NEIU) and African American (Chicago State)—in the metro area and across the country (30–31).

14. Six months after releasing the initial report, the Consortium on Chicago School Research released an update based upon new reporting by institutions. As a result, I cite, as appropriate, the conclusions from the initial report and the data from the update.

of NEIU and CSU, in addition to being featured at the Illinois Legislative Latino Caucus hearing, were reported in *The New York Times*, the *Chicago Tribune*, and other newspapers across the country, and were criticized by national and local figures, such as Jesse Jackson.

In response to this national attention, NEIU and CSU administrators argued that part of the problem is transfer students who, whether transferring to or from, are not considered graduates, and part-time students who obviously need longer to graduate. However, neither transfer nor part-time student numbers can fully explain these graduation rates when comparable institutions, such as CUNY-Lehman College, which has a similar campus ethnic diversity,[15] reportedly has a graduation rate that is twice the rate of NEIU (Finder 2006).[16]

THE EDUCATIONAL CHALLENGES OF ETHNIC DIVERSITY

Clearly, ethnic diversity benefits the institution by providing national recognition and additional funds, as well as an explanation for limited educational results, and yet this ongoing act of identity politics also produces educational challenges for the institution where students struggle, some more than others, to complete their courses and earn their degrees.

Retention and graduation rates have received recent national attention, and researchers have concluded that retention and graduation rates and other outcomes exhibit systematic disparities related to class, ethnicity/race, and gender even when controlling for high- school GPA, ACT/SAT scores, and demographics (Bowen, Chingos, and McPherson 2009, 222–225, 233–235). As such, these results raise questions about social equity that have been central to education and literacy, as Catherine Prendergast (2003) demonstrates, since *Brown v. Board of Education* decisions in the 1950s that required the desegregation of schools across the Unites States.

In many ways, these demands are still relevant, especially at NEIU where so many CPS students come after leaving a socially segregated CPS system. Between 1970 and 1980, the white enrollment in CPS decreased by almost 60 percent as these students increasingly left for parochial or suburban schools, and when desegregation initiatives failed to integrate CPS, the threat of federal intervention resulted in a 1980 consent decree

---

15. In 2007, CUNY-Lehman, according to *U.S. News*, had a campus ethnic diversity of .61 with 51 percent Hispanic students.
16. In response to this report, I argued, in an article for the campus newspaper, that these conditions should not result in lowered expectations but rather realistic reevaluations of literacy and education in the twenty-first century, which reappears in Different Standards, Part I of this book.

and a court-mandated school desegregation plan. However, conditions in CPS continued to deteriorate so much that in 1987 the then U.S. Secretary of Education William Bennett declared CPS as the worst in the country (Rury 2005a). At that time, a coalition of community groups, in conjunction with then Mayor Harold Washington, prepared proposals that, as a result of state legislation in 1988, became the Chicago School Reform Act, which established local school councils, consisting of parents, educators, and community members, for all CPS schools (Rury 2005a). Still, white enrollment decreased 75 percent between 1970 and 1990. In the 1990s, between six and seven in ten (66 percent) of white Chicago students attended private schools, and many of those who remained in CPS attended magnet schools on the north and southwest sides of the city. As a result, CPS is largely African American and, increasingly, Hispanic with between seven and eight in ten (75 percent) in 2000 from low-income families (Rury 2005b).

These social and cultural conditions constitute the backdrop for NEIU, especially given its connections to CPS and the Chicago community where court oversight of both the CPS desegregation consent decree and the CPS bilingual program was recently terminated. In arguments before the court, CPS suggested that rather than race, it might use socioeconomic status for its selective-admission schools although these processes are still being determined.

Regardless, these conditions create numerous challenges for this institution, which are described by the NEIU Center for Teaching and Learning in this way:

> Despite our attribute as the "most diverse university in the Midwest," NEIU has been struggling with effectively utilizing the educational benefits of its diversity. Our academic calendar is marked by many campus events that allow students and faculty to hear about issues of diversity. We have three academic programs with a focus on ethnic and gender diversity. Many of our faculty incorporate diversity issues into their courses. Our new First Year Experience program attempts to integrate a "Diversity in Chicago" theme into every course section. And yet, we still seem to lack an overall concept of how to address diversity at the curricular level as well as translate it into our overall campus climate. Examples of that include:
>
> • Students on campus largely keep to their own ethnic group when socializing in between classes.

- There is a lack of public communication between people from different backgrounds regarding their experience (on or off campus) of disrespect, intolerance, and injustice.

- Many students have little knowledge about what it takes to function effectively in our global society.

- Many students (and probably faculty) are ill-equipped with conflict resolution skills when it comes to sensitive interactions between members of different ethnic and racial groups.

- There is probably little agreement on the university's role in not only helping students acquire critical knowledge but also *acting* on this knowledge and the resulting beliefs and values. (Center 2007b)

Those who attended workshops on diversity and the curriculum offered suggestions for better integrating diversity into the institution, including creating more media coverage of diversity issues and renaming campus buildings for individuals who have promoted cultural diversity. They were encouraged to consider the characteristics of a multicultural curriculum, which was defined as content that accurately represents underrepresented groups and materials that reflect multiple perspectives, as well as having other characteristics, including critical inclusivity, social and civic responsibility, and ongoing assessment (Center 2007b).

While a start, these suggestions conspicuously neglect issues of language and literacy, which are places where educational access and social equity are contested and negotiated. To find any mention of these issues, a NEIU faculty member would first have to use the featured URL to access a Web site entitled 20 (Self-)Critical Things I Will Do to Be a Better Multicultural Educator, and then he or she would have to scroll halfway down the list:

> I will build coalitions with teachers who are different from me (in terms of race, ethnicity, sexual orientation, gender, religion, first language, disability, and other identities). These can be valuable relationships of trust and honest critique. At the same time, I must not rely on other people to identify my weaknesses. In particular, in areas of my identity around which I experience privilege, I must not rely on people from historically underprivileged groups to teach me how to improve myself (which is, in and of itself, a practice of privilege). (Gorski 2008)

And yet such coalitions alone, given the allure of social assimilation and the compulsion of cultural (auto)colonization, cannot guarantee greater educational equity, especially when linguistic discrimination persists as an acceptable proxy for ethinic or economic discrimination (e.g., Milroy and Milroy 1999, 2). However, such conclusions about educational equity, and the contributions of literacy instruction, cannot be reached until the experiences of NEIU students are considered. To these, this account turns.

Appendix

THE PRESIDENT'S COUNCIL
AUGUST 27, 2008

DIVERSITY AT NORTHEASTERN ILLINOIS UNIVERSITY: WHAT IS IT?

During the strategic planning process in the spring and summer of 2008, these questions were frequently asked: What is diversity? What does diversity mean at NEIU? How do we define diversity? Do we have a shared understanding of how significant it is for Northeastern? In consideration of this, the president's council developed this reflection to provide a response to the university community. It serves as a complement to the planning process.

Northeastern Illinois University is the most diverse university in the Midwest. This diversity affects the core of the institution—we learn, teach, and work in an environment that is made richer, more relevant and more rewarding by the deeply diverse group of individuals who make up our University community.

Our demographics reflect the urban environment of Chicago and the greater metropolitan area. Individually, we vary in ethnicity, race, age, and gender. We also vary in areas other than these traditional demographic measures. Nearly 50 languages other than English are spoken as a first language by our students. We come from various cultures and observe many different religions. Our students, faculty, and staff have a variety of economic backgrounds and bring a breadth of values, experiences, intellectual interests, and sexual orientations.

Our community is diverse in every sense and this transcends not only all that we do, but how we do it. We welcome, accept, respect, and embrace our differences because we value learning from others. We support divergent perspectives and expect our community to voice their differing views of history, politics, and world events—that is how we add value to our educational experiences and grow as individuals. We recognize the broad array of experiences and knowledge of cultures that our communities bring to the University and our learning experiences. These experiences transform our individual and institutional lives.

Diversity is at the core of all we do. This is illustrated by the inclusion of diversity among the core values adopted and embraced by the University community in our Statement of Values:

Diversity — NEIU values the inclusion of a broad spectrum of students, staff, and faculty in the life of the University. We celebrate and foster global perspectives. We encourage the open and respectful expression of ideas and differences in thoughts, experiences, and opinions.

The University, therefore, is a collection of values, ideas, experiences, and thoughts. As a community, we incorporate this diversity into how we learn, teach, and provide service to our metropolitan region. We feel that consciously weaving this diversity into all that we do is what makes Northeastern unique.

Different Standards
PART II

When the first plane struck, I had just arrived in my office and begun streaming the radio.

I called home several times before our campus was closed, and my commute, typically twenty minutes by bus, took more than an hour. Inbound lanes toward Manhattan, and the rest of the country, were empty except for an occasional fire truck or ambulance, while the outbound ones to Long Island were endless trains of vehicles interrupted only by traffic lights. Huddled around the television, we watched the sickening events occurring just miles away, and from our backyard, we could smell acrid smoke in the air and see fighter jets against the blue sky.

This experience changed Rani's mind, but for me, it merely reinforced a fear I had even before I officially started my new position as coordinator of a campuswide writing program. After being hired, I moved my pregnant wife and one-year-old daughter to Long Island. Then one of my new colleagues offered, even before I assumed responsibility for coordinating the program, to edit a manuscript for me, only to mention on returning it that if I had provided it in the interview, I probably wouldn't have been offered the position.

My fear, however, wasn't finalized until one brown-bag lunch in a series I had scheduled. For this session, several colleagues from across the campus had agreed to offer short position statements on good writing and then lead a discussion about disciplinary standards. At the event, the attendance was higher, and the debate was livelier, than I expected, but as I stood silently in the back of the crowded conference room, listening to history and philosophy professors argue over commas and clarity, I realized I couldn't continue as writing program administrator.

The problem, I knew, was me. I still believed in the importance of integrated writing instruction, but while I found the administrative obligations to be challenging, I was almost overwhelmed by the intellectual dissonance. No matter how many times I thought through the tensions, I still couldn't reconcile my role in the campuswide writing program, as outlined in the official and unofficial duties of the position, and my reading about situated literacies and teaching of sociolinguistics and cultural linguistics courses. Administrators and colleagues expected standardization, and yet my research and teaching emphasized differences.

At first, I only applied for a few other positions, including one at a public university in Chicago that seemed ideal. I had always wanted to work in a public university, and Chicago had been home away from home. Also, the university emphasized its ethnic diversity and community partnerships, and the job involved no administrative responsibilities.

Although I had declined the initial invitation to interview because Rani wasn't ready to leave New York, 9/11 changed her mind, and when I checked I found that the position hadn't been filled. I contacted the search chair, who informed me that if I would be willing to accept a certain salary, I could still interview for the job.

I was going to Chicago in a couple of weeks for a wedding, so I offered to meet then with the search committee, which readily agreed because, I was told, it had already spent its budget. While others rehearsed the wedding ceremony, I talked to department members and campus administrators, and by the time I returned to New York, an offer had been made. As a result, I had six weeks to pack our possessions, sell the house, and move to Chicago before the new semester started.

Before I could leave New York, I was contacted by a campus administrator who explained that he had budgeted some money for a part-time writing-across-the-curriculum person and wondered if, with my experience, I'd help him start his program. Although apprehensive, I recognized the opportunity to collaborate on a campuswide writing initiative for a culturally diverse academic community. I might not make an effective administrator, I reasoned, and maybe I would never resolve my ambivalence about conducting faculty development workshops, but at the very least I could use the concerns that caused me to resign as a WPA to contribute to a campuswide writing program that emphasized greater educational equity.

Soon after starting this new position, I was appointed to the Language Skills Assessment Task Force (LSATF), which had been established to evaluate literacy instruction on campus. Here, I met two others who had created the English Language Program and collaborated on *Proyecto Pa'Lante*, as well as had attempted several campus-wide writing initiatives.

Along with these, several others—three of us from English, two coordinators of the Writing Lab and Assessment and Testing, and an assessment specialist from the Center for Teaching and Learning—met regularly. The meetings were sometimes contentious, and my efforts to articulate my uncertainties about institutionalized literacy instruction were sometimes shouted down. This was their third, and final, attempt to bring WAC to NEIU.

As we conducted surveys and drafted reports, I started the institutional case study I am describing in this book. Each time I saw, between building or at meetings, the administrator who had contacted me in New York, I asked if he had hired anyone for the WAC work. Each time, he said he hadn't.

Part Two

EVERYDAY EXPERIENCES AT NEIU

2

PROYECTO PA'LANTE STUDENTS

When we started at NEIU, the Proyecto Pa'Lante (PP) students and I had no way of knowing that the university would soon be recognized as the most outstanding member institution within the Hispanic Association of Colleges and Universities (HACU), an association of more than 450 institutions in the United States, Puerto Rico, Latin America, Spain, and Portugal that, as described by HACU, are champions of Hispanic success in higher education. Nonetheless, they and I likely would have been encouraged to know that with this award, the university we had selected would be identified, in 2007, as the one that best fulfills the goals and missions of HACU, including improving post-secondary education for Latino students and collaborating with government, industry, and business (Hispanic Association).

In choosing NEIU, these PP students and I had selected an institution where they would have many similarities to their peers, yet most of their professors would be different from them and more like me:

NEIU Ethnicity Profile

ethnicity	Undergraduate Students Fall 2004 (n=9305)	T/TT Instructional Faculty Fall 2004 (n = 287)
African American	12.1	07.0
Asian	10.8	13.2
Caucasian	44.0	70.7
Hispanic	29.1	07.3
Native American	00.3	00.3
Unknown	----	01.4
Nonresident Alien/other	03.7	----

Source: NEIU Office of Institutional Studies and Planning

While these PP students would be part of the minority majority among NEIU undergraduates, more than seven in ten of their tenured/tenure-track teachers would be Caucasian.[1]

---

1. Another difference, and one that cannot be separated cleanly, is gender: while more

Despite these differences, the PP students seemed to have a slightly better initial semester than their institutional peers:

Fall 2004 (average)

	PP (n=103)	Gen Adm (n=758)
term hours attempted	12.3	12.9
term hours earned	10.6	10.4
term GPA	2.86[26]	2.67
cumulative GPA	2.92[27]	2.67

Source: NEIU Office of Institutional Studies and Planning

This relatively strong start continued in their second semester:

Spring 2005

	PP	GA
term hours attempted	12.2	13
term hours earned	10.1	10.2
term GPA	2.37	2.52
cumulative GPA	2.78	2.68

Source: NEIU Office of Institutional Studies and Planning

By the end of their first year, these PP students had accumulated levels of institutional currency similar to their institutional peers:

Retention Rate from One Term to the Next (percentage)

	PP	GA
fall 2004 to spring 2005	89.3	87.3
spring 2005 to fall 2005	78.6	68.7

Source: NEIU Office of Institutional Studies and Planning

After the initial semester, these PP students were as likely to return for a second semester as their institutional peers, yet after the first year, they were more likely to return for a second year than their institutional peers in spite of, or perhaps as a result of, their status as students in the Proyecto Pa'Lante program.

---

than six of ten undergraduate students (62.7 percent in 2004) are female, between four and five of ten T/TT faculty (45.3 percent in 2004) are female.

2.   NEIU uses a four-point scale.

3.   The difference between the term and cumulative GPAs in the initial semester suggests the presence of additional credits, such as ones earned through the Summer Transition Program.

THE PROYECTO PA'LANTE PROGRAM

Latino students are challenged by poor college preparation and rising tuition rates, according to Teresita Díaz, the Director of PP and Project Success and a former NEIU student, and the PP program permits many of these students to attend college. In general, the goals of the PP program, Díaz explained, are to recruit Latinos who have academic potential but do not satisfy general admission requirements—the top half of their high school graduating class and a minimum ACT composite score of 19 or a SAT of 890—and to support these students with academic advising and career and personal counseling, as well as to encourage the development of their self-image and their campus connections. While PP serves a limited number of students, it could be expanded, if funding could be increased, into the city and, following population migrations, the suburbs.[4]

For the fall 2004 cohort, the PP program considered 294 candidates, conducted 154 interviews, and admitted 110 students (Fuentes 2005). Given their status in a special admissions program, most, if not all, were likely in the lower half of their graduating class, and their average composite ACT scores fell below the NEIU admission requirements:[5]

Average ACT Scores[6]

	Proyecto Pa'Lante (n=99)	General Admission (n=703)	National Peers (2004)
composite	16	19	20.9
reading	16	19	21.3
English	15	19	20.4

Source: NEIU Office of Institutional Studies and Planning

For their first two years at NEIU, the PP program advises and tutors these students, as well as offers them a support system, as they adjust to the institution. To remain in this program, PP students must demonstrate academic progress and participate in support programs, including a special first-year seminar course taught by PP staff.

---

4. For more, see Rivera (2007).
5. For these PP students, the mean ACT = 15.96; median = 16; and mode = 14/15/16.
6. As a further comparison, the 2004 average ACT composite score for Mexican American/Chicanos in the United States was 18.4 and for Puerto Rican/Hispanic students was 18.8, both of which are closer to the PP students' institutional peers. While this and other ethnic distinctions are sometimes useful, these are usually not used by PP or the university.

To better understand their experiences in this seminar, I conducted classroom observations of one of these seminar courses. One Friday early in the semester, the PP students had been given the choice of whether to read silently to themselves or to listen to Neida, their PP seminar instructor and a former NEIU student, read to them.[7] Earlier in the week, she had assigned an article entitled "How I Started Writing Poetry" by Reginald Lockett (2006), a poet and teacher who worked with Latino and Asian students at San Jose City College until his death in 2008. In this short autobiographical piece, Locket explains that with a "façade of daring-do, hip, cool, con man bravado so prevalent among adolescent males in West Oakland," he completed a serendipitous creative writing class in seventh grade that transformed him from "raiding Rogers Men's Shop, Smiths and Flagg Brothers Shoes" to "stealing books by just about every poet and writer Miss Nettlebeck read to the class," which marked the beginning of his life as a poet.

On this day, the PP students challenged Neida about her feedback on an assignment about general education requirements, for which they had to list completed courses and select others to demonstrate how they could complete their NEIU general education requirements. Then they explained they hadn't brought drafts of their own autobiographies, which they were to write after reading Lockett's autobiography. Two claimed they had lost their handwritten versions. One said he lost his when his book bag was stolen. Another explained that he never had time to type it.

Neida announced that instead of reading, they were going to play the Diversity Game. She asked for someone to remind them of the rules. After some debate, they agreed that each person had to generate as many words for each letter—D-I-V-E-R-S-I-T-Y-G-A-M-E—as they could in a limited amount of time. These words, Neida insisted, had to be relevant.

Then they argued over how to win. Two of them offered options. A third suggested they could arm wrestle. "So what," said another, "the most creative wins?"

One of the students complained that Neida had played before.

"Can they be in Spanish?" said another.

One student voted against using Spanish. Another said he was neutral. "I can read Spanish," he said.

Neida asked me for an *A* word. I suggested *affirmative* as in *affirmative action*.

---

7.   Neida, who earned undergraduate and graduate degrees at NEIU, is also the primary focus of the next chapter.

After explaining how my suggestion would earn two points, she told them to begin. While they scribbled at their desks, Neida monitored the time, and when it had elapsed, they began compiling results:

D —different; Dominicans; destruction; dependent; differences

They argued over whether *dependent*, as in needing each other, should qualify as an acceptable word. Neida couldn't resolve the dispute, so she asked me. *Dependent*, I said, seemed appropriate, at least in the sense that diverse societies could be *dependent* upon their members.

I —independent; international; individual; interesting; illegals; interactive; infinite

"You think we're diverse in here?" Neida said.
"Somewhat," said one of them.

V —various; Vietnamese; variety; vast; violence

"Are we going to finish in time?" said another.
They raced through the remainder:

E —ethnicity

R —regions; Russian; roots

S —separate; sins; sexual orientation; society; Spanish; stereotypes; sensitivity

I —individuals; inequality; Italians; indigenous

T —traditions; traits; terrorism

Y —youth; you; Yugoslavian

G —groups; Greek; government

A —affirmative; American

M —mixed; Mexican; military

E —ethnicity; ethnic; environment; emotions

Then one of them rattled off a list of ethnicities he had generated. A second yelled that a third had thirty-three words on his list, so he should win. "You had no wrong," he said to his classmate, "did you?"

According to the PP program, the official purpose of this three-credit required seminar is to introduce students to college success strategies through developing thinking and learning abilities, self-awareness and self-assessment, and institutional and educational awareness; those PP students who do not earn a C or better either in this seminar or for the semester must repeat the seminar, which according to PP staff, is the same course.

The unofficial function of this seminar, as this incident suggests, is so much more. When asked, Neida explained the relation of this course to their university education in this way:

> There will always be groups of people that are learning and striving to improve their lives. When speaking about many of my students, I see that they represent a segment of society that is transition. They are on a life-transforming path. What I hope is that through their college education, learning, and ultimate increased earning potential, they will naturally flow into a more benefit-reaping segment of society. I believe that through the seminar classes that I teach for *Proyecto Pa'Lante*, I am able to condition and coach students into learning life skills, like skills that are tailored to NEIU and becoming a successful college student, which I hope will eventually influence their lives as professionals and becoming productive citizens.
>
> My students, regardless of their grade, will undoubtedly be exposed to cultural knowledge that often cannot be learned in books through our class sessions. The mere task of holding a conversation with actively engaged students should be seen as a success, because we are all exchanging meaningful ideas and the students are learning how to engage in a conversation with a person of authority, or of a different gender, of a different age and of so many other characteristics that point to our differences. They are learning. Learning how to interact with me and each other, something that is not in our textbooks or in the official requirements of the designed course objectives. I see this type of learning more practical and useful towards the students' success as individuals. It is through these conversations that I also get to know my students more intimately.

In addition to these informal conversations, Neida used formal assignments, such as writing their own autobiographies after reading Lockett's, to learn more about the students.

In his submission entitled "New Life after Elementary School," Manuel identified three educational experiences—attending elementary school, starting high school, and beginning his second year of high school—as significant educational experiences. In addition to describing the difficult transition to U.S. schools, he expressed his anxiety about the gangs that attended his high school—the same school that Neida had attended—and his fears about high-school classes. While his first year was challenging, his interest in English, he explained, helped him with his interests in other areas, from foreign languages to music, and then he discovered soccer. In the end, he suggested that while soccer might have motivated him, his English, and school, enabled him to become the person he is.[8]

Although this assignment, as their resistance suggests, challenged these students, it seemed to challenge Neida as well, as suggested by the fact that her responses were largely limited to writing short comments at the end and supplying them with rhetoric handbooks. In, for example, her response to Manuel's draft, Neida split the remaining white space at the end of the last page into two sections, which she connected with a curving line:

¡OJO!
  Have, Has & Had—be careful using the right one. Your periods & commas—Careful w/ run-on sentences. And double check your tenses—Are you talking about the past, present or future?

Manuel,
  ¡Que bien! Your story flowed very well. It had good structure!! I am proud of you. Now you need to work on your final draft!

Besides these endnotes, Neida's only other comments are in a brief note near the introduction—"This beginning is classic!"—and some sentence-level edits.

In addition to this autobiography assignment, other projects included a midterm exam about the university and an academic plan. In the session before the exam, they reviewed possible questions, such as the number of hours for gen ed requirements or the term for dropping all their courses. She often interrupted their review to encourage them to eat the doughnuts she had brought to their classroom. After reviewing for some time, she announced that they were prepared for the exam. One student asked if, now that the review had been completed, they could go home. Neida said that they could not, that she was first going to describe their next project, the academic plan assignment.

---

8.   The entire draft is reproduced in the appendix to this chapter, and it reappears in the next chapter.

"Are you taking notes?" she said, turning to look over her shoulder at the students sitting in their desks. "This is how I want it to look."

She continued sketching, on the chalkboard, a notebook page, which she divided into six rows. Each was labeled a different semester—Fall 2004, for example, and Spring 2005. She told them they were to list the classes they had already taken and planned to take until graduation. They could get extra credit, she said, if they used a word-processing program to complete the assignment.

At this point, one of the students proposed that they should move the midterm to Monday instead of Wednesday, and he called for a vote. Neida refused to vote on the midterm but offered to vote on other issues. Then he said his mother wouldn't provide him with the necessary tax documents to qualify for financial aid.

"What about financial aid," said another, "when I work and support myself?"

Financial aid dominated the discussion for the rest of the session.

After class ended, she stopped the student who said his mother would not provide the necessary tax documents to discuss a campus job. The job, Neida explained, would last the rest of the semester. She told him he should introduce himself to the supervisor who was hiring for the position, and he complained that his appearance wasn't good enough. She suggested that he could go home to take a shower and then come back to campus. He mentioned that this supervisor had called his house but that he couldn't get the correct number from the caller ID. Both agreed that he should list her number because his wasn't reliable.

After the midterm exam the following week, she returned their tests and announced that everyone had passed, that everyone had done quite well in fact. They reviewed the questions and answers in class.

"All in all," she said, "I'm proud of you guys."

When a late student arrived, Neida and he reviewed his exam, and then she reminded them that their academic plan was due next session.

"I thought that you were going to help us," said the student who arrived late.

"I've given you the skills to do this," she said. "I sent you to Leticia to practice."

"She didn't tell us if it was right or wrong," he said, "if we did good or not."

Neida agreed to make the submission for next session a working draft, which they could revise together in class.

"I have a comment," the student said. " 'It's good being with you guys.' "

Neida laughed. "You're so bad," she said.

Besides the autobiographical essay and the academic plan, the last major assignment was a PowerPoint presentation about themselves. On the day they began preparing for this assignment, the session started with jokes about their attendance, questions about remaining deadlines, and admonishments about summer plans. Students at Ivy League schools, Neida explained, schedule summer internships, so these students should schedule some too.

Then she asked them to review her comments on their educational autobiographies. One of the students said he thought she was going to help with their revision. She motioned to the different rhetoric handbooks she had brought to class.

"Any questions," she said, "*me pregunten.*"

Before the session ended, she passed out the assignment sheet for the PowerPoint presentation that would be the focus for the remainder of the semester. As indicated on the assignment sheet, this project had to include a minimum of eighteen slides, or screens, in a particular order:

I. Your Past
   A. Childhood & Adolescence
   B. Family
   C. Life Events
II. Your Present
   A. Young Adulthood
   B. Interests & Pastimes
   C. Beliefs and Outlook on Life
III. Your Future
   A. Possible Career
   B. Field/Industry Facts
   C. Personal Reasons to Pursue this Career
   D. Personal Goals (not work-related)

On a separate sheet, she indicated that students should "[i]nclude graphics, images, sounds, recordings, video clips, personal photographs, etc. . . . CREATIVITY will only improve your overall presentation and is a good idea." A central component was their "*FUTURE*—include concrete facts about your professional field or dream alongside your personal goals," as well as "*[i]nterviewing professionals in the field,*" which "will also enhance your power point presentation" (original emphasis). Also, they were urged to bring "personal items from home"—"*'Show and Tell' can be incorporated into your presentation,*" and they were reminded to use "the public speaking tips offered in class."

Near the end of the session, she again asked, in Spanish, the student whose mother wouldn't give him the necessary tax documents to stay after class. While not all of the students understood her when she used Spanish, he did.

After the others left, she informed him, again in Spanish, that she knew he hadn't been doing his assignments in his art class. When he explained that he couldn't afford the sketch books, she offered to buy them, as well as other items he might need for the course. Then he told her he still couldn't convince his mother to give him the tax documents for financial aid. Without these, he said, he might have to attend another school, one that had offered him a scholarship to play football.

Switching back and forth between Spanish and English, they finished their conversation. She suggested he recruit his little brother to help him obtain these forms. He said he couldn't apply himself in his classes because he knew he might not return next term. She told him about another job, this time at a nearby grocery store, that paid twelve dollars an hour, and she urged him to register for at least one class rather than drop out for the entire semester.

What none of us knew was that this student would receive a D in this course. The student whose PowerPoint presentation about his past, present, and future was the strongest, would earn a C in the course. In his presentation, he told us that he had been a part of ROTC in high school and that he was involved in community activism in his neighborhood.

When Neida asked him, at the end, how he gave back to his community, he cited a CD that he had produced, as well as his volunteer work at the community center where he DJed every Friday and his work with undocumented immigrants and community marches against violence in his neighborhood of Humboldt Park.[9]

"Everything is fresh," Neida said to the class. "He took it to a new level."

Another student who earned a C called her about obtaining a higher grade, Neida told me, but she informed the student that if she were to give him a B, she would have to *give* it to him because he hadn't *earned* it.

One student who had legal problems disappeared before the semester ended and failed the course.

---

9.   Humboldt Park figures prominently in Reymundo Sanchez's (2000) account of his experiences as a Latin King gang member, and it is marked today by iron sculptures of the Puerto Rican flag.

Before grades were released, the student whose mother wouldn't give him the tax documents stopped by Neida's office in Proyecto Pa'Lante to tell her that her class was his favorite, that she was his favorite teacher. As they talked, Neida wondered why, she told me later, he didn't complete his presentation and whether he was trying to convince her to change his grade.

After the semester ended, Manuel's father called to see how his son could remain at NEIU or, if not, at least attend a community college. He scheduled an appointment, and she told him he had to bring his son. Neither showed for the appointment, but, Neida learned after returning from vacation, both appeared one day just before the office closed. His father, according to her coworker, wasn't angry, only concerned about what they had done for his son and what he should do next. Another coworker told her, Neida explained to me, that there were emotional problems at home, but she had no sense of what they were.

THE NEXT THREE YEARS

In spite of these difficulties, the overall impact of the PP program seemed positive, especially given that more of these PP students were likely to return for a second year. However, this second year marked the beginning of two trends that persisted over the next three years. First, the PP students generally completed fewer hours and earned worse grades even as their institutional peers, who were also attempting fewer hours, generally earned better grades:

Averages for Fall 2004 PP and GA Cohorts

	Hours Attempted		Hours Earned		Term GPA		Cumulative GPA	
	PP	GA	PP	GA	PP	GA	PP	GA
fall 2004	12.3	12.9	10.6	10.4	2.86	2.67	2.92	2.67
spring 2005	12.2	13.0	10.1	10.2	2.37	2.52	2.78	2.68
fall 2005	12.5	12.7	09.0	10.0	2.32	2.62	2.71	2.82
spring 2006	12.1	12.4	09.0	10.3	2.26	2.71	2.67	2.88
fall 2006	11.4	12.0	08.7	09.6	2.40	2.70	2.69	2.90
spring 2007	10.6	11.7	07.3	09.4	2.31	2.77	2.69	2.94
fall 2007	10.8	11.7	07.6	09.5	2.46	2.84	2.72	2.97
spring 2008	10.3	11.4	08.4	09.6	2.56	2.96	2.70	3.00

Source: NEIU Office of Institutional Studies and Planning

Second, the higher retention rates also disappeared over years two, three, and four:

Retention Rate

	PP (%)	GA (%)
fall 2004 - spring 2005	89.3	87.3
spring 2005 - fall 2005	78.6	68.7
fall 2005 - spring 2006	72.8	60.3
spring 2006 - fall 2006	60.2	50.4
fall 2006 - spring 2007	53.4	46.3
spring 2007 - fall 2007	48.5	42.5
fall 2007 - spring 2008	39.8	39.4

Source: NEIU Office of Institutional Studies and Planning

After four years, fewer than four in ten of the PP students *and* their institutional peers remained at the university.

Over these four years as the PP students were taking courses and earning grades, the percentage of Hispanic students who graduated remained relatively consistent:

Undergraduate Degrees Conferred by Ethnicity

	FY2005 (%) (n=1247)	FY2006 (%) (n=1364)	FY2007 (%) (n=1364)	FY2008 (%) (n=1503)
African American	10.6	10.4	11.2	10.5
Asian	10.1	10.1	10.0	09.8
Caucasian	52.6	52.3	53.7	50.2
Hispanic	22.2	22.1	20.3	23.4
Native American	00.2	00.1	00.1	00.0
Other	04.3	05.0	04.8	05.7
TOTAL (degrees)	69.1	69.6	69.3	72.8

Source: NEIU Office of Institutional Studies and Planning

However, the PP students, along with their institutional peers, constitute a fraction of the degrees awarded after four years (see table "Spring 2008"). Although low, these graduation rates are not inconsistent with institutional graduation rates, as reported to the U.S. Department of Education: not only did slightly more than three in ten of first-time full-time NEIU undergraduates in 2002 transfer elsewhere, but also fewer than two in ten (18 percent) graduated within six years (150 percent of "normal time" to completion [2008])—3 percent in four years (2006) and 26 percent in eight years (2010)—with Hispanics having a lower six-year graduation rate (13 percent).

Spring 2008

	PP (n=3)	GA (n=26)
graduation rate (%)	03	03
mean grad GPA	3.50	3.56
mean degree hours	131.7	128.5

Source: NEIU Office of Institutional Studies and Planning

EDUCATION AND LITERACY

Together, these data offer an overview of the educational experiences of the PP students at the most ethnically diverse master's granting university and an officially designated Hispanic-Serving Institution. Although these PP students generally have a better first year in terms of earned credits and grades, they are less successful over the next three years than their institutional peers.

Just as these results would not have surprised me if I had not surveyed the PP students, the results, in all likelihood, would not surprise my NEIU colleagues who, similar to our colleagues across the country, believe that incoming students are underprepared, if not unprepared, for college courses. When asked, five in ten of my NEIU colleagues reported that half the students in their lowest level courses are not "reasonably proficient" in reading and speaking and almost three in ten indicated the same for writing proficiencies. Nonetheless, most of my colleagues—nearly seven in ten—believe they help NEIU students confront these "deficiencies" in their classes, and almost eight in ten assign a "fair amount" of writing—seven to ten pages or more—in these and other courses, often as individual or group projects that involve papers and presentations (53 percent), as well as short papers (26 percent), term papers (14 percent), projects with drafts (13 percent), and reflective journals (12 percent) with the amount of writing increasing, as might be expected, from general education to 300-level and then graduate courses (Center 2006).[10]

10. According to the director of the Center for Teaching and Learning, 600 surveys were distributed, and 116 responses were received for an overall response rate of 23 percent. Most of the respondents were tenured or tenure track (76 percent), which represents a within-group response rate of 33 percent, and most had been teaching for more than six years (60 percent). Moreover, these respondents were distributed across the Colleges of Arts and Sciences (75), Education (24), and Business (7) with several from Academic Development (Center 2006).

Given such perspectives and expectations, some might attempt to explain these results by referring to the admission status of PP students, including the nine in ten who scored below the required composite ACT score, or the cultural differences of these students, including the seven in ten for whom English is a second (or subsequent) language. As such, these conclusions would be consistent with larger social narratives of education as the means to improve lives for all students, including ethnic minorities, and such explanations, as we have seen, lead to questions about retention and graduation rates, particularly as they relate to the obligations of educational institutions, particularly those that emphasize identity politics. However, such accounts are inconsistent with other observations. In particular, these PP students brought similarly strong histories with reading and writing for themselves as their *national* peers, and stronger beliefs in and attitudes about literacy than those peers, and after a similarly successful first year as their *institutional* peers, they consistently attempted fewer hours, which could offset any increasing difficulty in their course work.

These and other inconsistencies suggest the need to examine more closely these students' encounters with language and literacy as they attempt to earn credits and grades and to complete their degrees. In addition to the long-standing relationship between education and literacy, recent research has suggested that one significant educational obstacle encountered by contemporary college students is institutionalized philosophies of academic literacy (e.g., Cox 2009, 140–156). Such scrutiny seems all the more appropriate given that almost ten in ten PP students enrolled in a remedial or regular writing course in their first semester, as did more than eight in ten of their institutional peers with nearly nine in ten of both these PP students and their institutional peers returning for a second semester.

PROFICIENCIES AND PLACEMENT

All NEIU students complete placement assessments in reading, writing, and math to assign them to the appropriate courses that, as explained in the catalogue, will enable them to develop "college level performance" in these areas (*Northeastern* 2004, 31). Similar to other institutions, NEIU offers these placement assessments only in English although the Coordinator of Assessment and Testing wishes that these assessments could be offered in other languages, such as Spanish, as well as that these tests were computerized, which could measure other aspects, from listening to structure, that would make the placement process more accurate.

As part of the placement process, the PP students and their institutional peers completed a language survey that asked whether they considered themselves to be native or nonnative English users as well as other questions about language at home and in school:

Selected Questions from the NEIU Language Survey

(Fall 2004 PP and General Admission Cohorts)

English first Language?[11] (%) (n=110-815)	*Yes*		*No*							
	PP	GA	PP	GA						
	29	53	71	47						

age learned English? (%) (n=85/460)	*1-6*		*7-9*		*10-12*		*13-15*		*16+*	
	PP	GA	PP	GA	PP	GA	PP	GA	PP	GA
	44	54	32	17	09	11	14	12	01	06

how long spoken English? (%) (n=85/442)	*10+ Yrs*		*6-9 Yrs*		*4-5 Yrs*		*2-3 Yrs*		*1 Yr or less*	
	PP	GA	PP	GA	PP	GA	PP	GA	PP	GA
	68	64	13	15	13	15	06	07	00	00

language of high-school courses?[12](%) (n=86/436)	*Mostly or Entirely English*		*Mostly or Entirely Another*		*Bilingual, English and Another*	
	PP	GA	PP	GA	PP	GA
	81	87	02	04	16	08

English with friends and family? (%) (n=86/436)	*Usually (80-100%)*		*Frequently (60-79%)*		*About Half (40-59%)*		*Occasionally (20-39%)*		*Seldom (<20%)*	
	PP	GA	PP	GA	PP	GA	PP	GA	PP	GA
	44	43	17	24	21	16	13	10	05	07

Source: NEIU Assessment and Testing

As predicted by my preliminary survey, the PP students were more likely to consider English as a second (or additional) language even as these multilingual students, at least according to these results, had similar histories to their multilingual institutional peers. For example, most of these had two

---

11. If English is their first language, then students are instructed to skip the remaining questions although obviously not all do. Nonetheless, these results suggest that almost three in ten PP students consider English to be their first language, and generally of those who do not, between four and five in ten of those students who use English as an additional language learned English by the age of six.

12. This question includes a range of instructional options for students. In addition to English Only, other secondary school options are newcomer programs (self-contained and intensive ESL), ESL, sheltered (i.e., specially designed English instruction in subject areas), and subject matter for English Language Learners (see Valdés 2001b, 15–16).

first languages—another language and English—by the time they were nine years old, yet most use English with family and friends.

In addition to these self-reports about language, other predictions can be made about their literacy proficiencies as a result of their composite ACT scores. As Norbert Elliot (2005) explains, standardized tests have a complicated relation to placement and performance, yet ACT claims that test scores can predict college readiness. Based upon their ACT scores and the College Readiness Standards, PP students, when reading, should be able to

- identify straightforward main ideas and purposes of paragraphs but not infer them;

- recognize functions of straightforward passages and locate simple details but neither identify important details nor infer the function of these details; and

- reach simple conclusions and make simple generalizations about straightforward texts.

At the same time, PP students, when writing, generally should be able to

- identify the main purposes of phrases and sentences and delete obviously irrelevant clauses and sentences but neither identify main ideas in straightforward texts nor determine the relevance of a variety of sentence-level details;

- add sentences to appropriate places in paragraphs but not essays and delete obviously redundant information but not when the form of this information is a different part of speech;

- use appropriate forms of commonly confused word pairs (e.g., *there* and *their*) but not idiomatic prepositions, particularly in combination with verbs (e.g., *long for*); and

- punctuate straightforward, awkward, and fused sentences but not participial phrases, relative pronouns, and misplaced modifiers; use appropriate tenses and voices; and delete commas that disrupt flow but neither delete unnecessary commas that might reflect incorrect readings of sentences (e.g., between verbs and direct objects) nor use commas to distinguish parenthetical phrases. (ACT 2008)[13]

---

13. These college readiness scores presume a particular notion of literacy, which is an issue that will be addressed in more detail later in chapter six.

Based upon categories from the ACT College Readiness scale and mean ACT scores of NEIU students, significant differences in reading abilities can be expected of NEIU students (scores ranging between 16 and 19) and others across the country who score higher (20–36), and significant differences in writing abilities can be expected among the PP students (13–15), their institutional peers (16–19), and those across the country who score higher (20–36).

At NEIU, the placement process has been the cause of some concern. For example, two reports were presented in 2004 to the NEIU Language Skills Assessment Task Force, which led members, who had been charged to evaluate literacy instruction on campus, to question why almost seven in ten NEIU students are placed into remedial reading courses or remedial tutoring while almost the same number are placed into regular writing courses:

2001–2003 Placement Results (%) of NEIU Students (n=4,462)

	reading[14]			*writing*	
	remedial	*tutoring*	*none*	*remedial*	*regular*
nonnative English courses	*32.0*			*17.5*	
native English courses	*17.4*			*12.6*	
total	*49.4*	*20.9*	*29.4*	*30.1*	*69.9*

Source: NEIU Assessment and Testing Center (Kasai 2004b, 2; Kasai 2004a, 1)

Rather than expecting these different placement results, some of my colleagues suggested that successful readers likely would have internalized the conventions of written English (Language 2005, 8).

At the time these assessments were conducted, reading placement was based upon scores from the Nelson-Denny Reading Test, a timed multiple-choice test designed to measure vocabulary and comprehension, and writing placement was the result of a direct assessment—a brief personal essay on an assigned topic that was holistically scored. After reviewing the results of 4,462 NEIU students who completed the placement tests between January 2001 and August 2003, the Assessment Coordinator calculated the mean ACT scores for placement into remedial courses.

Based upon statistical analyses of these results, he concluded that ACT reading scores of 20 could reasonably distinguish between students who needed remedial reading instruction and those who did not although those with a score below 20 would need further evaluation before a final recommendation could be made. Also, he concluded that

---

14.   Of the reading placement results, 4 percent are unknown (Kasai 2004b, 2).

the ACT English scores would inaccurately place students into writing courses (Kasai 2004a, 6; Kasai 2004b, 7–8).[15]

Mean ACT Scores and Placement Results of NEIU Students (n=4,462)

	ACT Reading-reading placement			ACT English-writing placement	
	remedial	tutoring	none	remedial	regular
nonnative English courses	12.8-14.9	18.1	22.8	10.5-13.7	18.2
native English courses	13.0-15.2			13.4	

Source: NEIU Assessment and Testing Center (Kasai 2004b, 4; Kasai 2004a, 3)

As these reports might suggest, these PP students were more likely to be assigned to remedial literacy courses:

Fall 2004 Placement Results

	PP (%)			GA (%)		
	total	NNES	NES	total	NNES	NES
remedial reading-tutoring	91	95	81	58	77	42
remedial writing	47	54	31	26	40	14

Source: NEIU Assessment and Testing

As these results indicate, more than nine in 10 of these PP students were assigned to remedial reading courses, and almost five in ten were assigned to remedial writing courses—more if they used English as a second (or additional) language—while their institutional peers were less likely to be assigned to remedial literacy courses regardless of whether they consider English to be a second or first language.

LITERACIES AND LEARNING

Similar to other institutions, NEIU offers different remedial writing courses for nonnative and native English users (e.g., Phillips, Stewart, and Stewart 2006). For example, those who self-identify as individuals who use English as a second (or additional) language, if placed into remedial writing courses offered by the English Language Program,

15. The reading placement requirements changed just after these students started at NEIU. As of January 2005, NEIU students with an ACT reading score of 20 or better were not required to complete remedial reading courses while those who had an ACT reading score below 20, or those whose reading scores were unavailable, had to complete the reading placement test. Even with this change, between eight and nine of ten (84 percent) of these PP students would still have had to complete the reading placement assessment, as would slightly more than five of ten (53 percent) of all fall 2004 incoming students.

can be assigned to one of several courses that must be completed in sequence—the English Language Workshop I, for example, leads to Workshop II and then Workshop III—while those who consider themselves to be native English users, if placed into remedial writing, have only one course to complete.

Despite these differences, the official mission of the English Language Program is to enable students "to acquire the level of oral and written English language skills expected of university students," and the goal, at least at NEIU, is the same, insofar that both options— the sequence for multilinguals and the course for native English speakers—share the same outcomes (*Northeastern* 2004, 43).[16] In particular, the last course in the ELP-ESL sequence—Workshop III—offers "[p] ractice and instruction in writing expository essays, with emphasis on paragraph development, increased fluency in written English, and proofreading skills," and the only ELP-DEV course—Developmental Writing—"provides native speakers of English with intensive work on basic writing skills such as planning, organizing and revising an essay, and emphasizes the development of sentence level skills and proofreading techniques" (*Northeastern* 2004, 43–44). Moreover, both of these courses share the same outcomes, as determined by the core ELP faculty and the Writing Lab staff:

- Pre-Writing: Planning—Use a variety of planning strategies to effectively develop academic topics as well as an individualized approach to generating ideas for college-level writing assignments.

- Drafting: Fluency—Write both in-class and out-of-class essays to develop academic fluency in written English.

- Revising: Topic/Genre—Write multi-paragraph essays in academic modes based on sources, unified around a thesis, and organized by self-generated frameworks.

- Revising: Support—Develop paragraphs that include both generalizations and support, that move coherently from abstract to concrete and vice versa, and that integrate sources into the text.

---

16. Reading placement results are, I was told, more like recommendations, insofar that the sequence of reading courses is not enforced, and the tutoring placement is unsupervised and ungraded. In general, the Reading Program was consistently uninvolved in both the institution and this project. For example, its absence was criticized by members of the Language Skills Assessment Task Force, and its members mostly ignored my invitations to participate in this project.

- Editing: Proofreading—Proofread essays that show good control over verb forms, spelling, and sentence boundaries, as well as syntactic maturity appropriate to college-level writing.

- Editing: Length—Demonstrate readiness for the next course in the sequence by writing at least one in-class essay of 400–600 words and one multi-draft, out-of-class essay of 700–800 words (2 ½–3 typed pages) that meet other outcomes.[17] (English 2004)

As these suggest, the goal for both tracks is a relatively autonomous set of skills in English, as the name of the program suggests.

Despite different linguistic histories, PP students have experiences in remedial literacy courses similar to those of their institutional peers. As the surveys suggest, the PP students in the remedial literacy courses are more likely to use English as an additional language:

Relation to English in Remedial Literacy Courses

	remedial reading-tutoring		remedial writing (%)	
	PP (n=101)	GA (n=471)	PP (n=53)	GA (n=211)
nonnative English (%)	74	61	81	71
native English (%)	26	39	19	29

Source: NEIU Assessment and Testing

Nonetheless, they have similar successes:

Remedial Literacy Courses (Fall 04-Spring 08)

	PP				GA			
	mean	median	mode	pass %	mean	median	mode	pass %
remedial reading courses								
total (n=83/237)	2.84	B	A	83	2.88	B	A	84
ESL (n=63/184)	2.95	B	A	84	3.01	A	A	85
DEV (n=20/53)	2.50	B	A/B	80	2.43	B	A	77
remedial writing courses								
total (n=86/319)	2.67	B	B	87	2.72	B	B	84
ESL (n=73/260)	2.64	B	B	86	2.80	B	B	87
DEV (n=13/59)	2.85	B	A/B/C	92	2.34	B	B	71

Source: NEIU Office of Institutional Studies and Planning

17. See the appendix at the end of this chapter for the full matrix.

In other words, PP students are more likely to be assigned to remedial literacy courses, especially if they consider English to be a second or additional language, yet they have strikingly similar experiences in these courses, at least in terms of earned grades and passing rates, to their institutional peers.

However, their experiences in the required writing courses, which are offered in the English Department, are different although some contextualization is needed to frame these results. As suggested previously, the relationship between ELP and English reflects an institutional history in which the responsibility for instruction was originally assigned to linguists after the institutional reconfiguration of the 1960s, many of whom contributed to the formation of academic support programs, including Proyecto Pa'Lante and the English Language Program. At that time, no writing courses were required, and the institutional function of the English Department was to teach literature courses, at least until the 1980s when administrators proposed required writing courses to be offered in the English Department. In response to this proposal, ELP faculty who were concerned about the treatment of nonnative English-speaking students in the English Department, initially supported a single required semester, which was expanded over time to a second required semester only for those students whose majors are offered by the Colleges of Business and Education and not the College of Arts and Sciences.

Although, in the current institutional configuration, both ELP and English are responsible for introductory literacy instruction, each seems to understand these responsibilities in different ways, which could reflect disciplinary differences some have sought to unify (e.g., Matsuda 1999; Silva and Leki 2004). These differences, in practice, can be seen in the different approaches to training teaching assistants, which typically occurs over two days near the end of August just before classes begin.

When I observed these sessions (2005), the first day was a joint meeting in the Writing Lab that was conducted by faculty from the Linguistics Department, whose assistants teach ELP courses, and the Writing Lab staff. At this joint session, assistants from both areas were introduced to the policies and procedures of the Writing Lab where all of them would work as part of their duties, and they observed a mock-tutoring session. After lunch, they practiced tutoring each other—they were encouraged to work with partners from their respective areas—until they were asked to negotiate training schedules and then tour the library. In contrast, the second day consisted of separate sessions, ELP assistants in one classroom and English assistants in another, where they reviewed sample syllabi and assignments, which, when juxtaposed, highlight these differences. In particular, the sample ELP syllabus had scheduled activities involving the use of the dictionary and word lists to improve vocabulary, and the assignment packet contained collocation and CLOZE exercises. In contrast, the sample English syllabus had scheduled activities involving assessments of grammar and mechanics—colons and semicolons, apostrophes and commas, and complete sentences—and the assignment packet contained recommendations for writing effective dialogue and avoiding logical fallacies.

In order to enroll in Writing I, NEIU students must be placed into this course or earn a C or better in either Workshop III or Developmental Writing—the English Department does not designate certain sections for ESL students—and in this course, students receive "[s]pecialized instruction and practice in beginning writing. Work in usage, grammar, style, paragraphs, and short essays" (*Northeastern* 2004, 102). Without an official writing program at that time, the English Department had established shared course outcomes, at the same time that the PP students started at NEIU, through a departmental poll and vote:

- how to read and write for a variety of formats: multiple modes, genres, and purposes
- how to use strategies for invention and revision
- how to edit for grammar and spelling
- the fundamentals of argument
- how to critique writing
- how to document bibliographies when appropriate. (Language 2005, 3)[18]

Those who were required to complete Writing II had to earn a C or better in Writing I, and this course would consist of a "[c]ontinuation of practice in composition with emphasis on a variety of forms of writing and longer essays, culminating in the annotated research paper" (Northeastern 2004, 102). In particular, this course requires students to

18. One result of the multimillion dollar writing grant was the creation of a first-year writing coordinator, who scheduled a series of workshops with faculty who taught multiple sections of Writing I in order to standardize the course. However, the new outcomes were established in fall 2008 and implemented in spring 2009 after most of the students at the center of this project had completed this course.

- write in a number of formats (modes, genres, purposes)

- respond to sources

- construct successful arguments

- incorporate research materials into these arguments

- improve analytical skills

- learn to revise essays and edit them for grammatical error

- produce an extended research essay according to codified national techniques. (Language 2005, 3)[19]

Throughout this project, slightly more than half these required writing courses were taught by full-time faculty:

Fall 2004-Spring 2008 Required Writing Courses[20]

	Tenured/ Tenure-Track (%)	Full-Time Instructors (%)	Part-Time Instructors (%)	Graduate Assistants (%)
Writing I (n=230)	14	43	31	13
Writing II (n=174)	12	49	39	00

Source: NEIU English Department

Between five and six in ten of the Writing I courses were taught by full-time faculty, and slightly more than six in ten of the Writing II courses, which were fewer, were taught by faculty with the same institutional standing.

Unlike their experiences in the remedial literacy courses, the PP students' experiences in the regular writing courses were different from their institutional peers. Once again, the PP students—more than seven in ten—were more likely to use English as an additional language than their institutional peers—fewer than five in ten—and yet in the remedial courses, the PP students had similar results to their institutional peers'. However, they had somewhat different results in the regular writing courses:

---

19. Some English faculty maintain that the outcomes for Writing II have not been established or approved by the English Department.
20. These figures exclude summer sections, which are noncontractual and, as a result, often excluded in reporting by the institution. Also, graduate assistants have since been removed from the role of primary instructors of these courses.

Regular Writing Courses (Fall 04-Spring 08)

	PP				GA			
	mean	median	mode	pass %	mean	median	mode	pass %
ENGL 101 (n = 100/705)	2.28	C	C	85	2.37	B	B	81
ENGL 102 (n = 53/468)	1.77	C	B	62	2.20	B	B	71

Source: NEIU Office of Institutional Studies and Planning

While more than eight in ten of these PP students and their institutional peers passed the first regular, and required, course, they generally earned lower grades, and if they completed the second regular semester, they were more likely to earn lower grades and to fail this course.

GENERAL EDUCATION AND THE ECE

These and other introductory courses over their first few years are believed to be helpful to NEIU students, at least according to a faculty panel that, while these PP students were taking classes and earning grades, reviewed writing samples from before students started at NEIU and after they completed most or all of their general education requirements. In general, incoming NEIU students, according to the report, consistently struggle to provide coherent reasoning for their assertions. From the writing samples, the faculty panel concluded that the strongest aspect was the clarity of the thesis, with white and African American students obtaining the highest mean scores in this area, and style and conventions, with white and Asian/Pacific Islander students obtaining the highest mean scores. At the same time, Hispanic students had lower mean scores, which were attributed to "[s]econd language issues."

Despite these differences, the proficiencies of NEIU students after these introductory courses, according to this faculty panel, had generally improved:

Mean Scores on Entry- and 300-Level Writing Samples

	Entry Level Samples (n=150)	300-Level Samples (n=149)
thesis clarity	2.6	2.9
organization	2.5	2.8
support/reasoning	2.4	2.9

| style | 2.4 | 2.8 |
| conventions | 2.5 | 2.9 |

Source: NEIU Committee on General Education (2005)

In addition, the faculty panel, after comparing the samples from NEIU students to a national academic profile of 50,000 students from master's (comprehensive) colleges and universities, found no significant differences between the writing of NEIU students and the writing of college students at comparable institutions across the country (NEIU Committee 2005).

These findings seem inconsistent with the results from the English Competency Exam (ECE), which is required of all NEIU students. According to the university, the ECE measures "baccalaureate-level skills" or "college-level competency" in reading and writing (*Northeastern* 2004, 31; Writing Lab 2008). The purpose of the ECE, according to the Assessment and Testing Center that administers the exam, is to identify students who need "to improve their English skills" for both academic and professional success, and while the exam, the Center acknowledges, is no longer required by many institutions, it is "beneficial" for NEIU students in two related ways. First, different sections of Writing I have significant instructional differences,[21] and second, the campus has a substantial number of nonnative English users who might need a different (i.e., an ESL) approach to writing instruction (1). Given these conditions, the ECE ensures a consistency of ability – some writing instructors even suggest that successful completion of it is one of the unofficial goals of Writing I.

To complete this exam, NEIU students have 150 minutes to produce a handwritten essay of 500–700 words in which they "take a position on a social, educational, or business issue," such as whether financial support should be provided by husbands and wives or husbands alone or if the campus activity fee should be assessed of all students or only those who use these options. In preparing their exams, NEIU students are expected to use "proper essay format," consisting of an introduction and a conclusion with two to four body paragraphs, and they are encouraged to plan their approach—outlining, diagramming, or an alternative method—for an hour and to draft for an hour and a half. In addition, they are provided with sample outlines and essays with evaluations (Writing 2008).[22]

---

21. These differences have likely been reduced as a result of the $2.8 million HSI grant that, among other purposes, is to standardize the first-year writing program.
22. For most of the PP students, the ECE will be only a writing assessment. When this

According to NEIU, all students are expected to attempt the ECE by the time they have earned sixty credits (sophomore status) and to pass the exam by the time they have earned ninety credits (junior status), and more than eight in ten in the year (2003) before these PP students started at NEIU passed on their first attempt. As might be expected, those whose first language is English or who earned better grades in Writing I tend to do better on the ECE: between seven and eight in ten nonnative English speakers passed the ECE while more than nine in ten of their native-English-speaking peers had the same results. Almost nine in ten of those who earned an A in Writing I passed the ECE while between six and seven in ten of those who earned a C had the same success although those who completed this course at NEIU were somewhat less likely to pass on their first attempt (76.9 percent) than those who took the course elsewhere or otherwise had this requirement waived (85.6 percent). Finally, those who still cannot pass after exhausting all recommendations can submit a portfolio consisting of a self-assessment, an essay from the last writing course, an in-class writing sample, a researched writing project, and one of the failed ECE attempts (Writing 2008, 12–13; NEIU, *Northeastern* 2004, 31).

Even after four years, few of the PP students and their institutional peers attempted this exam:

English Competency Exam and Fall 2004 Cohorts

	PP (%) (n = 114)	GA (%) (n = 859)
attempted ECE	12.3	13.4
passed ECE	07.9	11.8
pass rate	64.3	88.6

Source: NEIU Assessment and Testing Center

Although few of these students have attempted the ECE, these initial results suggest another educational challenge for these PP students, who have much to do before they complete their degrees.

---

project started, the ECE also had a reading portion, which allowed thirty-five minutes to complete a standardized test divided into a vocabulary section of eighty words and a comprehension section of thirty-eight questions about seven passages. However, this portion was eliminated by the Provost, upon the recommendation of the Faculty Council on Academic Affairs in 2007, and as of spring 2008, almost nine of ten of these students had yet to attempt the exam. See the appendix to this chapter for these samples. At the same time, the ECE requirement was reduced in 2010 to an option for students who started before 2008, which could also be satisfied by completing a writing-intensive course with a C or better, and it was eliminated for all students who start at NEIU after spring 2012.

ETHNOLINGUISTIC DIFFERENCES AND EDUCATIONAL OBSTACLES

Once again, PP students bring as good and, in some cases, better expe-riences with and attitudes about literacy than their *national* peers, yet they are more likely to be placed into remedial literacy courses than their *institutional* peers. In remedial courses, the PP students, who are more likely to be multilingual, succeed in similar ways to their institu-tional peers, which could reflect the accuracy of the placement process, yet in the regular writing courses, the PP students, who again are more likely to be multilingual, struggle more than their institutional peers, especially in the second-semester course where the results, regardless of linguistic proficiencies, suggest larger problems for PP students. Finally, fewer PP students who have attempted the ECE have passed this gradua-tion requirement than their comparable institutional peers.

Clearly, these data are limited, and more analysis and research are needed to understand the experiences of ethnolinguistic minorities at this institution. For example, these data could be disaggregated in terms of relationship to English in order to analyze the statistical significance or correlated with other data, such as GPAs, zip codes, and median income, to develop analytic dimensions. (Staffing changes reduced access to institutional data, and multiple requests were unfulfilled or otherwise ignored.) Nonetheless, these results raise difficult questions about education and literacy for an official Hispanic-Serving Institution and the most (ethnically) diverse university in the Midwest.

In particular, these data suggest several ways this institution poses par-ticular problems for multilingual students. In general, more than seven in ten of these PP students (and almost five in ten of their institutional peers) are prevented from performing in the languages they identify as most central to their everyday lives. While some might argue that these performances must be conducted in English, such arguments at the very least presume conclusions to ongoing debates over language policies, as well as a misunderstanding of possibilities (e.g., Schmidt 2000).

At the same time, many PP students must expend additional resources, such as time and money, to complete required literacy courses, and thus their degrees, even as their access to these resources, as suggested, for example, by the economic and educational status of their parents, is often less.[23] In general, PP students are more likely to be

23. Some NEIU students might be unaware of how their answers to the question of whether English is their first language can affect placement options and degree requirements.

placed into remedial reading and writing courses regardless of whether English is their first or additional language, and they are more likely to be assigned to complete a sequence of remedial literacy courses, given their multilingual abilities, than a single remedial course, which only increases the costs, in terms of both time and money, of their degrees. While these students and others who are placed into remedial literacy courses can count these credits toward their overall degrees, they cannot be used for general education or major requirement, which was a "hollow victory," in the words of one faculty member, at least until the approval of a minor in Interdisciplinary English Studies shortly after these PP students started at NEIU.[24]

In addition to extra costs, another potential problem is the institutional misrepresentation of multilingual students, who often find their experiences and expertise reduced to binary terms.[25] At NEIU, institutional identities are established, at least initially, by self-reports on language surveys and placement performances although such institutional and disciplinary designations, such as ESL or ELL, can reflect tactical and emotional choices of students that can shape experiences in significant, and sometimes unexpected, ways (e.g., Harklau 2000; Starfield 2002). While some have suggested other options, such as Generation 1.5 (e.g., Harklau, Losey, and Siegal 1999), that can better recognize the complexity of experience and expertise, others have argued that even these more informed designations still essentialize differences and suggest deficiencies (Ortmeier-Hooper 2008, 410–412).

In these and other ways, PP students face educational obstacles, especially in their introductory literacy courses where they likely encounter faculty who add to these demands by denying ethnolinguistic differences.[26] In this instance, the issue is not that faculty fail to recognize cultural differences. For example, many define *diversity*, as in the most *diverse* university in the Midwest, as a *diversity of experience*, or a "flexibility of thought," according to a full-time English instructor who has taught at NEIU for seventeen years even as for this instructor the U.S.-born

---

24. Shortly after this minor was approved, the minor as a graduation requirement was eliminated.

25. For more, see Canagarajah (2002, 10), Leki (2006), Matsuda (2006), or Valdés (1992, 92).

26. In preparing these questionnaires, I started with the more generic term—*diversity*—used by the institution, and while a couple asked for clarification, most defined it as *ethnic diversity*, as the institution generally does. After distributing fifty-two questionnaires to colleagues in the Reading, English Language Program, and English, I received fifteen responses, for a response rate of 29 percent.

students need more "thought-diversity awareness" than their foreign-born counterparts.

Rather, the problem is that most of these instructors seem to believe that ethnolinguistic diversity interferes with reading and writing. For example, a member of the Reading Program, and a graduate of NEIU, suggests that diversity goes beyond "different ways of knowing" to include "different styles of questioning as well as different patterns of interaction" that can shape "learning styles, content, and instruction styles," and yet she insists that she mentors "Standard American English" in her responses to students, albeit in green, and not red, ink. In a similar way, a tenured English faculty member explains that she refuses to teach the second-semester writing course because she cannot overcome the impact of cultural differences upon reading even as, in advising other instructors, she recommends greater toleration of more personal writing styles that nonetheless must be counterbalanced with "the conventions of academic discourse."

Even if some recognize diversity of practices, most stop short of diverse standards, particularly for writing. For example, another faculty member insists that "a good essay" is "not a matter of diversity" but rather "a matter of communicating effectively," and still another rejects "a lot of diversity in writing" in favor of "a style of writing that is effective as literary criticism," which is defined as "economical syntax, careful and considered word choice, correct grammar, and consistent purpose." One tenured English professor who has taught at NEIU for almost forty years expects "clear, grammatical understanding English" (sic)—in his terms, "No more no less"—and a part-time instructor who is also a writer emphasizes the importance of recognizing the need for remediation, especially for ethnic minorities.

Among those who responded, only one suggested the possibility that ethnolinguistic diversity could be productive. Often people encounter problems, she explained in her office, when talking to others who don't use English often, and sometimes this situation can be exciting. "When you're talking to somebody," she said, "who has a really heavy accent so you have trouble understanding them. Or they don't quite know the language, and you're sort of . . . they'll say something, and they'll kind of reach toward you to get the word they need, and so it can really be very stimulating and create a certain—I don't know what you'd call it exactly—a feeling of intimacy." She had shut her door to ensure that we wouldn't be interrupted. "Like you're struggling together," she said, "like it becomes a collaborative effort to make the conversation." However, she rarely has this experience, she explained, only a few times with people who have recently arrived in the United States and never with NEIU students.

Such experiences persist beyond the introductory literacy courses. For example, an administrator who came to the United States at the age of eighteen responded to a question I asked concerning his predictions about the experiences of ethnolinguistic minorities at NEIU. After he sketched an overview of institutional requirements, I asked about his experiences.

"From my experience—you know I take courses here from time to time—I have had pretty bad experiences from some classes. Some instructors lack sensitivity to other cultures or individuals' differences. And they—well some instructors obviously don't know how to deal with these things, how to handle situations that they are not familiar with, so I'm sure some—well not only minority students but mainstream students too, I think—might have a difficult time."

I asked for an example.

"Well how about English?" he said. "ESL students. They go to a writing class, and depending on how the instructors perceive their skills, or well let's say their mistakes or their errors, [they succeed or not]. . . . [S]ome instructors say 'Your English is so awful you can't—you don't belong here. Look at this. You can't even make a sentence.' That may be the case, but you know the students might be very mature, and they can think intelligently and maturely despite their English, but if the instructor failed to see that, the students might not have a good time. Or [be] motivated to stay at school or proceed."

As these responses suggest, ethnolinguistic differences are often framed as educational obstacles to overcome, which can be found not only in introductory literacy courses but also in the English Competency Exam. While the PP students in my study were taking classes and earning credits, this graduation requirement was debated in the campus newspaper. In an opinion column in the campus newspaper, a student suggested that the ECE was "an undue burden" for students who use English as an additional language, that English proficiencies are better certified in ENGL 101 classes, and that standards arguments are "code for neo-conservative rhetoric" to establish "dominant Anglo, middle class, English-speaking American culture as the norm" and to marginalize "non-Native English speakers" in schools and throughout society (López 2007a). In published responses, a math lab supervisor argued that such a position is an extreme form of anti-intellectualism and that English proficiency cannot be certified through ENGL 101, and an English professor argued that the ECE and other language proficiency requirements, as forms of "de facto discrimination," prevent some students, especially "non-middle class, non-native students," from competing for jobs that both these and the middle-class students are qualified to have (Martindale 2007; White 2007a).

Clearly, these responses raise questions not just about educational obligations of an institution to the students it admits, which had been debated in a national forum, but also about the intellectual and social impact of linguistic policies and literacy philosophies upon students, especially the ethnolinguistic minorities that constitute its institutional identity, the ones it ostensibly serves. These larger implications, which extend beyond the results from the experiences of the PP students, are the focus of the next three chapters.

Appendix A

Manuel
March 14, 2005
Seminar II

New Life after Elementary School

The things that happened when I arrived to the United States were useful towards my life and towards my education skills. The three most important times that changed my life were when I attended elementary school, when I started high school, when I started my second year in high school and so on.

While attending elementary school, I was learning how the English language worked. My English speaking was very poor, and my other classes I was doing bad also. To tell you the truth, my two years in elementary were nothing at all, I went there to learn, but I didn't learn that much. I was a lazy student and didn't participate at all because back then I didn't had that skill to learn fast and being able to recognize the things that the teacher went through the last day. In my math class we were doing fractions and decimals, and I learned that math in 5th grade back in Ecuador; unfortunately, I wasn't learning nothing new. In science, social studies, and in English my learning wasn't that good. Back then, my importance of learning these subjects weren't something fun to do. As my first year flew, the second year was just around the corner. In my second year, new challenges were coming as I learned new thing, but it wasn't enough for me, and I couldn't face them because of my skills in my education. These two years were good, but not very good at all; however, at the end of the school year I was put to go to Roosevelt H.S. Everybody said that this school was pretty bad and that gang members attended there. I felt kind of scared and at the same time nothing in life because of my laziness towards learning. Fortunately, I decided not to give up and keep up studying because I knew it was up to myself and not to the school system.

I though that the classes were going to be harder than the classes from elementary school, but I though wrong and realize that it was much easier. During my first year I was beginning to form some kind of understanding to teachers and being able to do my homework easily than before. As the days past in the school, there was also an interlude while studying, like going to practice for the school soccer team. This hobby motivated me towards learning because if I didn't passed my classes, I couldn't be in this team anymore. I also did poor during my freshman year, my grades were low except for one, my English class. I began to develop my English skills and to understand more to the words that make the English language hard to learn. After a while, this class became my favorite one and from that time to now, in all of my English classes, I have been doing pretty well. My absorption of learning became really high and at the same time learning new things in life became a really fun thing to do. After my first year came to an end, new challenges began to appear and that time I could face them easily and with a good improved English understanding. I knew that the second year was going to be harder, but I was just starting to learn and to keep it to my mind for the rest of my life.

After I was done with my freshman year and became a sophomore, new things came to my life, so I was ready to challenge them. Since that moment, all classes became easy and very understandable for me, my professors were real nice with me forcing and advising me that learning is the success of becoming a professional, and a well educated person in life. Many things became interested for me such as foreign languages and learning how to play the guitar. All these cool classes carry me to become a good student towards the end of high school. I loved electronic things like computers, video games; however, my passion was a sport. I think that playing a sport keeps you motivated and energetic in going to school to learn something new because you feel free and at the same time you have two important times in your life. My education went from poor to excellent, I learned a lot of things attending four long years in high school. My professors and family played a really good role while I was going to school, but I think that my prestige and guts of learning was the main key to graduate from Roosevelt H. S.

Learning new subjects and especially English helped me a lot on going to college and start like an average student would start. Going from seventh grade to twelfth grade was a good experience for me because I didn't just learned math, English, and other subjects, I also learned how to be a respectful, honest, and educated person as the years passed. Passing from elementary school to high school was a challenge for me, too. Before going to ninth grade, I was lazy and I didn't learned nothing; however, during the next years in high school I learned a lot of things and important things, so I could defend myself and also because of me, I was the one who dedicated to study hard, so I could start my career attending a college.

Appendix B
ECE INSTRUCTIONS AND SAMPLE RESPONSE

SAMPLE ONLY: THESE ARE NOT ACTUAL ECE QUESTIONS!
Exam # XXXXX
English Competency Examination
Essay Topic Sheet

Instructions: Choose one of the following statements, circle the number of the statement that you have chosen, and write a well-organized, multi-paragraph essay of 500-700 words supporting that statement. Be sure to develop your essay by giving logical arguments and specific details, and remember to proofread your work for grammar, punctuation, and mechanics.

You may use the attached color sheet to write notes, ideas, or an outline. You will be graded only on what you write in the lined essay booklet.

1. Children should be allowed to have computers and televisions in their rooms.

2. Children should not be allowed to have computers and television in their rooms.

3. It would not be a good idea for office workers to bring their dogs or cats to work with them.

4. It would be a good idea for office workers to bring their dogs or cats to work with them.

5. There are many advantages to being a returning adult student at Northeastern.

6. There are many disadvantages to being a returning adult student at Northeastern.

THE ENGLISH COMPETENCY EXAM TOPICS, ANSWER SHEETS, AND RELATED TEST MATERIALS ARE THE PROPERTY OF THE NORTHEASTERN ILLINOIS UNIVERSITY ASSESSMENT CENTER. ALL MATERIALS MUST BE RETURNED TO THE EXAMINATION SUPERVISOR BEFORE YOU LEAVE. NO COPIES MAY BE MADE.

Sample Essay

This section includes the instructions you will receive for your ECE, as well as sample topics, a sample outline, and a sample essay. Following the sample essay is a brief discussion of its strengths.

Instructions: (This is the exact wording you will find on an ECE booklet.) Choose one of the following statements, circle the number of the statement that you have chosen, and write a well-organized essay of 500—700 words supporting that statement. Be sure to develop your essay by giving logical arguments and specific details, and to address the topic fully. Also, remember to proofread your work for grammar, punctuation, and spelling.

You may use the attached color sheet to write notes, ideas, or an outline. You will be graded only on what you write in the lined essay booklet.

Sample topics: These are not real ECE questions; they are examples of what you can expect to receive.

1. TV has a positive impact on children's development.

2. TV has a negative impact on children's development.

Sample outline: The following is a sample outline for essay topic #2:

I. Introduction
II. T.V. interferes with progress in school
   A. discourages doing homework
   B. discourages outside reading
III. T.V. interferes with social development
   A. discourages interactive communication skills
   B. discourages use of social skills
IV. T.V. interferes with physical fitness
   A. discourages physical activity
   B. encourages poor eating habits
V. Conclusion

Sample essay: The following is a sample essay for topic #2

Watching too much television can cause children to not have enough time for development of other skills and activities which are important for any child's growth, as well as important for creating successful and

healthy adults. These negative effects on a child's growth include reasons such as the fact that TV could interfere with a child's progress in
school, with a child's social development, and could also interfere with
a child's level of physical fitness and eating habits.

First, TV interferes with progress in school. My kids, for example,
would rather watch TV than do homework anytime, and from what
they tell me, so would their classmates and friends. However, without
the reinforcement that homework provides, it takes children longer to
grasp important concepts which they are learning in school. Doing their
homework thoughtfully and carefully helps a child do better on exams
in class, and to be a better student not only in early grades, but also in
high school and college. In addition, kids can do much better in school
if they read in addition to the material in their textbooks. Not only does
additional reading foster better reading and comprehension skills, but
reading offers more knowledge to the child than what is offered only
in class. For example, I learned a great deal of history and geography
through reading historical novels, some basic logic through reading
mystery novels, and anthropology and philosophy through science fiction. Unfortunately, TV lures children away from homework and from
outside reading, and their performance in school suffers. It is important
for parents, therefore, to encourage their children to watch less TV and
to spend more time on activities such as homework and reading so that
they can develop intellectually.

Second, TV can interfere with children's social development. When
kids watch TV, they are being passive recipients of what they see, instead
of talking to each other, responding to questions and thinking about
ideas and new ways of looking at things. Sometimes, I have to yell or
step in front of the television to even get my children's attention, and
to try to get them to talk with me. It is important for children to learn
how to interact with others and to express their ideas, and it is important
for them to learn to use their imagination and to share their thoughts
with others. Many television programs offer nothing but the same old
plots, the same characterizations and story lines, and do not encourage
the imagination or questions about our world or human behavior. In
addition, children do not sit together after a TV show and discuss what
happened in the program, come up with their own ideas of what they
just saw, or take time to agree or disagree with the outcome of the plot
or the "moral of the story." Instead, they just continue to watch another
television program, accepting what they see as reality. Not only do their

intellectual and imaginative skills suffer, but also their basic social skills. Instead of sitting passively in front of the television, children should be playing together, and learning basic social skills such as waiting for a turn, sharing, or asking for things politely.

Finally, TV negatively affects children's development physically as well as intellectually. With TV's dominance of our lives we have come up with the phrase, "couch potato," to describe people who spend much of their time sitting in front of the TV instead of exercising. Children need to engage in physical activities such as playing games, running, and walking in order to develop fitness habits which will last a lifetime. In addition, while they are sitting for hours watching television, television commercials encourage a desire for snacks such as candy, sweetened cereal, soda pop, chips, and other high calorie junk food. The combination of no exercise and lots of junk food eaten during TV viewing results in children who are unfit, overweight, and sluggish. If a child does not learn the necessity of physical fitness and a balanced diet when they are young, they will most likely be unfit and overweight adults.

In order to create adults who are intellectually, socially, and physically fit and developed, it is important to encourage all the necessary habits and skills early in life. TV, because it encourages little attention for school work and intellectual growth, almost no social interaction, and no physical activity and healthful dietary habits, has a negative effect on a child's possibility of becoming an accomplished and healthy adult.

Basic strengths of this essay:

- The introduction has a strong organizing thesis, as well as a brief description of the reasons that will be used in the body paragraphs.

- Each body paragraph has a topic sentence.

- The writer uses examples and illustrations for each point.

- The writer also uses good techniques of persuasive and argumentative writing.

- There is frequent use of transition and connecting phrases (for example: first, second, finally).

- The conclusion restates the main idea of the essay, but does not simply repeat the introductory paragraph.

- There are very few grammar, punctuation or sentence structure errors.

- The essay meets the length requirement of 500-700 words.

Different Standards
PART III

Throughout the fall, the Language Skills Assessment Task Force completed its review of literacy instruction on campus, and I started my survey of the Proyecto Pa'Lante students. Meanwhile, the union was negotiating a new contract, which had been extended, month by month since the summer, and when negotiations slowed, a strike was authorized and then called.

For almost three weeks, the university more or less stopped, after which the semester was extended, and the break was shortened. We returned in the spring to a tense campus and an unexpected hire—someone with an educational psychology PhD and a dissertation in second language suprasegmental phonemes—to lead the WAC efforts. As I analyzed survey results, the others on the LSATF and I were preparing our final report. In our ongoing deliberations, I occasionally expressed my concerns about institutionalized literacy instruction, which seemed validated by the data about experiences with and attitudes about literacy of the PP students.

After submitting our report and concluding the semester, I moved to Oak Park, which is known throughout the area for its cultural diversity and its public schools. In 1973, Oak Park approved its first Diversity Statement, and in 1997, it reorganized its schools to "enhance" its social diversity (Village 2001). In the most recent version of the Diversity Statement, its authors acknowledge the tensions between cultural differences and shared identities, as well as the need to respect the past and change the future, and they encourage residents both to celebrate their differences and to find consensus for the future (Village 2003).

When I mentioned the move, colleagues from the College of Ed or who lived in Oak Park praised my kids' new elementary school, which was named for Horace Mann, the public school advocate who argued in 1848 that public education, if "universal and complete," would "do more than all things to obliterate factitious distinctions" throughout society. Adjacent to a public park, the central building rose over neighborhood homes while more modern wings stretched from one end of the leafy block to almost the other.

As I settled into a new semester, my kids adjusted to new teachers and new friends, and soon, I received notices of their first parent-teacher conferences. On the appointed afternoon, they led me through solemn hallways where a few other parents walked, heads bowed over folders in their hands.

We waited outside the classroom door. Once my daughter's teacher finished with previous parents, she ushered me into her classroom where we lowered ourselves into small seats around a circular table near the back of the room. For most of our conversation, I listened to her impressions of Mahal's abilities and reviewed samples of her work. Her teacher showed me benchmarks from the beginning of the school year, and she explained her goals and expectations for my daughter.

At the end, she slid a special education consent form across the table for me to sign. Your daughter, she said, needs speech therapy.

Surprised, I asked how she had reached that conclusion.

The speech therapist can better explain, she said. You'll want to meet her before she leaves for the day.

She led me into the hall—I motioned for my kids to continue sitting—and into another room where she introduced me to the district speech therapist. After her classroom teacher left, I asked the same question, and the speech therapist turned to a metal filing cabinet and withdrew a piece of paper, which she handed to me. It consisted of a speech chart with English sounds—between forty and forty-five depending on how you count—and acquisition ages—in years and months—at which children should demonstrate their mastery of these.

She is behind other kids her age, said the speech therapist, but with a few sessions, she can easily catch up.

When I asked about the source of this chart, the speech therapist said she would get back to me. Several days later, my daughter dutifully delivered a sealed envelope, which contained another speech chart, this time with a bibliographical citation highlighted in bright yellow.

After confirming that the article was available in the campus library, I clutched the citation as I climbed three flights of stairs and then scanned the stacks for the journal and the volume. Flipping through the issues to the article, I reviewed the abstract, which indicated that this 1980s article, based upon monolingual speakers from Iowa, was actually a replication of a 1930s study of monolingual speakers from Nebraska.

After copying the article, I contacted the speech therapist, who refused to discuss the relevance of this study or other issues, such as the homogenization of English, for a district committed, in the language of its mission statement, to the needs of a diverse population. Then I scheduled a meeting with a school administrator, an ethnic minority woman who also had young children, and I explained, at a small table in her cramped office, that while I didn't object to speech therapy for my daughter, I couldn't determine whether she needed it. She assured me that she understood my concerns because she too cringed when her husband mispronounced certain English words around their children.

At that point, I realized something wasn't clear, so I withdrew my consent and contacted the district administrators, as I had been encouraged to do. While the first never responded, the second indicated, weeks later, that this sound chart was only one of several factors in the speech evaluation although two of the four criteria, according to the evaluation rubric I received, invoked "developmental guidelines" for determining whether a child's speech had an "adverse effect" upon cognitive development or social interaction.

As these discussions continued into the spring term, local activists and others across the country had been publicizing a nationwide protest they were calling A Day Without Immigrants. The week before the planned march, President George W. Bush proclaimed that the national anthem should be sung in English, not Spanish, although his wife Laura later admitted she wasn't troubled by other languages for this song as long as the tone was respectful.

On the morning of the march, I called my kids' school to report their absences, and then we walked with friends to the Green Line for a ride to the rally. We got off the train at Ashland and descended from the platform into an eddy of thousands listening to local leaders argue for the rights and, when Barack Obama spoke, the responsibilities of immigrants.

Then the tides reversed, and we flooded into the streets—some say 400,000 in Chicago alone, some say many, many more—and flowed downtown. Waves of sound—*si se puede*, from César Chávez and

Dolores Huerta, and *el pueblo unido jamás será vencido*—crashed against big buildings. As we ebbed and flowed, I thought about the immigrants in my life, including those at the university where even the undocumented only pay in-state tuition as long as they attended an Illinois high school.

Several weeks later, my son's teacher, at his spring parent-teacher conference, recommended a speech therapy assessment for him. Later, a colleague whispered to me, at commencement while we waited for degrees to be distributed, that her friend, a speech therapist who sometimes consults for my kids' school district, told her that Filipino students are often referred to speech therapy. On the basis, apparently, of monolingual speakers in Iowa and Nebraska from decades ago.

3
ONE OF THEIR TEACHERS

with Neida Hernandez-Santamaria

When Neida told me she wanted to be a lawyer but her LSAT scores weren't good enough, we were sitting around a table near the coffee stand in the noisy student union, discussing the session of her PP seminar class I had just observed.

I had realized, soon after starting these observations, that she was part of a larger story about education and literacy, so I had asked if she wanted to collaborate on this chapter with me. "You'll have to show me the ropes," she said. I mentioned Richard Rodriguez's *Hunger of Memory* (1983), which was in the campus bookstore because I was using it in one of my writing courses. She said she probably wouldn't read it.

We were sitting at the same table at the end of the semester when she mentioned she had not only read Rodriguez's book but had also tracked down a PBS interview he had done. "You should be shocked," she joked. "I don't read." As we discussed her reactions, she mentioned she had also attended the recent campus dinner for Nilo Cruz, the 2003 Pulitzer Prize-winning playwright who, like her father, had come from Cuba. After dinner, Cruz had read from *Anna in the Tropics* and other works, so I asked if she liked his use of language. "You know at the moment I don't think I was in the mindset," she said. "I was just ready to go." Agreeing that it had been a late evening, I tried to explain what I liked about his lyrical language.

Neida and I often discussed her experiences and this project as I tracked the PP students through the institution. From time to time, she shared reflections she had written for this chapter. Then, eighteen months after we started our discussions, she notified me in an email that she was "out of fuel for this project":

> So although I loved the idea of seeing your project through to the end, I have found that the end for me has to be sooner than the project's. Now, I will

> understand if instead of using me to co-author a chapter you simply use me
> as having been part of your research.

At this time, the PP students from Neida's class and their program peers had just completed their first semester after the PP program (fall 2006), and they, according to traditional expectations, still had eighteen months before graduation. By NEIU standards, they could have years.

When I started this project, I had also volunteered to tutor PP students. For the first three weeks, I sat alone in the PP conference room during activity hour—an officially designated time free of classes for meetings and other uses—while the Proyecto Pa'Lante and Project Success advisers and administrators used the microwave and refrigerator that, along with the long conference table, filled the room.

Although I often overheard Spanish and English conversations in the nearby offices, I sat in silence until one day a work-study student, an older woman with rectangular glasses and highlighted hair, came into the conference room and asked if I was waiting for students. I introduced myself, and she told me her name. "They need to know," she said, "that it's a service right here." Then she left. A few minutes later, another person came into the room and asked if she could complain about her PP students' English. She told me her name was Neida. Once she finished describing her complaints, we discussed popular beliefs about English and culturally specific ways of speaking and writing. Then the work-study student returned. She said she had overheard our discussion and wanted to say that even Spanish-English speakers could be condescending to other Spanish-English speakers whose English wasn't as strong.

The following week, one of my students stopped when, passing the doorway, she saw me sitting at the table. Soon, she was telling me about watching political debates in English while her father watched in Spanish on another television in another room. She explained that as the oldest, she was the family translator—from English to Spanish for her parents, from Spanish to English for her brothers.

Neither the work-study student nor my student returned, but Neida did. Over the weeks, we discovered some surprising similarities. She was a conflicted Catholic who was interested in liberation theology, for example, and I was a recovering Catholic who was only interested in liberation theology. Often, we discussed the escalating tensions between the union and the administration. By the middle of the semester, a strike was authorized and, a month later, called. For twenty days, we marched around the campus perimeter. I sometimes saw other Proyecto Pa'Lante employees zoom through a break in the picket line, and I wondered how the strike might affect this project.

Once a new contract was approved, we returned to an extended semester and a shortened break, and after the new semester started, I met with the PP Director in her office to discuss the future of this project. When I mentioned the failure with tutoring, she explained that the PP program had attempted multiple models to provide tutoring that also were unsuccessful. One of the reasons, she suggested, was that in addition to completing classes, more than nine in ten of the PP students work, sometimes two jobs. Another reason, she thought, was the social stigma of tutoring, as well as the expectation to keep problems within families. These families, she told me, were the target of recent PP outreach—a PP family orientation program to address the unique circumstances of first- and second-generation Latinos who want a college education for their children or themselves.

At the end of our conversation, she suggested that I continue this project by observing their seminar course—one of them was scheduled, she told me, for Mondays, Wednesdays, and Fridays from 9:00 to 9:50 am. Its instructor, she said, was Neida.

For one of my initial observations, I walked to the learning center on the fourth floor of the library. Once a month, Neida brought her students here to work on study skills with Katherine, the Learning Center Coordinator, whom the PP Director had also suggested I contact.

No one from the seminar was there when I arrived, so I asked Katherine about her work with the PP students. As we sat at a study table in front of looming library stacks, Katherine explained that she often worked on time management. I mentioned my first-hand familiarity with Filipino Time (and PR and Egyptian Time) and asked if she thought this "study skill" had a cultural component.

Katherine started a story about a friend who worked on PR Time when Neida arrived. I interrupted her to explain to Neida that I was recording the conversation because after initially agreeing to have her classes recorded, Neida had changed her mind. As Katherine finished her story, Neida listened, and then added that she knew professional people who would sometimes keep others waiting and then charge them for the time.

On the walk to the student union after the class session, Neida explained that she hadn't wanted to interrupt Katherine and me because she heard us talking "white," which always intimidated her. Later, I would learn that a Latino colleague had criticized her English when they had been co-teaching a course; this was why she had changed her mind about being recorded in class.

Neida did agree, however, to recording our conversations after class, which often addressed her uncertainties about education and language. Once over coffee at our usual table, she told me she had contacted a Catholic school to see if her MA in educational leadership, which she had also earned at NEIU, would enable her to teach there, but she was told it wouldn't.

She hates telling people she is a teacher, she explained, and she hates teaching because it's not what she wanted to do. I asked about her activities as an undergrad at NEIU, such as her work as a peer leader for first-year orientation sessions. These sessions, she said, involved "facilitating," not teaching, which, she explained, would require the completion of a teacher-education program. "Again, I wasn't trained to be a teacher," she said, "so you know I picked up on certain things." She mentioned her Loyola University graduate assistant—"a classically trained English teacher"—who helped her.

Despite these uncertainties, she was confident of her conclusions about Latino students. When, for example, I suggested that sometimes students are blamed for performances in ways that ignore larger institutional and social contexts, she quickly challenged me. "I have to say this," she said. "From my experience—I don't know if this is for every Latino in the world or whatever—*that* doesn't happen. It's someone else's fault. I think that students think that too. It's ingrained."

Intrigued, I asked her to tell me more. "The Latinos," she said, "we. That is my experience. There is something wrong, something failed— someone or something failed; somewhere along the process someone should have done something better or provided an opportunity bet-ter—a better opportunity, and then I have to say that there have been a few instances where parents have said, 'This is a rotten apple' or 'a bad seed,' but that's much rarer, that's . . . I don't know."

She mentioned her husband, an auto mechanics instructor at a local community college. "I know that that sounds terrible on my part," she said, "but he truly and deeply cares and interacts with students, and you should just see the way the students interact with him and I think admire him. You can—it's very weird. My students couldn't—wouldn't never be—I don't know."

At some point, she became "disillusioned" with teaching, she explained, realizing that "it's just work," while her husband sees it as much more than that. "That is why I say," she said, "that I need to do something else. Although I guess on the outside it may look like I do a good job and I'd say okay, yeah, I guess by certain standards I'm fulfilling the requirements of my job, but it's work. I don't know if that made sense."

I said that from my experiences in her classroom, she seemed quite committed to, and invested in, her students.

"You see and that's what I'm saying—that's what's so weird—I'd just—but inside my heart I think it's work," she said. "Maybe that's just me saying—well that way I don't have to invest so much, and then I don't get all bent out of shape when things don't go well. I don't know."

Early in our collaboration, I asked Neida about the way the institution responds to the cultural diversity of its students. "In terms of PP responding to the diversity of its students," she wrote, "that is easy."

Every student is assessed one on one. As advisors we develop relationships with the students individually where we encourage sharing thoughts, ideas, challenges, needs, etc. . . . We are sensitive to the environments that the students have come from and continue to learn from the students as we develop deeper relationships, which helps in addressing each student's needs. Taking into consideration the fact that we are promoting Latino students success, we are morally required to be aware of environmental and social factors that impact the diverse members of the Latino community. By being aware we can more effectively help our students succeed in college and eventually as professionals by tailoring for example the Seminar classes to meet specific needs.

NEIU in general I think would be proud of the way it responds to diversity. NEIU provides a forum for different groups to be represented in classes topics and programming. I think that NEIU has a challenge in that because of its diversity, it cannot make any one group fully satisfied. Everyone always wants more. However, achieving balance is the key to a basic sense of peace. As long as NEIU is taking proactive measures to satisfy and represent its diversity in all areas, honestly and genuinely and is able to provide legitimate evidence of the efforts and results supporting [and] promoting diversity as a number one priority, then NEIU is on the right path in terms of responding effectively to the diversity of its students. I think that we still have work to do in having NEIU staff, faculty and administrators reflect the students' diversity, but this is not a problem specifically for NEIU. I think this is a multifaceted and complex issue in higher education.

This sense is shared, she indicated, by others in the Proyecto Pa'Lante program and across NEIU.

Perhaps her uncertainty was the result of her experiences as an instructor and adviser for the PP program. After her seminar class had concluded, I asked for her perspectives on and predictions for the students enrolled in it:

In terms of success stories, or who I have the most faith in terms of graduating and "becoming someone" as the students and I say, is Arturo.[1] After the seminar II, he requested to have his advisor changed. I have been his advisor ever since. He makes me proud because I can feel how much he wants to do well in life. He may not have the perfect grades and may still get distracted every now and then, but he is going to make it!!!!! I don't know if you remember, but I expressed to my students that I want them to want to do well and finish school. Frequently, I say, 'I want you to want to want it.' Arturo has truly demonstrated to me how he has grown and matured.

Ricardo seems to be lost forever or for a very long time. He has completely disappeared. The issues he was having with the legal system and his immediate environment seem to have required more of his attention than college. He might be a late blossom.

Javier might be fine. He seems to have needed a lot of love. Something he was not getting from home. He wanted and required a lot of attention. The issue with Javier was that I think he may have confused my empathy and willingness to listen to the challenges he faced as a way to excuse him from producing in class. I saw him from a distance last week, and he immediately looked away.

Manuel might do okay. I don't have much to say about him since he was so quiet. The most I can comment on was his writing. He stuck around at NEIU.

1.   This student graduated in August 2010.

Oscar had lots of potential. However, I attributed some of his distractions to his involvement with a grass roots organization and his level of maturity. I think he was still testing the different worlds he could become a part of based on his interests. I don't know if he remained with the PP or NEIU.

When Manuel's father asked what Proyecto Pa'Lante had done for his son, he was expressing, Neida explained, a common expectation. "The expectation is there," she said, "that we are going to do something more, and I don't know what that more is other than maybe be ourselves and maybe be *Latino*, if you get what I'm saying."

After her PP seminar course had ended, Neida agreed to return to the essay that Manuel had written in response to the intellectual coming-of-age story she had assigned. In her initial response to it and him, she offered two brief and general comments—"¡Que Bien! Your story flowed very well. It had good structure!! I am proud of you. Now you need to work on your final draft!" and "¡OJO! Have, has & had—be careful using the right one. Your periods & commas—Careful w/ run-on sentences. And double check your tenses—Are [you] talking about the past, present or future?"—and this time, I asked her to reconsider it in relation to negotiations with Spanish.[2]

We had selected the same round table in the student union. Before turning to this text, she contrasted it with another submission from Manuel, which is why, she explained, she suspected he had gotten help with the introduction to this assignment that, she claimed, didn't fit. Then she worked silently through the first few lines until she reached a sentence—*I was a lazy student and didn't participate at all because back then I didn't had that skill to learn fast and being able to recognize the things that the teachers went through the last day*—that she had edited for Manuel in the version she had returned to him. On his draft, she had crossed out *had that* and inserted *have the* above it and underlined *being able to recognize* with a squiggly line. "He was thinking in Spanish when he wrote it," she said, "or whoever wrote it." Spanish, she explained, uses *being* obsessively,

---

2. Such a request resembles Tom Fox's (1999) efforts with a basic writer, and it reflects recent theories of negotiated literacy (Canagarajah 2006c; Schroeder 2001). At the same time, I wanted to know if Neida could use her own linguistic resources to reread her students' efforts (e.g., Canagarajah 2006c; T. Fox 1999, 61–70; Horner and Lu 1996; Kells 2004; Schroeder 2001). Again, this essay, in its entirety, can be found in the appendix to the previous chapter.

which was something she often saw in drafts from other students, and even in her own drafts, but she had heard from an English teacher that "you don't use *being* ever."

She continued working, sentence by sentence, until she reached another one—*I felt kind of scared and at the same time nothing in life because of my laziness towards learning*—that would be "a deep thought," she said, in Spanish. "Sound very eloquent in Spanish," she said. "In Spanish you could pull that off . . . sound like something you could read in literature, but it didn't work here."

None of these was marked in the version she had returned to Manuel.

She pointed to another sentence. Manuel had written *In my math class we were doing fractions and decimals, and I learned that math in 5th grade in Ecuador; unfortunately, I wasn't learning nothing new.* In her response, she had struck the semicolon, capitalized the first letter in *unfortunately*, and inserted *anything* above *nothing*, which she had crossed out. "That is weird," she said, "but I don't know why."

After some silence, I asked if the difference between negation in Spanish and English—*Lamentablemente, yo no estaba aprendiendo nada nuevo* perhaps—could be one explanation for why Manuel had written what he did.

"After doing this," she said, looking up and smiling, "I could decode *The Da Vinci Code.*"

I asked how she thought Manuel might be read by others. What might seem imprecise from an English reader's perspective, I suggested, or even illogical—*These two years were good, but not very good at all*—could be read differently by a Spanish speaker.

"It would pass as poetic," she said, "a sign of sophistication."

Or the opposite, I explained, if the English reader didn't know Spanish.

"Or boil it down to just not knowing the language," she said.

I asked if it suggested a broader knowledge of different Spanish varieties.

"Exactly," she said, "because he must know—or at least if he doesn't know how to write it . . ." She started over. "He missed out on the most sophisticated type of writing over there, but . . . the form of expression is sophisticated enough already in Spanish."

When we returned to the draft, she asked if I would object to an utterance she had marked—*I though that the classes were going to be harder than the classes from elementary school but I though wrong and realize that it was much easier*. She had inserted two *ts* on Manuel's manuscript to change *though* to *thought* near the beginning and end of the sentence.

I explained that the verbs were more marked for me, which might make me wonder about the timing of his realization—at a distinct point in the past as opposed to over time in the past or even in the present as he was writing—and I asked if she would shift to the present if she were using Spanish.

"It depends on how he is thinking," she said. "I could say it in the past or in the present. It's a matter of what he is thinking at the moment. It could work either way. And it would still get the same point across."

After translating it into Spanish, she said it had to be in the past, which means, she concluded, that he was thinking in Spanish. "A common mistake actually," she said, "that people like me would actually make in Spanish in reverse."

Later when we resumed our review, she seemed more immersed in her impressions, which she couldn't quite express. "I'm having a hard time switching to Spanish," she said.

She explained that for the past two weeks while she had been away from campus, she didn't use Spanish at all. In fact, she uses more Spanish at work, she said, than she does at home. She blames her husband's mother for his inability to use Spanish. While she doesn't use Spanish with their daughter, she said that she feels as if she needs to teach her Spanish in order to be a perfect mother.

Returning to the manuscript, she pointed to another sentence—*This hobby motivated me towards learning because if I didn't passed my classes, I couldn't be in this team anymore.* "That is totally in Spanish," she said. "I don't think you'd say that in English 'motivated me toward learning' but in Spanish, it would be '*me motivó asi a something,*' so that's exactly what he was saying—he was thinking in Spanish when he wrote it."

Then we discussed the differences between the Spanish *en* and the English *in* and *on*. "I realize I can't speak when I'm switching back and forth," she said. "Do you notice? I stumble."

She said that Manuel's Spanish vocabulary is better than hers.

I asked about Spanish expectations of what, in English, would be the *given-new* contract. The *new*, I said, seems to my nonnative ear to come much later in Spanish than in English.

"It's true," Neida said. "We always have this background—the need for this background information, and you're right because I grapple with that in English. Sometimes, I'm like, 'Okay Neida, now shut up, you really didn't need to do all that and say all that to get to the point.'"

Her teachers, she explained, tried to tell her about this and other expectations of English. Then she referred to Amy Tan's (2003) "Mother Tongue," an essay she found in the rhetoric handbook for her husband's writing course—he had gone back to school to earn his bachelor's degree—and said that some people are better than others at teaching others to make these shifts to an English self.

She explained that sometimes Manuel is thinking in Spanish, literally translating from Spanish, and sometimes he seems to think English is a certain way. She also suggested that he probably got help from someone, who she added might have been a native Spanish speaker. "I'm no expert," she said, even though her undergraduate major was Spanish. She suggested that I check with someone who is.

After rereading Manuel's manuscript, I later asked for her general impressions, and she emailed this explanation:

A theme emerged in Manuel's essay, "My Life after Elementary School". Manuel seems to be trying to figure out how things work. First he mentions in his essay that in elementary school he was ". . . learning how the English language worked." Then on page 2 of his essay, he states that he ". . . was beginning to form some kind of understanding to teachers. . ." he goes on to indicate being able to do his homework with greater ease, once he feels he has figured out how some things work.

Manuel has been focused on figuring out how systems work, like the English language, teacher student relationships, and the American schooling system. In attempting to figure out the systems, he then is unable to internalize and make meaning of the English language. This in turn impacts his academic performance negatively as he notes during his elementary school years and his freshman year of high school in Chicago. There is more to learning and performing academically well in schools and exams than the English language.

Another interesting characteristic from Manuel's essay was his use of the word "absorption" in relation to his learning. I think this speaks to a quality in my own learning that I have not been able to quite define and articulate in its entirety. This absorption implies other ways of knowing or learning more than the mechanics of the English language. Once Manuel felt he had absorbed sufficient knowledge about how the systems he was involved in worked, he is able to articulate that he learned at a higher rate and enjoys learning new things.

Although Manuel and she had attended the same high school, his experience, Neida insisted, was different from hers. When she was there, the school, she explained, was about half Latino, and now it's almost all Latino—90 percent, she said, or more.

Unlike Richard Rodriguez (Mexican American) after he started school, Neida still uses Spanish with her father (Cuban) and her mother (Costa Rican) but English with her sisters although she sometimes switches to Spanish with the older one who grew up with Spanish even though English, in Neida's opinion, is her older sister's stronger language. In high school, Neida used English, and while she could use Spanish with her friends, it was, in her own words, "an uncomfortable thing."

While earning her BA in Spanish at NEIU, Neida used English in her classes, at campus events, and with her friends although she had an undergraduate adviser, another Cuban who also earned her undergraduate and graduate degrees from NEIU, with whom she only used Spanish. Although this adviser, according to Neida, often criticized Neida's Spanish, at least she could understand Neida's English, which was something her father couldn't always do. Nonetheless, Neida and her father sometimes used English to exclude her mother—his wife—from their conversations.

When asked to describe the differences, Neida explained that Spanish is "wordier" in both speaking and writing and doesn't "get to the point." "Whereas English," she said, "this is what I'm going to talk about. Here is why or this is why it's important. And I'm done."

To illustrate, she offered an incident with her mother.

"Okay, so my mother—you go to the doctor and you say what you are feeling, and my Mom will go through a *history*, I swear to God, of when she was born to now. And she, let's say, needs to focus on the central nervous system, and she is talking about the peripheral first and then maybe this way and then maybe that and then maybe she comes to the central nervous system maybe. But then what happens—the doctor picks up on something else. Then she leaves the doctor's saying, (sigh) "Well, they didn't do . . . ," and I'm like, "What do you mean?" Well, because I'm thinking, yeah you probably gave him one of those really long stories, and the doctor's trying to pick out key symptoms or God knows what—you know I'm not the doctor—so it didn't work.

"Whereas I learned—I was the same way—I modeled—you know, didn't have any other experience so I had this new health insurance when I finally finished graduate school, so I go in with a piece of paper with three bullets of what's wrong with me. And then if the doctor chooses to ask more or wants a more descriptive story, then I will provide one."

This approach, she acknowledged, does have its limitations.

"I'm a little bit annoyed with this way," she said, "that is, because sometimes you need a little bit of the story, but that could be just an issue I have with health care. That is a whole other conversation."

She also indicated that these experiences provide some perspective for students. "I wouldn't be annoyed," she said, "but I would say, 'You know what? With me, I get it, but with other teachers, you're gonna need to'—and I do that a lot with them."

These differences exist, for Neida, in classrooms and with writing. "I'm like, 'Look, I know what you're saying, or you know I understand how you feel, but'—even with their behavior— for instance, maybe they're sitting like this, and I'm like, 'You understand—do you realize the impression you're giving?' And I don't tell—I'm not scolding them. I'll maybe talk to them later. I'll say, 'You know, I'm sure that is not what you want to do. That's not the message you want to convey because when you have someone else, what are they going to think about you? What are they going to think? Ah, lazy. Or not serious. You know? Is that what you really want to send out?' So that's what I do. And that's the same with the writing. They could dance around, and I'll say, 'Well yeah, but what's going to get you the grade is probably bam bam bam.'"

In part, the difference, she explained, is structure—"sticking to a nice framework, a structure, a familiar structure"—that she had been taught in schools. "The structure that at least in grade school I learned about," she said. "And obviously I've been rewarded in a lot of ways because I wasn't a bad—a horrendous college student. I got decent grades."

This structure is different from sentence-level features. "I'm not asking you," she said, "to have a sentence with all the the different pieces to it. I'm not asking you to use semicolons. Or colons. I'm just—*Jane went to school.* Period. You know. There's the beginning, middle, and end. The subject. All that stuff. I don't know."

In other words, some of these features transcend different languages. "That's why even for the nonnative speaker—the person who's still learning—I say, 'Think about it, even if you were talking about it in Spanish—if you kinda start changing the subject, it's time for a new paragraph.' But then a lot of my kids that are the nonnative didn't get formally educated in their countries anyway, so they don't really know the mechanics or whatever you call it in Spanish, so they don't have a structure."

These issues are obvious, from her perspective, in the personal statements prepared by students that are part of the Proyecto Pa'Lante application process, which come from native and nonnative English users. "Native speaker to me," she said, "means you were born here and learned English from day one or you came when you were really really really young and it's— you switch English-Spanish like it's not a big deal."

These distinctions help her, she explained, when she reads drafts from students although native-user status is no guarantee. "You know," she said, "I have plenty of native speakers that it's like Lord have mercy Jesus Christ please again somebody just kill me—I'm sharing that with you not again to say that I'm not being considerate of them as I'm doing it—I am being considerate—but when I step away, it's like Oh God, why, why."

This link between language and status, however, is no easy equation. With her daughter, Neida mostly uses English although her daughter hears Spanish from her parents, who watch her while Neida is working. (She laughs, she said, when she hears her parents using English with her daughter.) Although we mostly use English, Neida is Latina with me, she explained, but at her doctor's office, she is, in her own words, American.

Over the summer, we continued our conversations about her students, which often made her think of her own experiences.

I am thinking about linking Javier's experiences as I know them and a bit of my experiences, since we both went to the same high school and essentially grew up in the same neighborhoods. I realize of course, they are different times, but that is kind of the whole point of what I'm thinking about. Being successful in terms of education, and material wealth, and acquiring or "discovering" cultural knowledge and competencies (which also include language) based on where one starts on the *number line*, can have a monumental impact on one's life path regardless of the times. It is more one's immediate circle or [one's] resources or lack of resources and knowledge and time invested in figuring out systems of society that influence our life's direction.

Without explaining further, I would like to know what meaning you gather from my idea of the number line. I do have a detailed explanation of this idea, but would like to know if it is even needed.

I did ask for more, so she offered this elaboration:

You see, I was born to immigrant parents who did not know English. They did not know anything more than the idea that in the US one must work hard to live at least at a level that is presumably better than that of their native countries. Their lives were consumed with the day to day responsibilities of caring for children, keeping house, and earning a paycheck to stay afloat. What I have just described is the fact that in terms of material wealth, language, cultural knowledge, and competencies, my parents were at a major disadvantage compared to other segments of society that already possessed these essential skills and knowledge. Therefore, if I had to place my parents, during that time on a number line, they were probably at a negative four or five.

By the time I was born, I had the advantage of being exposed to English immediately. My sisters had finally learned English. Still, I was limited in terms of cultural knowledge, but I had one mighty tool available, my English language. I see myself somewhere between negative one and zero on the number line. Although, I am slowly inching along the number line in a positive direction, with every day that goes by, yet [I] always feel and probably am behind others of the same age from the same time.

I can confidently say that my daughter has already begun her life on the positive side of the number line, because she will not have to invest all the time that I have had to in figuring things out from society, in that I will hand down this information and be her resource.

As I collected, sifted, and synthesized, I was struggling to assemble these pieces into a coherent picture. Part of the problem was that in talking with Neida, I often got more than I anticipated, which only raised more questions.

LITERATURE IN MY HOME?

I was thinking about the kind of material that was read in my home as a child growing up and the impact that it has made in my life as an adult. A few of the least embarrassing kinds of "literature" read in my home were the Bible, *Reader's Digest*, the *Old Farmer's Almanac*, and "how-to" books. There were also the regular *Mad* magazines, photography magazines, and Spanish-language newspapers. What these publications, with the exception of the Bible and some of the Spanish-language newspapers, had in common was that they offered a window into "American" life and into mainstream culture for my father. It was a safe and interesting way to learn and gain knowledge about this relatively new world he was now a part of, at least geographically.

I recall seeing my father reading often. I can hear my mother comment on how my father was so smart. In the same breath, she would also say what a shame it was that he did not complete his higher education back in Cuba. My mother often made these comments when she was at her wits' end trying to tidy the house and organize the piles of books, newspapers, and magazines left behind by my father. It was as if she was thinking it was too bad he didn't devote the same time to more scholarly pursuits, implying that if he had done so, he could have potentially secured a better employment situation to improve the family's living conditions. After all, an education equals better employment opportunities, therefore a better life, right?

As an adult, I have determined that my reading habits and tastes are quite similar to those of my father. Although, I made no conscious effort to mimic his reading preferences, and he made no effort to explicitly state what I should read and like, it undoubtedly shaped me as an adult reader. Instead of reading scholarly material like literary novels that one might expect a college-educated person to do, I choose to devote my limited time to reading magazines and other material that offer practical information and/or inform me of current events. This kind of reading allows me to feel connected to the world I was born into, and become a more authentic bridge or window to "American" life and mainstream culture for my parents and family. Since my time is very limited, I feel that I must invest my time wisely into learning everything I can about the world I live in today, and not waste my time reading academic or literature-type material that feels so removed from my everyday experience. After all, I am not in college anymore and can freely choose what to read.

The point I am trying to make with this long-winded description of what was read in my home growing up is that although I am not reading the exact publications my father did, I read in a similar way and with a similar purpose. It is quite striking for me to realize that both my father and I are nuts and bolts kinds of readers. We are simple, practical persons who are seeking knowledge about our surrounding world.

FIRST WRITING MEMORIES

One of my first memories about writing is when I was in kindergarten. My sister would sit with me at the dining room table spelling out my name, N-E-I-D-A. I would sit listening to her say the letters and watching her write my name on a writing tablet over and over again. This extra help in learning to read and write my name came after some emotionally hellish first weeks of kindergarten.

Besides going through the normal separation anxiety, being abandoned by my Mami, I could not read or write my own name. Imagine for a moment that you are five years old and it is time to start kindergarten. You have never before read your name or written your name. Actually, you may have seen your name, but just did not know it was your name spelled out: N-E-I-D-A-H-E-R-N-A-N-D-E-Z. After several minutes of crying, wailing, and vomiting, you walk into a place that is completely foreign, the classroom. It is a classroom that is full of other children standing in a straight and orderly line. Also, standing before you is a tall old white lady with gray hair and glasses. As you look at her from a distance, you notice her blue eyes, then dark polyester pants, and finally her Buster Brown gummy rubber platform-soled tan suede shoes—very hip for the time. Finally, it is your turn to step up from the line towards the bulletin board. There are many index cards with big letters written in black permanent marker. You are asked to identify your name, pull it off the board, and drop it in a "present" pouch. The fear and anxiety overcomes you and you start to feel another wave of nausea. This was my daily kindergarten routine for the first couple of weeks in school and one of my first memories about learning to read and write. I have come to the conclusion that this kindergarten experience actually shaped how I feel about my name.

I have always focused on the negative aspects of my name. The fact that my name did not adhere to the English language rules regarding pronunciation made it all that more difficult for me to understand and learn how to write my name. I always wanted to have pencils or stickers or anything personalized with my name, but never was able to just go to a store and pick something up. My name did not exist in the world that I was living in beyond my family. Why could my name not have been Linda, Lisa, or even Maria? At least those names were easily written, read, and existed in the market place. My entire life, people have mispronounced my name terribly. I have been called Nadia, like the Olympic gold-medal-winning gymnast; at least that was someone special. But who the heck are Needa, Nidia, Eneeda, Anita, and Nerayda? All I know is that they are common mispronunciations of Neida. Recently, I stopped hating my name. Neida is not bad or ugly. It is just Spanish. It is just too bad so many can't pronounce it. It is a name that can only be pronounced in Spanish. Therefore, my new perspective on my name is that I have forced all those who have met me to learn and know a little bit of Spanish and a little bit of me. Yes, I was born and raised in Chicago, but I am more than geography and an unpronounceable name.

A year after my initial surveys of the Proyecto Pa'Lante students, I outlined the emerging connections between our collaborative chapter and the larger project, and then I asked Neida for her perspective:

The central problem that I see being addressed according to your proposal, is persuading people to appreciate (or at least acknowledge) the abilities or talent used when producing a meaningful message within "competing textual and cultural practices". So, maybe it is not so much about literacy or degrees of literacy, but presenting cases for describing instances showing the complexity (depending on how you view it—complexity or confusion?) of what individuals who are bilingual must manage.

Gosh, I don't know if this makes any sense. It is the same feeling I had when I left your office that other day. It is like I can't find the right words to describe THIS phenomenon.

I must say that you are much more positive than I when it comes to the experience and impact that being bilingual has on language and writing. The funny thing is that had you not presented your ideas to me, I would have always viewed the differences in our writing as deficient. I can confidently say that now, at least I can appreciate what you are trying to do—aha!!!! I think I have it!!!

I am a member of the bilingual group. You have not been, at least not naturally. Therefore your job as the "outsider" is to show using quantitative and qualitative methods (you know, a legitimate scientific approach) that "bilinguals" are as intellectually capable as anyone else—and what better tangible tool can we use to exemplify this point but writing? My job as an "insider" is slightly different. I believe that my job is to prepare "bilinguals"—Spanish/English—to expose them and act somewhat as a bridge between cultures, seeing as that I am a natural combination of both cultures. I would like to think of it in this way. What do you think about this last idea I presented? Could this be that "something" we were having a hard time encapsulating?

Within days, I received in the campus mail a photocopy of a newspaper column by David Brooks (2005) from the *New York Times* that Neida had gotten from the Director of *Proyecto Pa'Lante*. Neida had marked these passages on the photocopied page:

> College graduates earn nearly twice as much as high school graduates, and people with professional degrees earn nearly twice as much as those with college degrees.
>
> Now we live in a society stratified by education. In many ways this system is more fair, but as the information economy matures, we are learning it comes with its own brutal barriers to opportunities and ascent.
>
> Educated parents not only pass down economic resources to their children, they pass down expectations, habits, knowledge and cognitive abilities. Pretty soon you end up with a hereditary meritocratic class that reinforces itself generation after generation.
>
> A lot of it has to do with being academically prepared, psychologically prepared and culturally prepared for college.

The highlighted areas," she wrote in blue ink, "are points that to me seem to be a form of literacy. This is why I keep saying that college/writing (to me it is the same) equals more opportunities in life." Next to her signature was a hand-drawn smiley face with an extended hand, and beneath it, she had written, "ENJOY!"

Between sessions of her course, she had told me that she knew why her PP students had asked her to read Lockett's "How I Started Writing Poetry" to them but that she wasn't going to tell me. Later, she explained that she thought they had asked her to read to them because they had never been read to. The reason she hadn't told me, she explained, was that she thought I would steal her theory. "Oh you can have it," she said, "you can write about it, it's yours."

For our next discussion, we had agreed to meet in the new Proyecto Pa'Lante conference room, which along with the rest of the program had been relocated to the fourth floor of Lech Walesa Hall. She gave me a tour of their new offices, and then she took me across the hallway to the conference room that still smelled of new carpet.

After we swapped stories about our families, we turned to our chapter. At one point, she mentioned she had recently attended a Mission Weekend where, she explained, she had been introduced to the others in her new graduate school cohort—her concentration, she explained, is Latino Studies. "The issues with why we're coming to college," she said, "and why we're basically so academically underprepared."

Although we had been meeting for more than a year, she had never mentioned that she was, after abandoning plans for law school, considering an EdD program where she would concentrate on these issues. Nonetheless, she wanted to know more, she explained, about these conditions and their causes. "Which, in my mind, I think I know the answers. I hear all the social problems, all this, but it would be nice actually—okay, I did the research, now I know. This is really what's happening. This is really what's not happening. We can't blame this."

Part of the appeal, she told me, is the promise by the program that she will discover much about herself. "I need to have a purpose," she said, "and this I think will help me, and maybe it'll answer why I maybe perceive myself to have been academically underprepared, and I don't always feel up to par as it is, so you know always trying to keep up, trying just to stay up at a minimum."

She'll need three years, she explained, to finish the program. "I'm curious to see who I'm gonna be by the time I'm done," she said. "Not that I'm going to be a completely different person, but I'm excited to just be able to make more links and understand more things. And just from that one weekend, from having gone through some readings and experiences, sitting here at some presentation, I was already thinking, 'Oh that kinda goes with what we were talking about'—or doesn't go, or whatever."

Her family, she explained, is supportive, but others have teased that she is less worried about the academic challenges and more concerned about the social consequences, including the two weeks over the summer when she'll be away from her family.

That fall, she returned to campus fully immersed in her graduate education program. Near the end of the semester, I suggested that perhaps I could draft this chapter over the break, and then she and I could revise it throughout the spring. "Neato-frito!" she wrote.

I think that I like your plan about bouncing it back and forth. Can we make a point somewhere to clarify that I am a work in progress and so is my thinking and thoughts? As I continue to read, learn and experience more in life and school, I just feel like I keep growing in all directions. I will be checking in with e-mail during our break and stuff so this should work.

I realize that I have given you some written thoughts and have had many e-mail exchanges with you. Would it be appropriate to ask you to pick the ones you would like to expand on? That way I could put together more and we could respond to each other's thoughts. Do you plan on working in our conversations or was that more a tool to spark your ideas?

Hey, I want to be able to plug this into my resume as something that I have been able to work on with you, whether or not it is published. DO I have your permission and if I do what can I call this?

I responded by explaining that our chapter could use some relevant background stories in order to better understand her perspectives on diversity and language at NEIU. "Great!!" she replied. "Thanks for the direction. That is exactly what I needed in order to put my thoughts in writing." She promised a draft in four weeks.

Four weeks later, she sent me her draft. "Here is the piece as promised," she wrote in the message. "I have adapted something else I have written and hope it can work. I think the organization of it reflects who I am and a style unique to me as a Latina first-generation American."

WALKING ON A TIGHTROPE

It does not matter whether one is eighteen years old or thirty-one years old, belief in one's abilities, or lack of, and going away to college, leaving behind one's family, will be a significant life-shaping force. This past summer I felt exactly that. June of 2006 was my first term in the doctoral program in adult education with National-Louis University. The program started with a fourteen-day in-residence experience. I had never gone away to college. In fact, as an undergraduate and graduate student I lived at home and attended a strictly commuter institution that was about four blocks away from where I lived at that time. Now, at the age of thirty-one, and as a wife and mother, I would be packing up to leave home on a higher-education adventure I could not begin to imagine.

Emotionally, days and weeks prior to my departure I had held it together quite well. I worried mostly about what it would be like to have a roommate other than my husband. I worried about leaving my two-year-old daughter and being able to manage missing her. I also worried about silly things. I worried about taking a bath/shower in a bathroom that was not my own. My toilet at home is awesome. Would the plumbing hold up? Should I bring a plunger? Should I pack deodorizer? Matches are better. Maybe it would be best to bring both to be safe. Thoughts like these kept me distracted from the real pain I would experience the day I actually had to leave my family.

The day arrived when I had to leave. My husband drove me out of state to what I like to call "camp college." I arrived at "camp college" to see steep hills, lots of grass, a pristine lake, and several cabins. My cabin was directly in front of the fire pit and lake. Harold, my husband, helped me settle into my cabin and then prepared to drive back home. I hugged him tightly and burrowed my face into his broad chest as I wept inconsolably. I thanked him for being so supportive of me and told him I would miss him and Miranda immeasurably. He told me it was a sacrifice for a better life for all of us. He wiped my tears away with his hand and, as usual, we blessed each other with a mini sign of the cross on each other's forehead as the final good-bye.

A couple of days passed, and I began to feel overwhelmed with the level of preparation that had been expected and number of readings that needed to have been completed prior to the start of the term. Often, I wondered if I would I be found out. I was never a "reader" and have often professed my lack of interest in reading in general, especially literature. Intensive classes and activities were planned every day and night. I felt like I was not keeping up during the term and possibly was not doctoral material. I yearned for balance in order to manage my readings and assignments with the distraction of my vulnerable emotional state caused by my yearning to be close to my family.

Then, as I was feeling like I might have made a mistake about pursuing my doctoral degree, I took part in an outdoor experiential leadership training program. This was the significant life-shaping force to forever change my life. I gained so much confidence from taking part in this activity that I wish I had experienced this sooner in my life.

After a day full of team-building activities, I took part in the high ropes (tree and pole course). There were three courses to select, an easy one, a harder one, and the hardest. I naively chose the hardest one. Envision this: a five foot three inch woman that weighs over two hundred pounds who never exercises making it through such an obstacle course. I climbed a rope ladder that hung from a tree up to a height of about fifty feet. At that point, I made my way over to a tightrope that crisscrossed in the middle, while holding on to a rope above my head. After about the half way point by the crisscross of the tightrope, I lost my balance and slipped. However, I still managed to stay on the rope. I thought, "Strength and balance are all I need to finish." I could not feel my hands and I was sweating unlike I have ever experienced in my life, so much so that I could even smell myself. The sweat stung my eyes as it dripped from my forehead and hair. My fellow scholars encouraged me to keep going. I hung on the rope for what seemed like forever. I was losing my energy. I thought I could not do it anymore. At one point, I thought I was going to vomit as I felt the nerves in my stomach take hold of my core. "Oh no! How embarrassing is this going to look if I vomit from all the way up here and it lands on someone?" Then finally, the leader up in the tree said to reach out for his hand, so that he could help me. I told him I could not do it. I was not able to go further. He would not take no for an answer. I calmly explained about four times that it was not for lack of desire on my part, but that I physically could not do it.

He said to me "*si se puede.*" It struck me that he chose to speak to me in Spanish after he had only been speaking to me in English, and yelling "you can do it." Then, I could hear Yolanda, the only other Latina in the doctoral program yell out "*si se puede.*" I chuckled because I thought, "What difference would it make to hear the same message in Spanish?" To my surprise, I did it! I reached the tree where the leader was and I was able to accept his help and words of encouragement. Maybe hearing the words in the language of my home made it possible? I don't know; but, what I do know is that I made it across.

I wanted to cry (but did not) after looking back at what I had accomplished despite my lack of self-confidence. After that moment, the rest of the course was a piece of cake. I climbed the tree five feet down to a platform where I needed to walk across a wooden beam. Then, I made it to the bungee zip line that I would attach myself to and go down into a ravine from about forty feet up. I made it down and was so proud of myself and simply in awe that I had it in me.

I discovered that it was okay to get help from others. It was okay to hear and accept the encouragement of others. Since then, as challenging and overwhelming as the demands of the doctoral program could be academically, and as hard as it is to balance family demands, career, and study, I now know in my core that I can get through this and anything successfully.

Before I started on my doctoral journey, the level of frustration I felt when reading my students' papers was immeasurable. It was all emotions and frustrations that I could not articulate. I was upset that the students could not write the way that I thought entering freshmen should write. I had many questions: "Don't they know the typical five paragraph formula for writing an essay? Have they ever heard of a topic sentence? Do they know what a paragraph is? Do they know how to construct a simple sentence? Okay, have any of them at the very least ever heard of spell check on the computer?" I was astonished at the fact the students would submit such poorly written papers to me.

The problem I had at that time was that I had tunnel vision. I could not get past the horrible writing mistakes and that caused me oftentimes not to appreciate the meaning behind the mistakes and the experience the students brought to their writing. The irony in all this is that I understood the meanings, just did not appreciate them. What I had not expected as a result of my first term towards earning my doctorate and critically reflecting on my own life is that I have become more and more aware that I am blessed with the ability to understand the students I work with on a deeper level. Becoming more aware of myself through critical reflection has helped me understand how I make meaning of my world. I now can see that the English and Spanish languages, in addition to my spirit as a Latina and first-generation American, enable me to understand my students' writing differently than others.

That is to say, I appreciate the thinking behind the words. I can pick up on the rhythms and subtleties of mixing the English and Spanish languages and cultures that are in the organization and sentence structure of my bilingual and bicultural students, including native and nonnative English speakers. I will never forget something one of my students wrote one day. He described himself as not having hairs on his tongue. My graduate assistant, who was not bilingual and was of

European ancestry, read the paper first. She was completely perplexed over the idea of hairs on the tongue. This is when I explained to her that this was how in Spanish we say one is blunt.

I am just now starting to embark on discovering how I may have learned and been taught. I can say that I learned how to write in grade school and high school quite well. I may not have been an Ernest Hemingway, but I could get my point across without too many distractions or major grammatical mistakes. I do remember lots of praise by my teachers for my writing abilities. This positive reinforcement and encouragement may have played a role in my writing abilities. However, now that I feel comfortable and confident that I have mastered writing at a scholarly level and am centered as a Latina and first-generation American, I have discovered that I have the right to express my authentic voice and have a responsibility to listen to my students' voices. However, the fact remains that I do not have an answer for how educators should teach or how learners can learn the written English language better or increase literacy levels. As an adult educator, I can only encourage my students not to give up and to be proud of who and where they are in their own development as future professionals and world citizens.

When we first met, Neida complained about her students' English, and after the initial classroom observations, she agreed to collaborate on this chapter. At the time, she asked to be shown the ropes, and then after hours of classroom observations, informal conversations, and preliminary writing, she offered an account of her high ropes experience in the summer institution for her nontraditional EdD program, an account she had also submitted to an edited collection on experiences of Latino students in higher education.

As I considered my response, she learned that this manuscript—"a slightly shorter and different version of what I wrote"—had been accepted for publication. She had been notified, she explained, on Christmas Eve, making it the best gift she had ever received.

Even more unsure of how to respond, I asked a series of questions, such as how this experience could be similar to those of her students:

Yes, I do have so much in common with many of my students. However, as I mentioned in my writing I have undergone a transformation unlike one I ever expected. The best I can do is to explain this at this time is referring to Richard Rodriguez, but I have no other words to finish this sentence. The book says a great deal alone.

I was reminded hard and fast that I am more than a woman, a mother, student, etc . . . . I am also a Latina during my "camp college" experience. Becoming educated does not mean forgetting who I am.

I also asked how this experience enabled her to conclude that her students might have more in their writing:

It was a realization that I had something else in me that I was not aware of. I needed to be challenged in a physical, emotional, psychological and social way. I am still processing the experience and how hearing the encouragement in Spanish seemed to have an impact on me. As I described in my reflection, I don't know if "Si se puede" had something to do with it, but I sure did make it across.

Sometimes, I think it is that feeling of "home"; hearing the language of my Mom and Dad, of my home that helped. That connection that only comes from being Latina/o. Maybe, my students just need someone to trust and know that they can be themselves without worry— maybe it is not language, but what it symbolizes and the assumptions that are made about it. (I am bilingual and express myself primarily, if not exclusively in English with my husband and daughter, the Spanish language and Latino culture is however a part of my core.)

I also asked about the ability of NEIU to address its cultural and linguistic diversity, as a follow-up to similar question I had asked when we first started collaborating:

This is a tricky one. I believe at this time that the question you are asking is valid. However, the society we live in and higher education has [sic] certain elements of life that are permanent. These elements are permanent because it is serving the interests of some particular group. Therefore, the fact that the data shows this and that NEIU "seems" unable to deal with these issues or people for me is not a big surprise. This is why I have had to learn how to navigate in different realms and believe that I have a personal responsibility to make sure that my daughter is resilient and able to navigate in multiple circles. My responsibility is also to do what I can within the framework that exists in society to help someone pursuing knowledge or guidance. Consequently, helping fellow Latinos is important to me.

Okay, so back to your question. NEIU is not going to do more than they already have. NEIU has done some things and that is fine for now. I think that even if more programming is offered or curriculum is changed, there will have to be some converging interests between the University and the urban student population it serves. As a non-white person, I will look forward to reaping some benefits as a result of additional programming, etc. . . . I don't expect things to change drastically. Maybe we will have to seek "creative" ways to help the university manage the beliefs, attitudes and linguistic and cultural diversity at the university. I'll need more time to think about a "creative" concrete solution.

I also asked what she wanted readers to take from her ropes story:

What I am running into is that I don't have anything else to say about literacy or teaching writing. I expect for readers especially those who research literacy and teach reading and writing to read between the lines. Maybe that is the trouble, it is an expectation that might never be met. Analyze what I have written and said as though it was some fine piece of literature written by the best author that ever existed. Look for symbolism. Listen for the story. Know that the words I have selected are purposeful. Know that I am full of different experiences. Know that I am a product of my family, school, work, etc. . . . and have an individual history in addition to a collective history. THEN, show me how writing, reading and communication works in YOUR (the Professor's) world using examples to contrast both cultures. So, what does this mean? It means that the person who takes on the challenge of teaching writing needs to have more than a superficial understanding of the cultures of his/her students. It means more than studying a culture like one would mice in a laboratory.

At the end, I suggested that her responses could be the basis for a revised version of this chapter that attempts to account for the shift within her, a shift that was nonetheless a struggle despite her access to Spanish and Latinidad. She explained that while she valued my suggestions, she was too busy with too many other projects and, as a result, wouldn't have any more time for this chapter.

The book she had said she wouldn't read is the book she cites to explain her transformation from someone who objects to her students' English to someone who could see, in it, an inherent intelligence of multilinguals. In effect, an argument for the distinction between public and private spheres seems to attest to the presence of private spheres within public ones.

From time to time, I hear from or see Neida, who finished her program more than four years after I first sat in her classroom. When I do, I ask about her family and the educational consulting business that she and her husband created. Initially, they started with two schools, and recently, they have begun working with one from Canada. Maybe her memories have made her hunger for more.

4
MARKED FOR LIFE

Sophia López

Time has not lessened the pain of my mother's humiliations. She came to this country as a teenager, not knowing the language. She'd been a straight A student in Mexico but found herself working a factory job in Chicago. She escaped a life of blistered hands on the assembly line by studying to become a secretary. She could almost pass for white—until her accent betrayed her. I couldn't hear it as a child and didn't know what having one meant to her.

At her first office job, a coworker, this white woman, asked her why she didn't go back to her own country. Stunned and unable to verbally defend herself, my mother was struck silent. Every time she tells me this story, it is always laced with anger. She knows her accent has cost her job opportunities in the past.

For my mother, success meant speaking perfect English. She was set on both me and my brother being bilingual. As children, she forced us to speak English when we were with her in public. We protested, but sharp pinches to our arms kept us in line.

Still, my childhood was a happy one insulated by intense family closeness. My grandparents lived on the first floor and I grew up on Mexican food, music, and traditions. We lived in a predominantly Latino neighborhood and I attended schools where all my classmates and teachers spoke Spanish.

When I was seven years old my family picked up and moved to Skokie, a northern suburb of Chicago. My parents were drawn to its good schools and promise of a better life. I was placed in the English as a Second Language (ESL) program. My teacher, a young blonde woman with pimples, scolded me for not pronouncing vowels exactly the right way. When I spoke in front of the class, revealing a slight accent, my classmates laughed, and made sure to correct me. I didn't know what to do so I laughed along with them.

While sitting at the kitchen table one evening doing my homework, my mom leaned in to inspect my work. She saw the accent mark I used in the *o* over López and asked me why I was still writing my last name that way, telling me I should stop. When I asked her why, she replied, in Spanish, "Because they're going to know you're not from here." I didn't understand, but I did as I was told. I was literally erasing a big part of who I was.

Later, for a school project, I was to interview somebody I admired. I chose my mother. She was the center of my world. To me, she was a giant, a strong and confidant woman. I confessed to her that when I grew up I wanted to be just like her. "I want to be a secretary too," I said. But my mother turned serious, looked at me, and told me I must never say that again. She said I was going to be somebody. I was going to go to college and be a professional. And it was at that exact moment I began to see just how powerless and vulnerable she really was. This Wonder Woman that was my mother was brought down to size. I couldn't look up to her anymore. The spell had been broken.

I began feeling ashamed of my parents. I would go out of my way to keep them away from the world of school, especially my father. I'd inherited his brown skin. He was a stern and proud man, a man of few words. He spoke semibroken English, and his writing was plagued by poor grammar and syntax. He had less formal education than my mother and worked downtown as a janitor. I only saw them reading bills, never a book.

Survival in my new environment meant suppressing my working-class Mexican ancestry, passing myself off as straight, and adopting the Anglo middle-class mannerisms of school. This deception came to be second nature. By the time I got to high school, I was tracked into lower-level classes and rarely made honor roll. I got detentions because my way of explaining confrontations with teachers wasn't in sync with those of the school's. They demanded respect they had not earned.

I was more afraid of disappointing my parents than anything a dean could ever do to me. I saw how hard they worked but still struggled to pay the mortgage, and I knew, almost instinctively, that the American Dream of equal opportunity was a romantic myth, a lie. But this awareness only pushed me further away from the world of school. And when all the messages you get is that you're not as smart or as talented as the affluent white kids in your classes are, you begin to believe it. So my way of surviving was shutting down. It hurt less that way. I grew to hate who I was and where I came from.

My classmates were making plans to go away for college. Many were attending private, elite, and highly selective state universities across the country. I, however, was the first in my family to go to university and knew nothing about filling out school forms or applying for financial aid. There was a college resource center, but the dusty shelves jammed with catalogs didn't help. I ended up at Northern Illinois University and was on my own for the first time in my life.

I was in the middle of nowhere, surrounded by cornfields and Wal-Mart. I was terribly homesick, but I wasn't allowed to come home. My parents had worked so hard and sacrificed so much so that my brother and I had the opportunities they didn't have. I felt trapped, caught in the middle of a nervous breakdown. The pressure was too much, and a suicide attempt marked the end of my semester. I came home a disgrace, a failure.

My mother, always pushing a college education, wouldn't let me take time off and made me enroll at a nearby community college. But I still wanted to end my life. What kept me from blowing my brains out was confessing to her that I was a lesbian. And when I didn't lose her love, I chose to live, not just survive.

Determined, I slowly got reacquainted with the rhythm of school and made plans to transfer to a four-year university. I needed a clean break, a fresh start, and Northeastern was going to give that to me. My brother was already a student there, and tuition was affordable. It was an easy decision. I was thrilled being at a new school.

I had to take English 101, and my professor, a white guy, said we could call him anything we'd like. But my sense of formality couldn't break with teacher as authority figure. My professor thought language was at the bottom of everything and asked us to see language as a game. Smiling, he said, "How many of you believe there's such a thing as Standard English?" A few hands went up, but I kept my hands firmly across my desk. I knew it was a setup, but the question made no sense to me. I thought to myself that of course there is a right and wrong way of talking. My mother had made sure of it.

The first thing my professor had us read was an autobiography of this girl who'd lived half her life on the streets. In jail she gets rehabilitated and eventually makes it to university. But she confessed to missing her own language and realized it'd been such a big part of who she was. She was caught between Standard English and the language of the streets. What freed her was recognizing the arbitrary rules surrounding

Standard English. This awareness allowed her to survive in the mainstream and love her own language at the same time. I wanted that freedom too, but I was afraid of where that search would take me.

But it was Richard Rodriguez's *Hunger of Memory* (1983) that forced me to see the terrible ways I'd been scarred by language. It was the closest to myself I'd ever seen on paper. Rodriguez is the son of working-class Mexican immigrants and chronicles his assimilation into American culture. Like him, I'd grown up in a middle-class environment, surrounded by white faces. His teachers asked his parents to speak only English at home. Wanting a better life for their son, they complied.

Relatives came to tease him for not speaking Spanish and started calling him *pocho*, a word I'd never heard before but sensed it somehow referred to someone like me. It was derogatory and basically means an Anglicized Mexican, a sellout of sorts.

To my parents, Mexico is home, and the umbilical cord to it will never be severed. But I was an American by birth, and I know that when I go to Mexico, the stay is temporary. I was caught between two cultures and had no real sense of place.

Growing up, I'd wanted to pretend that the transition from Spanish to English was no big deal. I'd tell myself that I never really had a mother tongue and protected myself with a shield of indifference. Until now, I could never admit to myself how much this loss had hurt me.

Rodriguez's differentiation between the middle class and working class struck at the core of who I was. His words made me see the privilege in my own life, which was hard because it didn't fit with the image I had of myself as an oppressed person. I wasn't vulnerable like a recent immigrant Mexican woman. I didn't have to worry about being deported and being separated from my family. I spoke Standard English and was fluent in all things American. I was also receiving a college education, a luxury some can only dream about.

The book shed light on why I felt different from other Latino students at Northeastern. Now that I was surrounded by brown faces, I didn't know what to make of it. Many of them had grown up in the city and attended Chicago Public Schools. They'd speak Spanish freely. Although my roots were working class, I'd grown up in a middle-class environment. Despite my miserable years in high school, I was fortunate to have attended well-funded schools and received an excellent education.

I felt this difference most when we posted to an online class journal. I tried to continue class discussions, but my classmates remained passive.

Many of them used poor grammar and wrote in short, incomplete thoughts and sentences. Some didn't write at all. And I wondered if this was because they didn't care or because they couldn't write at the college level. It might have been a little bit of both.

I couldn't help showing my enthusiasm, and I asked myself if there was something wrong with me. I'd never felt this connected to school. For the first time in my life, the classroom was relevant to my own experience. The nonauthoritarian style of my professor and the readings drew me in. I became fascinated by the interplay between language, culture, and power.

English 101 was also the first time I was exposed to the controversial nature of affirmative action. It was a key subject in Rodriguez's *Hunger of Memory*. He'd gained notoriety for his arguments against bilingual education and affirmative action. His words angered me. They made me choose sides. They woke me up. I saw him as a betrayer of his own people. It was perfect having a Hispanic criticize programs meant to benefit Hispanics. It gave him credibility.

The topic of affirmative action proved to be a divisive one. At the time, I wasn't sure exactly what it was, but I made sure to check off "Hispanic" every time I was asked my race on school forms. *Hunger of Memory* schooled me on it, and in class, I got into an argument with a whiteboy who said that affirmative action was "reverse racism." He added that minorities filed lawsuits when denied a job.

But he was failing to look at the history of racism in this country. There was no social context to it. I told him that blacks and Latinos didn't have the institutional power to discriminate against whites. And it takes a lot of energy trying to explain this to someone who isn't particularly interested in understanding. It wasn't about finding common ground or looking at the complexity of the issues; it was about winning the argument. I was being silenced no matter what I said.

Despite the occasional clashes, English 101 came to be my favorite class. We spent the semester looking at how certain ways of talking and writing are dismissed by institutions of power, like school. I always participated and did the required readings. But when the end of the semester came, and it was time to turn in my portfolio, I kept hitting roadblocks. I was choking on words. I felt like the fragile boundaries between American and Mexican, Spanish and English, working class and middle class, were blurring. The childhood I'd so carefully tried to protect from cultural assaults came crashing down. I'd been caught playing a double part and it made me physically sick.

The class was a shattering experience, ripping open old wounds and forcing me to see the consequences of my learned self-hatred. It's what led, in part, to my withdrawal from school, my depressions, a suicide attempt. I didn't realize how deeply wounded I'd been by language. I felt trapped by the power of labels, both institutional and personal. And now I was being moved by forces I don't think I'll ever fully understand. And it was a fight, always. Against myself, my environment, my past, my present, my knowledge, my thoughts. I ended up with an incomplete for the semester.

I spent winter break alone, shocked and numbed by the intensity of this crisis. My core self was shaken. I felt like I was being lied to this whole time and I needed to fill my self-doubt and insecurities with concrete knowledge. Clearing my incomplete became my primary preoccupation. So I enrolled in a sociology class called Race, Class, Sex, and Education. My professor was a white lesbian and led a nonauthoritarian classroom. She encouraged critical analysis and asked us to contextualize our lives within the readings.

The class was geared for students planning a career in education. Almost all of us were students of color. I wanted to be a teacher but felt wary going through the College of Education. To me, it seemed so restrictive and bureaucratic. A girl in my class said, "I hated school. That's why I want to be a teacher!" It sounded funny at first but in a way made sense. As someone who'd felt so alienated from school, she'd easily be able to connect with working-class students of color in the classroom.

And as obvious as it is to me now, it didn't occur to me that almost all my teachers growing up were middle-class white women. I sensed they treated me just a little differently. They probably bought into stereotypes about Mexicans, and I was a brown body in their classrooms. For me, being tracked into lower-level classes began at an early age.

I would have loved to have had a Latina teacher as a kid. I think it's important that young students of color have teachers who look like them and share similar backgrounds. I've heard it said that having minority teachers would help white students dispel racial stereotypes, but that is not my concern. What matters is that working-class students of color have teachers who believe in them, who respect them, and who see their brilliance.

I know that simply being black or Latino doesn't necessarily make someone an effective teacher of students of color and have no romantic notion of teacher-as-savior. I know there are problems kids face outside school that are beyond my control. But teaching working-class students of color allows the opportunity to reach those who most need a quality education.

I met with my sociology professor outside class, and she gave me an article she'd written about Northeastern. I found out that Northeastern was a federally designated Hispanic-Serving Institution, but I didn't know what that meant. She described its large working-class student population and how most of us were first-generation college students.

When she used the expression "lower-middle class/working-poor," I knew I'd found my family on the economic ladder. I'd grown up in the suburbs with kids who had college-educated parents. I knew their language, I knew their system, but I didn't belong to it. At the same time, my family didn't live in poverty. Even though there was never money left over, we lived a relatively comfortable life. My family was somewhere in between.

In class I learned about the power dynamics that impact the lives of working-class students of color. I began to understand why I felt so alienated from school growing up. For the first time, I saw the problem with school itself and not my family. My anger turned outward. I needed to know this shit when I was a kid, not wait 'til I'm in fucking college.

I started reading material we hadn't gotten to in class and invested myself in a feverish consumption of books, theory, poetry, and literature. It filled me, as if with new life. I carried around these books with me everywhere. I wanted to talk about them with friends but all I heard was "I don't read." I knew where that came from. School turned reading into such a dreadful thing.

When relatives saw me reading, they'd ask if school was over, and when I said "yes" they'd give me this look that said "So why the fuck are you reading?" It was kinda funny, but I couldn't talk to anyone about it. Reading came to be a solitary activity, a quiet world away. That summer, I fell in love with books.

I randomly stumbled on a book called *The Skin That We Speak* (Delpit and Dowdy 2002). It was about the politics of language and education and it introduced me to the concept of code-switching. It means shifting, almost unconsciously, the way one talks depending on the social context. It wasn't acting, it was adapting to whichever group had more power at the time, and it wasn't always white people. The idea helped me understand how I was able to navigate between my white middle-class schools, to Spanish-speaking family in Pilsen, to being openly gay at school and closeted at home. I didn't know there was a word for what it was I was doing. This was just me surviving and navigating below the radar.

And the more I read, the more I wanted to know. I still had my incomplete for English 101 hanging over my head and needed to get those words on paper. I knew it was past the deadline, but I didn't care. I had something to prove. I barricaded myself in my mom's small, un-air conditioned office and had books and packets of theory spread out across cheap gray carpeting. I'd never had a space, an outlet, to explore the power of language, class, and culture in my life. It went under the guise of academic purpose, but I was really writing for myself. It was such a personal thing.

This was me telling my story for the first time in my life and facing the contradictions of who I was. Everything just flooded together and I had to get all that shit on paper or else I would explode. Torrents of words filled the screen. It was a heightened consciousness. And when I finished writing everything I had to say, the essays totaled more than 300 pages. It was one of the most painful, difficult, and freeing things I've ever done in my life.

I kept telling myself that what I'd done was no big deal. I didn't want to admit to how much the class had affected me. When I finally met face to face with my professor, he felt I'd done advanced work, but said, "Unfortunately, the traditional university can't handle a student like you." I didn't know whether to feel insulted or flattered. He explained that English 101 carried certain requirements and that I hadn't quite met them.

And honestly, I didn't think it would hurt me. That's when I really felt it. I'd worked so hard, really pushed myself, dared to put truth on paper, but it wasn't good enough for them. I walked away with a C, but no grade on paper could ever show all the heart that went into those essays. Exhausted, I fell ill and was forced to take time off from school.

I returned to Northeastern a year later and started taking philosophy classes with Professor Sarah Hoagland. Her classes marked a critical turning point in my academic and personal development. My professor was an openly out lesbian, and this fact alone already drew me in. She had us read material written by radical women of color. The challenging material was made easier and concrete by bringing in our own experiences and observations. Suddenly, our lives had academic value.

When I'd first transferred into Northeastern, I was eager to check out its Gay, Lesbian, Bisexual, and Transgender Alliance (GLBTA) club. This was the first school I'd attended that had a visible queer community. I still wasn't used to the idea of being out, and when I finally mustered the courage to go to a meeting, I didn't know if I'd even want to go back. I was the only brown girl in the room and I didn't feel particularly welcome, but I also didn't want to just leave either. The club was closely associated with the Feminist Majority Leadership Alliance (FMLA). I became a regular member of both organizations.

But in time I grew tired of being the only Latina in these clubs. It didn't make sense that there weren't more women of color in a school as diverse as Northeastern. When I tried raising issues of exclusion, race, and class, I found myself alone. These white women were willing to have me around as long as I stayed in my place. As my anger and frustrations grew, I found myself even more isolated and was essentially kicked out of these organizations. Racism within feminist circles was not new.

Professor Hoagland was the only one who understood. Her support meant so much to me, but as a student I was on my own. This experience made me careful about what clubs and organizations I got involved with. I wouldn't find a true sense of community until much later.

In the meantime, I kept taking philosophy classes with Professor Hoagland because they were empowering to me. I'd grown up trained not to trust my own voice, but engaging material in these philosophy classes was giving me confidence as a student. I excelled in her classes and I began developing a critical consciousness.

One of the biggest things I got out of her classes was seeing the oppressed in a different light. Professor Hoagland asked us to see those living under oppression not as victims, but as active agents capable of resistance. I began seeing agency in the smallest ways and under the most coercive of conditions.

It was here that I was finally able to forgive myself for the shame I used to feel about my family. Given where I'd grown up, it made sense for me to want to suppress my working-class Mexican ancestry. That was my resistance, my act of survival. Seeing it this way allowed me to cut myself some slack. It wasn't my fault I was made to hate who I was.

I also began to understand why it was that my mother made me speak English when we were with her in public. It wasn't that Spanish was something lower class and shameful; it was that she knew her children would be judged by the way they spoke. By forcing us to know both English and Spanish, she was trying to protect us in her own way.

It was the same when she'd asked me to stop using the accent mark in my last name. She wanted me to be fully American and wanted me to be safe in this world. Because of the hard work of both my parents, I now had opportunities that were beyond their reach as newly arrived immigrants. I'm proud of what they have achieved since first coming to this country.

But I am an American by birth, and I can't deny having grown up in a middle-class environment. I was both Mexican and American, and ignoring either one meant erasing half my life. There are parts of American culture that I do not identify with, but sometimes I do claim the word *American* because that has been denied me.

I used to feel bad not fitting in anywhere, but Professor Hoagland's philosophy classes helped me value my ability to move in and out of different communities. I learned to respect the skills I'd developed by simply living the life I lived. I jokingly say that no group wants to claim me; I am the ultimate social reject. And yet, for me, this gives me the freedom and the space to create an identity on my own terms.

Overall, I think our generation is more fluid and permeable. Our identities are not static and are always changing, shifting, reacting to whatever is going on in the culture around us. There's stuff we like from both and stuff we don't. It's more than just a clash between Mexican and American. It's not Spanglish, not an equal split of both, but it's something new.

It's also important to keep in mind that the Latino community is not homogeneous, and there are many cultural and linguistic differences among Latinos as a people. There are Latino students at Northeastern who don't understand Spanish. Some are third generation. But what all of us seem to have in common is our education. It is something that cannot be taken away from us.

Professor Hoagland would tell us, "All of you have high IQs. That you've made it to college and gone this far in your education shows that you've been able to internalize the values of a very racist, sexist, classist, and homophobic system." There was a great deal of truth in this. We were the lucky ones, the ones who'd made it to university. We could survive in a system that devalued where so many of us came from.

Our success rested on learning Western ways of being. We had to learn their history, their language, and celebrate their heritage on a daily basis. It's so powerful it almost seems universal. White people, on the other hand, can choose whether or not they want to engage African, Asian, Hispanic, or Native American cultures. To them, that is multiculturalism and diversity. We, however, do not have that luxury. For us, there's really no way around the Western canon.

One of the philosophy classes I took with Professor Hoagland focused on the myriad ways women are silenced across different cultures. I was asked to reflect on my ancestry, on my grandmother and great grandmother. By Western standards, they would be considered largely illiterate, but they are a tremendous reservoir of oral history and knowledge. There were other ways of telling stories

My grandmother is a *curandera*, a healer, and people have come to her to help cure their illnesses. She'd also been a midwife in the rural part of Mexico where my father's family is from. I didn't know this until I was in high school and my science teacher started ripping on it, saying it wasn't as good as Western medicine. He was a teacher, an authority figure, and I had no way of defending my grandmother.

But Professor Hoagland's class taught me to see the greatness of my grandmother. Given the constant devaluation of Mexican culture, it's no wonder I had to be taught to value and respect my heritage. My confidence as a student kept growing and I was able to question who had the authority to determine what counts as knowledge and on what grounds. I experienced it right away when I registered for an American literature class.

My professor was the director of the English Department at the time and on the first day of class, he said, "How many of you believe in folk medicine?" Before anyone could say anything, he smirked, "I'd rather chew on aspirin." It's as if he were inflicting violence on my grandmother and entire family. He was dismissing non-Western ways of knowing and insulting the medicinal practices of my grandmother. This time, it wasn't shame I felt, it was a quiet rage and contempt. For the rest of the semester, I sat all the way in the back corner, passive. When I did participate, it was usually something sarcastic and smartass, trying to mess with the professor. It was the only way to endure such a class.

I then registered for a multicultural literature class. We were to read a Native American book, an African American one, a Hispanic one, and finally, a book on the Asian experience in this country. Although America is said to be a nation of immigrants and a melting pot of cultures, there is a generally accepted notion of what a real American is.

They are white, English speaking, and middle class. Everything that doesn't fit that category is considered "ethnic."

Because there was no book on the Caucasian experience, it was unwittingly the standard against which all other cultures were being measured. When my professor, a white woman, said that calling what happened to the Native Americans in this country "genocide" would be "too extreme," I knew I had to drop the class.

So I registered for a Chicano literature class instead. But I was afraid that doing so would alienate me from Chicano literature. I grew up learning about slavery, Jim Crow, and the civil rights movement, and I wasn't used to having my people under the microscope. I knew outsiders were going to be passing judgment on a community they had no idea about, except for whatever stereotypes they already had about Mexicans.

When we watched a documentary about Cesar Chavez and the United Farm Workers, a black woman said that the farm workers had "envy" and were asking for too much, too fast. She was implying that Chicanos had a false sense of entitlement, much like what was said about African Americans during the Civil Rights Movement. Our professor, a white guy, just chuckled and didn't say anything to address this comment.

Overall, the class was hostile against the Chicano movement. It might have been the strong nationalism that turned them off, but they weren't willing to look at how institutionalized racism trapped Mexican Americans under a tight system of oppression. Even a middle-aged immigrant Mexican man, someone who should know better, said he didn't understand what the Chicanos wanted. Frustrated, I said, "Well, what do you want? Good schools? Safe neighborhoods? Affordable healthcare? Respect? That's what they want." Chicanos just wanted a better life like anyone else.

I felt like I was taking on the class, the professor, and the material being covered. But this takes a lot of energy, and I didn't have backup. I gave up and sat all the way in the back, not saying a word. I missed a lot of class but still managed to get a decent grade. It was long after the class was over that I enjoyed the books on my own. I didn't have much faith in the ethnic literature classes at Northeastern and discouraged friends from enrolling in them.

I began sitting in on an honors class called Indigenous Ways of Knowing. My brother was enrolled in the class. Almost everyone was struggling. Students complained about the teacher and the class. These were honors students who had the grades on paper, but who weren't used to active learning and critical analysis. Engaging material that directly challenged the Western canon was foreign to them. They were lost. All that mattered to them was the grade.

In class, this whitegirl started talking about grad school and how she'd been denied a spot in the McNair Scholars program. It is a program meant to serve minority, working-class and first-generation college students. It offers mentorship, free GRE prep classes, a summer research stipend, and assistance in applying to grad schools. It's a great program but there are a limited number of spots.

Indignant, she claimed that even though she had better grades and tests scores, her spot was given away to a "minority" instead. First, there is no way she could've known this. Second, they're looking for more than just what's on paper. They are looking for students who have traditionally been underrepresented in institutions of higher learning. My brother was a McNair Scholar, and half his cohort consisted of white girls. If there's anyone who's benefited most from such programs, it has been white women.

She then said, "I feel like a minority at Northeastern. I mean, why do people (minorities) have to cling to their ethnicities? Why can't we all just be American?" I've heard this argument before, and it always irritates the shit out of me. Pretending to be color-blind fails to recognize how inequality disproportionately affects one group over another. Also, I do not like being denied my culture. I don't see difference as a threat. I am proud of being Mexican and am not going to give it up for what someone else thinks an American is supposed to be.

This wouldn't be the last time I witnessed the racial politics of well-intentioned programs meant to benefit minorities. When a friend applied to the McNair Scholars program, she was asked to prove her racial makeup, never mind she is dark skinned and comes from a Caribbean nation. Although many white women have been McNair Scholars, a blonde blue-eyed friend said she felt ostracized being in the program. I understood why she might feel this way, but I was surprised by how perceptive she was about race and higher education.

We were talking about students of color being admitted into elite universities, and she said these students were more likely to fail out. "Not because they're not smart, but because they don't have a support network around them. It's one thing to allow them in, it's quite another to ensure they succeed and make it to graduation. They have nervous breakdowns and fall through the cracks. They commit suicide. If they're lucky they'll be able to go to a community college. But how do you recover from that? That's not fair to them. They're giving them false hope to think they can compete at a level like these privileged people."

I agreed with her, but before I could say anything, she added, "Okay, I understand the whole 'lifting up the race' thing, and that Blacks had slavery, but . . . ." And that's when I knew this whitegirl was a little crazy. It becomes a hierarchy of oppression, of who has it worst. It's one of the side effects of such programs.

Another scholar, a white girl with a Hispanic last name, saw the program as a competition. When she told an English professor she was a McNair Scholar, the teacher said, "I guess they're being more selective now." She mistakenly took this as a compliment. Of all the McNair Scholars, which included working-class black men, Latino men and Latino women, she was the only one to claim discrimination as a Puerto Rican as a reason to want to be in the program. She was light skinned, half Puerto Rican, and came from a middle-class family. She was far from oppressed.

When she was awarded a minority internship, it became a mockery of the program. But I think most of the resentment came when she was propped up and praised as the ideal McNair Scholar. She was a "good" student on paper, but not in the true sense of the word. The traditional university was set up for someone like her. She would have sailed smoothly through college regardless.

Now there is a white guy in the program. I swear, he'd better be homeless or something. It's not so much him as a person, it's what he represents: privilege. Although it's true that working-class white men face their own struggles in this country, as a whole, white men have historically been a big part of the university system. Like the Hispanic whitegirl before him, he too is praised as the ideal McNair Scholar. This is offensive, and it undermines the efforts of those who truly struggled, worked hard, and succeeded because of such programs.

For so many of us who come from the working class and are students of color, simply getting to university is quite an achievement in and of itself. Programs like this are make-or-break and can determine whether a Latino student drops out or goes on to graduate school. A lot is on the line.

And I remembered what my English 101 professor said about what makes a successful student. He suggested that maybe the most successful students weren't necessarily those who attended class every day or always did their homework. Maybe it was those who'd learned to play the language game. But I found myself asking what kind of success he was talking about. Sometimes our hard work, challenges, and triumphs didn't always show. Those who got the best grades on paper weren't necessarily the most intelligent, even if the university saw it that way.

We were talking about grad school in Professor Hoagland's class one day, and she told us not to go for the name or how prestigious a school is but to go where you will flourish. She told us she had more respect for students who struggled and came out on top, than for those who always had it made. I'd done so much fighting just to claim my right to exist as a working-class queer woman of color in the university, and when I heard someone important to me say those words, it felt like such validation. I almost felt like crying.

I felt less alone knowing I wasn't the only working-class student of color who'd felt extreme alienation in school. We can't turn to our parents for help in navigating through university bureaucracy. We are usually isolated from the few Latinos we do see on campus. And there's a lot of pressure put on us by our families to fulfill the dreams they've spent a lifetime building. And when we fall short of such high expectations, the results can be disastrous. It's no wonder many of us have nervous breakdowns and commit suicide.

Professor Hoagland can teach anywhere, but she chooses Northeastern. She respects her students, which believe me, is no small thing. She didn't know how so many of us managed to work so much, take care of families, and still go to college. "It's incredible," she said.

I know Northeastern lacks prestige and is ripped on by outsiders who don't know what's going on inside it. This is one of the most affordable universities in the state and is open to pretty much anybody. This is a strength, not a weakness. I love that this place gives the chance of higher education to those who otherwise wouldn't have it. I've met and befriended all kinds of people, and I can't imagine being anywhere else.

But at the same time, this school doesn't always give you the information you need to plan your major and graduate in time. It's discouraging to those who are already alienated from the world of the academy. To address these problems, the chair of the Latino and Latin American Studies Program, Professor Victor Ortiz, began holding a series of informal meetings to discuss the status of Latino students on campus.

He explained that the Hispanic-Serving Institution designation simply means that at least 25 percent of its student body is Hispanic. It is enrollment ratios that make Northeastern eligible for certain federal grants, not an actual commitment to its Latino student population. One statistic showed only 17 percent of Latino students graduated within a six-year period. But this only measured incoming full-time freshmen who'd been consecutively enrolled. Northeastern has a large transfer rate and a significant number of part-time students. It also has a sizeable population of returning adult learners. Students around here tend to be a little older. Few seem to know about the undocumented students on campus. Needless to say, ours is not the traditional university.

Some might view Northeastern's low graduation rate as evidence that its students aren't capable of performing at the college level, but they fail to see all the factors going into it. It may take some of us a little longer than the traditional four years to earn a degree, but this doesn't mean we're not intelligent and don't work hard. It also doesn't mean we don't set high expectations for ourselves. Focusing strictly on graduation rates fails to see the whole story.

Because of the meetings which focused on the status of Latino students on campus, I got more involved with Latino organizations on campus. I became a member of the Union for Puerto Rican Students (UPRS), Chimexla, and the Latino Student Coalition. I'd finally found a true sense of community. It was with Latinos that I most strongly identified. I started writing for *Que Ondee Sola*, the first campus-based Latino magazine in the country. Its existence shows the long history of Latino student activism on campus.

I also became a staff writer for the campus newspaper. I started using the accent mark in my last name again. All those things that happened growing up, the ridiculing of my culture, my language, my past, all that had happened to someone else. This was to be my public voice. I had a knack for journalism and became the opinions editor. I also had the opportunity of doing the Voice of the Campus column, which was a space to address the entire NEIU community.

For the first edition, I wrote a last-minute article titled "English as a First Language: The Standards Debate." It was based off an idea two student government senators had proposed at a Latino student meeting. One of them, a Jamaican woman with a thick accent, suggested getting rid of the English Competency Exam requirement. She informed us that there were a lot of students, immigrant students in particular, who were failing this exam and argued that since we were already required to take English 101 and enroll in at least four years of college, this in itself should be enough.

Their idea was greeted with mixed results. A Latino advisor who worked specifically with Latino students opposed it and said Northeastern shouldn't be lowering standards. But even if they didn't succeed in getting rid of the English Competency Exam, they were well intentioned and wanted to raise awareness about Northeastern's immigrant student population.

After my piece ran in the newspaper, I received an angry letter from this white guy, an employee of the university, who ran the school's Math Lab. He said he was "disturbed" by my article and charged me with "anti-intellectualism,"'saying it was a new low for today's young people. He was shocked that I was the editor of a newspaper.

I was caught off guard and felt vulnerable in a very public way . Instead of looking at what the English Competency Exam really was, he came after me with personal insults. He knew nothing about me except my last name. Angry, I responded by saying that passing the English Competency Exam does not mean someone is competent in using English. It simply means that they were able to know a few vocabulary words and write a short essay. I said that people with ethnic-sounding or "black-sounding" names were less likely to be called in for job interviews and that there were statistics for those inclined not to believe first-person accounts, like him. I added that there are a lot of white people who are not competent in using the English language.

Up until that point, I'd never personally experienced how politically charged the nature of language really is. I'd heard about it from my parents, and I'd studied it in books, but this was the first time I'd been the target of such hostility. I knew there were people eager to write off someone like me. The newspaper was a public forum, and I was initially afraid to admit that I'd been in ESL as a child. I felt it made dismissing me that much easier, but I had nothing to be ashamed about.

I purposely wrote my next column in Spanish, in part, to show what it felt like not knowing the language. I addressed it to our new incoming university president. There would be no translation. I was afraid of getting angry Letters to the Editor, but I learned that it just comes with the territory. In a way, the white guy's letter emboldened me and gave me the confidence to trust my public voice. Now I was strong. Now I wasn't afraid.

I established the tone of my column as a serious one. I always had to be proving myself to be a competent person. It's just the way it was, except now I felt armed with the words, the weapons, to win these battles. I used my column as a place to raise issues that weren't being addressed on campus. I figured I had little to lose and put myself out there, unafraid to challenge those in positions of power.

Because Northeastern had a new university president, there was a general feeling of excitement in the air that changes, however small, could come to Northeastern. Members of the Latino community saw it as a perfect opportunity to raise issues of retention and graduation rates. We rallied behind the idea of bringing a Latino Cultural and Resource Center to Northeastern. We wrote countless articles in *Que Ondee Sola* and named the problems, cited statistics, and offered solutions. I used my column to help give voice to our concerns. We wanted the Hispanic-Serving Institution label to actually mean something and knew no one else was going to be fighting our battles for us.

As a group, we learned to work with the administration, striking a delicate balance between working with power and fighting for students. We wanted to build a support network and make things a little easier for the next generation of Latino students. We know that progress works slowly and sometimes it's a matter of give and take, but this doesn't mean we are going to settle.

A core group of us knows how Northeastern banks on its diversity. We know the game they play. High-level administrators are happy having the Hispanic Serving Institution designation because it makes them eligible for multimillion dollar federal grants, but they oppose building a Latino Cultural and Resource Center. One administrator suggested having a "Diversity Village" instead, which would essentially turn Northeastern into Disney's Epcot Center. This school once had a Latino Cultural Center, but it was torn down by the administration in the 80s. Another administrator suggested calling Northeastern the "Ellis Island of the Midwest," but thankfully, this patronizing idea was quickly shot down. Around here, everyone wanted to talk about diversity and multiculturalism, but no one wanted to talk about issues of race, power, and inequality.

Back at the newspaper, morale was at an all-time low. There was no leadership at the top, and people had gotten sloppy. One day, a white guy entered the office and identified himself as an English instructor. After engaging us in small talk, he started pointing out all the grammatical errors in the latest edition. He joked, "I mean, are these ESL students!?" But it wasn't funny. Why couldn't all the errors be plain laziness on the part of its writers? Like many people, he confused English with intelligence and probably didn't think highly of the immigrant students in his classes. It bothered me because he was in a position of authority and was carelessly dismissing the ESL students in his classroom.

Later, in the newspaper office, I talked with a blonde, blue-eyed girl from the affluent suburb of Highland Park. She was doing her student teaching in Humboldt Park, a mostly working-class Latino neighborhood. "I love my kids," she told me. But the next time I saw her, she was visibly upset. She'd had a confrontation with one of the students, who'd told her, "Get outta my face you white bitch!" I'm not excusing such disrespect of a teacher or anybody else, but she didn't understand that when you're a kid coming from a working-class community of color, the last thing you want is some whitegirl from the suburbs trying to put you in your place.

To make matters worse, the Puerto Rican teacher of the classroom said to her, "You know they hate you cuz you're white." It was wrong on her part to have said this. Instead, she could have tried to explain to the student teacher that she was coming from a different background than the kids and that earning their trust and respect would take time. And I debated with myself if it was worth my saying something. I felt bad for her, but I knew this was a future teacher, and I was afraid she might one day be saying some stupid shit to a student of color and not even know it. So I asked her, "Well, do you respect them? The kids?"

"No," she admitted.

"And they know that, so they don't respect you," I told her. Kids pick up on it, and this is going on even before getting to the material being covered. She continued by saying that she'd overheard a conversation between some of the parents and was shocked by the occasional curse and slang. She said this was wrong because they were "instilling these values at a young age." She was faulting these parents not just for the way they were speaking, but for the way they lived, the neighborhood they lived in, and the communities they belonged to.

I kept trying to explain to her to just be aware that she's coming from a different community, but then she got angry and said, "Just say it Sophia! I'm white!" Part of me knew she was going to react this way. It's easy getting defensive. She wasn't used to being the outsider.

Later, she joked that she was teaching "*cholos*," meaning gangbangers. These were elementary-school children, and she was already seeing the working-class Latino students in her classroom as criminals. She also assumed she had the right to use that word. Sometimes it is used affectionately within our own communities, but when it is said by someone outside of that, it is insulting.

It's not easy seeing the privilege in your life. It's uncomfortable. It can change you, which is why it's easier not to self-reflect and think about what it means being white in this society. It's up to white folks to begin unlearning the insidious prevalence of racism in this country. And maybe here lies the possibility of true multiculturalism. Not the feel-good kind where we simply get to know each other's culture through ethnic food and traditional dances. No. It must be a serious endeavor that respects our differences and examines issues of power at the same time.

I know that white women continue to make up the bulk of teachers in this country. It's easier dubbing Latino children as deficient who need to be "fixed" and brought into the mainstream. But these future teachers should know that their way of being is not universal. It's partly what leads many children of color to be tracked into lower-level classes and receive harsher disciplinary actions. In a way, it's myself as a child I want to protect.

During our last semester at Northeastern, both my brother and I enrolled in a class called Puerto Rico and the Caribbean. Our professor's passion for knowledge was contagious, and he warned us that his was not going to be a traditional class. It would be challenging the history we'd been taught in school up until that point. He also required participation in Latino-based community events. Everyone in our class was Latino, and I assumed that since the course materials were more relevant to their lives, they would want to take it up. Unfortunately, most of them showed little interest and remained passive before the thought-provoking material being presented to them. Our professor was visibly frustrated and disappointed.

My brother and I didn't understand why our classmates weren't reacting to the class the same way we were. He suggested that maybe we'd had more prepping for such a class, but it was still sad to see nonetheless. We wanted to scream and tell them this was gold and that they weren't going to get this anywhere else. And I realized that by the time most students reach university, a real passion for knowledge has been tested out of us. Schooling is a slow death.

We came home one evening and sat talking at the kitchen table. We were graduating at the same time, and both of us planned careers as teachers. We were looking back at our time at Northeastern and saw how much we had grown and changed because of it. The Puerto Rico and the Caribbean class lingered in our minds. My brother told me, "I look at them, who just go through Northeastern unaffected. It's like how can you not get something out of a place like this? How would you engage someone like this? As a teacher, what could I do?"

I understood his frustration, but I told him, "Sometimes there's nothing you can do. You can try really hard to engage them, but not all kids are going to be responsive. And that's okay. There's nothing you can do up to a certain point. But this doesn't mean you don't try. And then there's those who'll get a lot out of it, like you and me."

There is truly something special about Northeastern. It is home to people from all parts of the world, fusing together to form an academic and cultural community. I came into consciousness and found a wonderful sense of community. I had a handful of supportive and brilliant professors.

For me, Northeastern has meant a radical process of self-transformation. It has meant healing. Because of it, I've found the strength to believe in myself, both as a student and as working-class queer woman of color. The spaces I've entered, the organizations I was a part of, the lifelong friends I've made, all these things helped me find a kind of peace in the anger that continues to fuel and sustain my resilience. I feel fortunate having had the chance to be a part of it. The beauty of this place, in a way, is hard to put into words.

5

LANGUAGE, ETHNICITY, AND HIGHER EDUCATION

Angela Vidal-Rodriguez

The professor started the speech to tell the McNair scholars why being McNair scholars was important. She started reading a beautiful fable and the literary analysis about it. She explained to us how this fable was an oral story that Mexicans in Texas used to tell. Mexicans in this region had a strong tradition of oral history which they kept after the annexation of Texas territory. She told us that much of this oral history had been compiled by a Mexican American women scholar who had lived at the end of the 1800s and beginning of 1900s. The author translated the stories so they wouldn't be lost. The same hope drove her to publish the compilation. The compilation however was lost in the libraries of Texas for many years. Finally, fifty years later, it was res-cued by another Mexican American, a low-income and first-generation scholar who found it in the library and got intrigued by it. Now, the professor giving the speech, a Mexican American and first-generation low-income student, was writing her doctoral thesis about the author and her writings. "Do you notice a pattern?" the professor asked us. This beautiful part of American literary history was there but nobody before noticed it. Nobody before gave it value, nobody before thought it was important, nobody before until somebody like us found it. "Do you understand now?" she asked.

Yes, I understood.

I understood how what I value and what I think is important, as well as the contribution to the world of my fellow Latinos, won't be valued by the mainstream academia because they cannot recognize its value. There is the obligation to show its value to the world. Many other anecdotes of this type I have in my life, yet this is one that depicts the best how it is that I understood that I had an obligation to myself to embrace my status as the Other instead of rejecting it. The reason is that I understood that I have to work for the advancement of my entire group so the group can show its real value to the American society, and then I would be valued as an equal.

INTRODUCTION

One of my main reasons to come to the United States was "to dominate the English." For me to dominate the language meant to lose the accent, speak quickly, understand all English speakers, learn all the idioms, read books in English, sing in English, and dream in English. Oddly enough, writing was not on the spectrum at all. The goal was to learn the culture to perfection and be able to replicate it perfectly too. My idea was to be an American when I was in the United States and be a Mexican when I went back to Mexico. In the meantime, earning a degree in the most prestigious educational system in the world wouldn't be a bad idea at all.

My master's in business administration was a result of the naive way in which I understood, or misunderstood, my migration. Entering Northeastern Illinois University (NEIU) was a blessing for me. I wanted to continue studying, but I didn't know how I would be able to afford it. Lucky enough, I met a professor in the business program at NEIU, and he was willing to help me. The professor proposed the best deal in the world at that moment. If I was admitted to the NEIU MBA program, he would hire me as a graduate assistant (a totally new concept for me). In this way, I could pay for my education. I never wanted to study business administration, but my qualifications as an economist were just perfect for it. Plus the graduate assistantship depended on the business program. As a result, I thought that was "the deal," and I took it gladly. My rush to keep studying English, to change my lifestyle, and to change my visa status were my incentives to enroll in a master's program, something I wouldn't have chosen otherwise.

When I came to United States I never considered myself an immigrant. I had no reason to leave my country, and I had many reasons to go back. I just wanted to be economically independent, travel the world, and learn many languages.

My desires were not very different from other immigrant desires. People come to this country for many different reasons, but rarely to immigrate. They come to visit their families, to study, to escape from war or a bad husband or a draft, to forget a love, to follow somebody, to save for a special item, to get training for a job, to learn the language. The majority of them, I will dare to say, believe that their pass through this country is temporary and think of their comeback as a strong reality. Yet when I migrated, I had no idea about this "shared wish" and I thought I was so different.

I arrived in Chicago by plane with a tourist visa and with three hundred dollars in my pocket. I was confident that I would survive and succeed in "my adventure" no matter what. After I smoothly entered the United States, I used to call myself a *mojada light* as a way to laugh about my obvious immigrant status, which I didn't acknowledge at the time. It was not because I wasn't faced with the immigrant life right away. In less than a month, I was working in a fast-food restaurant and cleaning houses. I even had my immigrant ID provided by the Mexican consulate. However, I never identified myself with my kitchen coworkers. Yes, we spoke the same language and had similar culture. We even came from the same country, but that was it. I thought I was a special case. I came with a bachelor's degree from one of the best universities in Mexico. I had two good jobs there, and my parents provided me with whatever I needed whenever I needed it. I knew how to read and write in English, and I was able to have a simple conversation. Furthermore, I was planning to go back to Mexico. I had come specifically to learn the language and perhaps to continue my education.

My self-perceptions were not aligned with my stereotype of an immigrant. I thought an immigrant was one who left home knowing he or she wasn't coming back, traveling through lonely parts of Mexico until getting to the frontier and finding a way to cross the border. An immigrant was usually a peasant, poor, uneducated, ignorant, with one motive for leaving their country: better pay. There was no way I could tune this stereotype to my self-image, at least not yet.

LITERACY, EDUCATION, AND ETHNICITY

The first semester of my master's reminded me about my story of the upper level of the bookshelf in my parent's library. My parents have a library at home. Its contents are the most appreciated objects in my house. The library is separated by sections, some of them unknown to me until now. There are different nonfiction sections with medical journals, books of social sciences, natural sciences, some statistics and management books, several encyclopedias of different themes, and general information books for which my parents have some interest or use. In addition there is a huge fiction section, the preferred readings of both of them. That section has the most mysterious arrangement to me, for I haven't read half of it, and it is always acquiring new selections. Of course, there is a huge children's section arranged in the lowest levels of the library, of which I was very fond all year long.

Although we could choose some books by ourselves, my mom and dad always acted as the librarians and tried to guide our reading. We asked for books, and they made an effort to give us something we could understand and might like for our age. I remember that when I turned twelve, I was still reading young adult books, but vacation time allowed me to read a lot and at a fast pace. After several books, and at my request, my mom took me to the library. She was browsing the book cabinet when she looked at me and asked: "How old are you?"

"Twelve," I answered

"I think you are ready to read books with no drawings," she replied, staring at me but speaking in voice that sounded more like she was talking to herself.

"What can you read?" she asked herself. Contemplative, she started looking at her collection. "Aha! Here it is! *The Black Tulip*. This book has only one drawing. Then, if you like it and do not get bored, you can read this other book with no drawings at all."

I felt excited, proud and little nervous. My heart was beating fast and hard. I could feel it inside my chest pumping blood to my neck, my ears, and my head. I was looking seriously at my mom, accepting the challenge and pretending I had no butterflies in my stomach. The truth is I had no idea that day that I would advance to an upper level of the bookshelf. To my surprise I enjoyed that book. From that moment on, I would devour my parents' fiction collection with an unsatisfied appetite, fearing the end of each novel but eager for the beginning of every new one.

When I got in the MBA program, I felt as if I had got myself into the upper level of the shelf again. The reason was that the amount of reading and writing that one was to do at the graduate level was completely unexpected for me. Reading in English took me, and I think it still does, two or three times longer than reading in Spanish.

Soon after I faced the quantity of reading needed to succeed in my classes, the English language became a tool instead of a goal. The dilemma was deciding between reading everything on time and understanding the meaning of the words through the context of the text, or reading even more slowly and translating every unknown word. I chose to use the dictionary only when the word gave the meaning to the text. Now I want to continue to a PhD, and I have to get a good score in Graduate Record Examination (better known as the terrifying GRE). I think of my decision as one necessary and practical but nearsighted.

Writing in English. Oh my God! The challenge was unbelievable. Writing in English made me feel as challenged as if the book my mom wanted me to read that day in my parents' library belonged to their medicine bookshelf. I had a bad relationship with writing already in my language. In general, the Mexican education system poorly valuates writing. Ironically, for many years (things are changing now) Mexican college seniors had to go through the difficult process of learning how to write doing a formal research paper guided only by their mentor. It took me one year and two mentors to finish my research project. My final mentor was great but strict. I had to handle it chapter by chapter, and I had to write and rewrite each part several times. This was my first encounter with the rewriting process. She was more concerned about content, so she used to correct organization, grammar, and spelling herself in order for me to keep advancing. The priority of the undergraduate thesis was the content and the structure that economic research should follow, and that I learned very well. Still my writing didn't improve too much, and that lack of skill would haunt me in the United States.

The first semester in the MBA program was the most difficult. As an international student, I was obligated to take three classes and maintain full-time student status. (According to the state, that rule prevents international students from having time to plan and carry out terrorist activities.) In just one of the classes, I had to write three papers of thirty pages each, plus the team project (paper and presentation) plus the final exam. I was writing like a machine. Nonstop was the rule. I just tried to put all my ideas into the paper and answer all the questions. I remember that while I was writing, I used many Spanish words to be able to develop an idea completely, and then I had to come back and translate them. (I still have to do that.) Again, I was happy just with handing in my papers. Although that semester I had the worst grades of my master's (two Bs and a C), I was satisfied that I could even handle it. The main priority was accomplished. I had endured the first semester and I was still in the program. I couldn't believe I had written and read so much—and in English at that!!!

My language also caused me some issues with my classmates. I really never had any issues with my master's peers. Although I had to work in teams frequently, which usually worked pretty well, working with teams only worked well with my master's peers. Somehow, by the last semester of my master's, I had skipped one of the master's core courses. To cut costs, the program administration had decided that graduate students could meet these requirements taking 300-level classes and doing a little more work so they could be counted as 400-level classes. The 300-level class I took was in the mornings and full of people younger than me. There were many more native speakers than in the master's class. My usually successful teamwork didn't go well at all this time. In that class, I had to change teams three times.

The first team fired me because they were used to having many meetings during the mornings when I was working, and I couldn't go. The second team fired me because my "work in process" language was perceived as lack of dedication and seriousness on my part. At the end, the team that accepted me was a team of friends, all guys who needed so much help, and they were happy with my cooperation. The class had many other individual assignments, and oddly enough, my individually written projects were the ones that assured me a final A. However, the experience taught me that my imperfect language was perceived as a lack of professionalism and commitment.

In spite of my language issues, the support of my classmates at the master's level, mostly international students, made my program a very enjoyable experience. At the end of the master's, I was *a straight-A student*, and my papers had been praised as "a fine piece of independent thinking." As in my story of the upper level of the book shelf in my parent's library, I didn't expect to do an MBA, but when I did I enjoyed it and I was happy and satisfied with my performance.

Although during the MBA program my objective to dominate the language became a secondary goal for me, it didn't become secondary to my other goals. I was trying to get in the history master's program at NEIU (again my naivete), so I went to see the master's advisor at that time. His name was Sharman; after my visit I named him Mr. Sharkman. He heard my case, and at the end of my monologue, he asked me how my reading skills were. I answered him that I had good understanding of the readings but a slow pace. He explained to me that right there I had a problem because the amount of reading in history was substantial. He also explained that he knew a little bit of Spanish and that he could hear that my English was better than his Spanish, but not good enough to be admitted in the history master's program.

"We are looking for a certain level of writing skills in English that, after hearing you, I don't think you have."

I wanted to cry. Maybe because it was true. Maybe because I assumed that he only knew how to say "*Como está, amigo*" in Spanish and that my

English was being compared to that. Maybe because I felt that I was being denied the opportunity to learn something I like because my native language was not English. Maybe I was just a little sensitive at that time. It didn't matter. I was already afraid. Yet I still took some history prerequisite classes and got As. Therefore I decided to apply to the program. The As were not enough, and I was rejected. The rejection letter said, "We encourage you to continue developing your writing skills." How could I develop my writing skills if they didn't let me in and give me a reason to practice? I did it in the MBA Program. I believed I could do it in history. Apparently they didn't. Now that I look back at this incident, I think I also felt upset because my capacity to learn the concepts and content of a discipline was being measured with my ability to use the English language, which I think it is an unfair assessment. Little did I know about the relation of my ethnicity and the perception of my cognitive capabilities that still carry a weight in this country.

I don't know if I'm a rare case. But I could bet I'm not. When I came to United States I didn't know that race matters. Don't get me wrong. I knew about Lincoln, about Martin Luther King and the civil rights movement. I witnessed the Los Angeles riots after Rodney King, and I have seen thousands of movies depicting blatant racism in United States, usually during a different time period. Of course I knew about the Ku Klux Klan and the new racist Skin Heads. I also knew about the killing of Chinos in the Wild Wild West, and the Cesar Chavez *jornalero* movement, about the Chicanos and their belonging to a lower class, and their problems with gangs. Still, I didn't know race matters. For me everything was in the past. The United States was the land of opportunity. If you wanted you could make it here big. I used to think that African Americans should get over it and move forward. Latinos, well, they were lower class, and their problem was a class problem. It took me several history classes and one year inside my job to understand how much I was mistaken.

My job is to increase the number of low-income, first-generation students and minorities attaining PhDs. When I started working for the NEIU McNair program, I didn't know I would acquire a broader view of the social system of the United States by learning about the higher-education system. The stories of my scholars about all the injustice, police abuse, neglect, and confusion they experienced because of their ethnicity increased my understanding and brought into my time period what I thought was in the past of the United States, a huge race problem among the dominant culture with minorities, and surprisingly, among minorities too.

Although Mexico, as any other, is a country full of inequities, I was in many cases protected from the consequences of its social injustice. I never faced the discrimination and bigotry that poor and indigenous people face every day. Sometimes my rich classmates at my university looked down their noses at me because I was upper middle class, but those behaviors never changed my life. Not even once did I suffer from closed doors in any advancement opportunities. On the contrary, I always had doors open all the time. I was a good student with a good attitude and full of ambitions. I believed my hard work would pay back always. I just needed to keep putting a lot of effort in anything I did. My parents had worked hard all their lives so I could have this freedom of becoming whoever I wanted whenever I wanted. The sky was the limit.

My class status allowed me to live in a bubble. Of course I was a strong critic of the system of inequalities. My parents were committed leftist activists during their youth. In general, through reading they empowered their young teens to participate in the political life of our country and more importantly in the usual after-dinner conversations with my close and extended relatives, which many times involved discussion of social issues. Although I was a critic, my activist peak was during high school, and after I went to a private college, I stayed as a spectator of injustice. I never suffered about it, so I could detach myself fairly easily from the problems that people in different class levels faced every day. When I came to the United States I thought I would be able to do the same.

I'm of the idea that an international student can live his or her life in the United States identifying themselves with their classmates and university mates and never feel the need to connect with the broader ethnic group to which we belong. This international student sense of belonging creates a bubble similar to the class bubble that protected me from the injustices of Mexico. The reason is that not identifying with other people means you are rejecting them as the Other, such as I rejected identifying with my fellow immigrants at the beginning of my stay in United States. However, I decided to stay in the United States and the understanding that I was the Other began to sink in.

Working inside the higher-education system helping low-income, first-generation and minority students helped me to understand how their stories of crude racism were only the most visible face and nasty face of a system as unjust as the Mexican one.

I remember one of my scholars telling me that her teachers at her school used to tell her, "You are very bright for a Mexican," or another scholar telling me that when she used to look for a job, during the interviews the employers used to praise her: "You have a commendable resume; when I got it I didn't think you were black."

As part of a bigger system, the world of academia is also shaped with this notion that some people are superior to others. The inertia of many years still shapes student, teacher, and administrator attitudes that express consciously or unconsciously a range of negative prejudices against minorities. The simple need for a program like McNair speaks about this issue. The cold numbers of minority students underrepresented in academia speaks even louder. However, the voices that spoke to me strongly were the voices of many professors and students indicating to me the visible and invisible ways academia fails to see the Other as equals or simply to see the Other.

The McNair program supposes that after attaining their PhDs, the students will come back to the universities, become faculty, and in this way diversify academia. A diversified faculty will help to improve the numbers of minority students at the college and graduate level. This cycle works under certain assumptions. The first one is that minority students need more role models. That idea is pretty evident. Students will perform better if they feel familiarized with the institution and with their professors. Yet one of our most committed mentors had a different notion of minority faculty as role models. Her idea was that minority role models are more important for the dominant culture students. Minority faculty help them to understand that the prejudices and stereotypes against minorities are only that, prejudices.

However, the students have baggage with them, and it is difficult to deconstruct an idea that has been sunk into their minds since they were young, as another professor would explain to me during a higher education conference. She was a young Latina who had written several articles and books already. In spite of her publishing record and her good reputation as a teacher, she still faced students questioning her syllabus. They often accused her of not teaching them what was "important" because they were reading about U.S. Latino history and problems. Both anecdotes made me understand that different from Mexico, even if I am educated and higher class in the United States, one day I will face similar stereotyping as any other Latino in the United States.

Maybe it was my upbringing as social critic that helped me to understand my dilemma here in the United States. As an international student, the latent plan of going back to my country allowed me to see *los toros desde la barrera* (see the things from the outside). This expectation allowed me to believe that, because my presence in this country was temporal, I could go through my life without understanding the country and without internalizing its complex problems. Yet, when I faced the reality of my immigration, I saw my dilemma. I could have decided to continue with my mentality of an international student, the mentality that wanted me to believe that I was not an immigrant, that I had nothing to do with my compatriots of America Latina, that because of my education and success I would be different than the Others. I would be the one who would blame the Others for their own misfortunes; the one who took advantage of the land of the opportunities and made it, and therefore was the strongest. As we say in my country: *el tuerto en el mundo de los ciegos* (the one-eyed in the world of the blind), as I know now.

On the other hand, I could learn, understand, and accept that even if I didn't know it, when I decided to come to this country I was automatically positioned in the category of the Other, in an eternal race to "overcome" my ethnicity that could play against me. Yet, embracing my "category," understanding that I belong to a group of people named immigrants, Latinos, Hispanics, or minority, allowed me to see that it is not my ethnicity that I have to overcome. My ethnicity is not the problem!! The problems are out there, waiting to be identified and addressed, and as an educated Latina, part of my duty is to address them.

Today I don't want to "dominate" English anymore; I just want to keep learning so I'm able to communicate clearly my ideas. I don't wish to lose completely my accent because I realize I will lose some of my personality with it. I will lose the flavor and the feeling that I put into my words in order to transmit different sensations as well as to get different reactions from people. I don't want to read or sing or dream only in English. I want to take advantage of the richness of both languages I know. I don't want to replicate the culture and be an American in the United States of America and Mexican only in Mexico, first because I cannot stop being Mexican (I love it!), second because after four years in the United States of America, moreover at Northeastern, I realize how naïve and ignorant I was. There is not just one culture that I can replicate so I can be an "American." America is full of different cultures and even languages (I think that is the part that I like the most about my life here). Finally, now that I understand this quest in academia for the original idea, I don't think I can be very original if I forget my culture and try to replicate another one. My way to see the world as Angela, Mexican, immigrant, Latina, women, sister, daughter, wife, friend, professional, citizen, permanent resident, *morena*, dreamer, traveler, and so forth, is what will allow me to offer something new to the body of knowledge.

Once again, such as it happened with my desire to dominate English, my desire to be more American than the Americans when in the United States disappeared, and I understood that I was a Latina in America and that was who I needed to be.

EPILOGUE

I answered the phone and my brother Camilo was calling me from Boston. He had applied to ten ivy league universities for his PhD program, and he had been rejected. He was bummed down; his Harvard master's hadn't helped him get in. He thought it was his fault. The English maybe, that could be the reason, he said, or his average GRE of 1200. "Well it was pretty difficult that I would have been chosen as the fifth Latin American in the political science PhD of Harvard. I would have to be a genius, right?"

The only thing I could see by that time was that he didn't understand that race matters. He was a freshman in this living in the United States. He was still thinking as an international student. The rejection letters were telling him "you are not a good fit with our department," and he believed the problem was him. However, he was far from understanding that the department didn't think he shared the characteristics or the research interests of the professors in that department. In other words, he would break the homogeneous research interests of those departments. There was nothing that Camilo had to offer to the departments, and then he was rejected. The truth is that Camilo needs to find a university and a department that believes that in order to have an accurate understanding of the whole world, it is necessary to bring to the discussion a broad diversity of scholars. The department that is committed to this inclusive belief would then have in place a selection process that values access more than selectivity. Then he will have to publish as many scholarly articles as he can per year to create value for his own research, and then, maybe then, we will compete for the same professorship positions as those who graduate from the most prestigious universities in America. It was not a question of being a loser or not. It was the question of finding the loophole in the closed system of the creation of knowledge and then expanding its boundaries.

Camilo's perception of the same problem is different from mine because I have understood that I'm part of a group that is disadvantaged in higher education. This awareness prevents me from internalizing prejudice easily and allows me to see how there are mechanisms in the academic system that block fair competition for minority students. The identification of this mechanism enables me to find the loopholes so minorities like me can achieve their maximum potential and eliminate prejudices.

Different Standards
PART IV

I later learned that after the Language Skills Assessment Task Force submitted its final report, the Faculty Council on Academic Affairs established another committee—the Writing Implementation Task Force—that reached similar conclusions: a need for better coordination among the Reading Program, the English Language Program, and the English Department and a goal of writing-intensive courses as major requirements, as well as the importance of adequate funding.

Aside from two members on this new task force, few in the English Department knew the details of these deliberations. Nonetheless, those of us who had been involved with previous writing initiatives on campus or had run writing programs elsewhere were asked to agree to an administrative rotation for the first-year writing program. One decided to await additional details about the proposed program while I declined the invitation, citing my previous conclusions about my administrative abilities.

While we awaited official information, we were sufficiently concerned by unofficial explanations and unverified rumors to express our reservations. In an email to department colleagues and campus administrators involved with the implementation task force, I explained that aside from the theoretical questions that motivated my resignation from WPA work, I was unsure about a planning process that had excluded not only those with WPA experience but also those with the most at stake—instructors, both full- and part-time, who together teach most of the introductory writing courses.

In response, our departmental colleagues promised a full discussion of the proposed program and our objections, which was delayed when one had a personal emergency. Then we all dispersed for the summer

Even before I had kids, I wanted to learn Tagalog, but first I had to finish comps and the dissertation. Then Mahal was born, and we left for Florida and later New York, and then Mateo was born.

After coming to Chicago, Tagalog became a regular experice in our everyday lives although my kids and I are learning it mostly on our own. Sure, their *lola* or sometimes their *lolo* or *nanay* will answer syntactical or lexical questions—sometimes their *lola* laughs and then is silent—but for now, we are working on our own, at least until we can plunge deeper into the conversations swirling around us.

At their house, their *lola* often uses Tagalog, but their *nanay* almost always responds in English. Sometimes, they turn to me, unsure whether I've tracked their talk, which some days seems easier. (At least I know now when they're talking about me.) At our house, Mahal is impatient with my Taglish. "Just use English," she insists, asking for the language of the playground.

These tensions seem more sensible when I consider historical and social conditions. In 1898, the Philippines, in the language of colonialism, was "acquired" by the United States from Spain, at the peak of nationalist identity movements, and by 1901, English was the language of Filipino schools. Although this archipelago acquired its independence in 1946, it has two official languages—Filipino, which is standardized Tagalog, and English—and two auxiliary languages—Spanish, which was the first official language of the islands, and Arabic.

Although Tagalog is the *lingua franca* among Filipinos in the United States and the Philippines, the islands, according to the Filipino governmnet, contain between 76 and 78 languages and more than 500 dialects. Most of these, except Spanish, English, Cantonese, Mandarin, Chavacano, and Hokkien, come from the Malayan-Polynesian branch of the Austronesian family of languages.

This linguistic contact shapes my experiences of learning this language. Tagalog, to my nonnative ears and eyes, seems to reflect this recent Spanish-English contact. For example, *mixed* in Spanish is *mestizo* or *mestiza* but only *mestisa* in Tagalog. Or *halo-halo*, which is also a sweet drink of shaved ice and condensed milk with fruit and beans that my kids' *lola* sometimes makes. Or even *white leghorn*, I've learned, if a person is more white than anything.

This contact also shapes my sense of syntax. Similar to English, Spanish is subject-verb-object (SVO) although its functional use of morphology and syntax allows for a more flexible word order—OVS, SOV, or OV (Sanz 2000, 7). Tagalog, as best as I can tell, has two basic structures—SVO and VSO (Thompson 2003, 132). For example, the same utterance—*the kids are mixed*—is *los niños son mestizos* in Spanish but in Tagalog is either *ang mga bata any mestisa*, which seems to resemble Spanish and English, or *mestisa ang mga bata*, which I'm told is more common and, for native Tagalog speakers, more comfortable.

Maybe it's my relation to English, but I must often wait—*mestisa ang mga bata*—to learn what or who is or are mixed. In this, syntax also becomes style and stance. Over the years, I've learned to sit back when listening to Filipinos using Tagalog, and even multilinguals using English, sometimes for one or more conversational turns, while meaning is made.

And yet such experiences make me wonder about those principles of clarity and grace—*open sentences with familiar units of information* or *begin sentences constituting a passage with consistent topic/ subjects* or even *push new, complex information to the end of the sentence* and *above all, write to others as you would have others write to you* (Williams 2003)—that I was taught and teach.

After returning to campus in the fall, I learned that a proposal for HSI funds had already been prepared and submitted. While everything in it hadn't been unanimously supported, I was told by my departmental colleagues on the committee, the proposed program could be altered later if it was funded. At that point, I was given a copy of the grant application with the proposed program and instructed to note my concerns but to invest my energy in the new search that had been authorized as a result of this initiative.

Five days later, I was informed that the application had been awarded 2.8 million dollars, which increased the urgency of the discussion about the proposed program, but first I had to read the grant application to discover what had been proposed. And at some point, I had to decide how to respond to my redacted email that had been published without my permission in the campus newspaper, not to mention the use of this email to accuse my colleagues and me of educational fraud.

As I was completing the data collection, the English Department was officially notified of the new campuswide writing program. The purpose of this multimillion dollar grant, according to the memo, was to support the new writing intensive requirement across the campus, a new Center for Academic Literacy in the library, and the coordination of first-year writing courses in the department. This coordination, we were assured, was the least significant aspect of the grant, and it merely required "uniform" but "not identical" sections as part of a "sequenced writing program" that prepares students, and faculty, for writing-intensive courses in the majors.

More explanation was provided at our next department meeting. While the grant required the institutionalization of these efforts by its end, the data collected through E-rater and other means would help administrators determine whether to continue funding this initiative once the grant money had been spent. Also, the grant would likely eliminate the current policy that all tenured and tenure-track English faculty should teach at least one section of first-year writing every academic year.

And maybe, once the grant was over, the writing program would be separated from the English Department, which would allow both, we were told, to have more productive meetings.

Part Three

CONNECTIONS AND CONCLUSIONS

6

PRACTICES, POLICIES, PHILOSOPHIES, AND POLITICS

Despite our difficulties with diversity, our belief in education endures, especially among ethnolinguistic minorities. For example, a recent editorial entitled "Educación para Toda la Familia" (*Hoy* 2008) in a local newspaper suggests that educational opportunities are available to everyone, including recent arrivals:

> *Quienes dicen que para un inmigrante latino con pocos recursos no es posible obtener una educación y una buena profesión, están equivocados. Aunque miles llegan a Estados Unidos sin dinero, con poca educación académica, y sin profesión, todos pueden mejorar sus vidas y las de sus familias si están dispuestos a pagar el precio.*[1]

At the same time, educational success is a family affair:

> *Sabemos que debemos presionar a las autoridades para que cumplan con su responsabilidad, sin embargo, no hay nada más efectivo que los padres se involucren en el éxito académico y personal de sus hijos.*[2]

For many, these opportunities, as almost moral obligations, bring social and political benefits:

> *Hay muchos ejemplos en nuestra comunidad de que el progreso está al alcance; son testimonios de "querer es poder". Quizá sea difícil, pero no hay que dejarse guiar sólo por el camino fácil. Como decía la mamá de Guzmán: "El que no estudia en este país, es porque no quiere". Tampoco olvidemos el mensaje sencillo y poderoso que nos heredo Cesar Chávez: "Sí se puede". Porque si otros pueden, nosotros también podemos.*[3] (Rebecca Sánchez 2008)

---

1. Translation: Those who say that for a Latino immigrant with few resources it is not possible to obtain an education and a good job, these people are wrong. While thousands arrive in the United States without money, with little education, and without a job, everyone can improve their lives and those of their families if they are willing to pay the price.
2. Translation: We know that we should pressure authorities to fulfill their responsibility. However, there is nothing more effective than the involvement of parents in the academic and personal success of their children.
3. Translation: There are many examples in our community that progress is within reach; these are testimonials that "want is power." It might be difficult, but there are none who must be guided only by the easy road. As Guzmán's mother said: "He

Especially for immigrants who come to the United States, education is the means to a better life for both individuals and communities.

While such perspectives might explain why ethnolinguistic minorities and their peers come to NEIU and other educational institutions, many, as these Proyecto Pa'Lante students demonstrate, struggle to complete their classes and earn their degrees. They arrive with reading and writing experiences that are as good as their *national* peers', and better beliefs and attitudes about literacy than those peers. In addition, they have similar success throughout their first year, and are more likely to return for a second year, than their *institutional* peers. Over the next three years, however, they earn fewer hours and worse grades while their institutional peers earn better grades. This can only increase the costs for the fewer than four in ten of these PP students and their institutional peers who remain after four years. Even when ethnolinguistic minority students earn better grades, they must confront cultural and linguistic challenges that can increase the emotional and psychological costs of completing their degrees, as the institutional autobiographies of Neida, Sophia, and Angela attest.

To explain these educational experiences, some turn to these students and their cultures. According to Katherine, the Coordinator of NEIU Learning Center, the institution serves a "whole Hispanic generation on the march," a "gathering political force" that understands the importance of college to their futures yet lacks the "luxury" of time to think. Over several conversations at the Learning Center and in the student union, she expressed her concerns about students who report, in for example entrance interviews, that they hate reading. "Their parents are working very hard jobs," she said, and while these students recognize the importance of school, they understand it as a job. "They fail to recognize the journey," she said, "and what is involved in it and the skills they must develop."

As an illustration, she described a student who bought two books for a class but didn't notice the connections between the chapters in the textbook and the profiles in the collection until Katherine identified them. Another student, she explained, emigrated from Mexico, enrolled in U.S. elementary schools, and wants to be an elementary Spanish teacher. When this student started working with Katherine at the Learning Center, the student didn't know that she should read and write differently in

---

who does not study in this country, it is because he does not want to." Nor should we forget the simple and powerful message that was given to us by Cesar Chávez: "Yes we can." Because if others can, we also can.

different situations, such as avoiding first person in classroom observation reports.

In contrast, she described her friend's daughter, who had a perfect ACT score but is "devoid of personality," or her son's friend, whose mother outlined textbook chapters for his high-school AP course. "You don't know the money that the people in Evanston[4] spend to get these scores on these tests," she said. Some parents, she explained, request schedule changes, such as PE exemptions, in order to enable their children to enroll in additional courses. "The manipulation at that level is pretty incredible," she said.

Others suggest differences between classroom performance and student perceptions that persist across the United States. "One of the biggest problems that we're up against, that we have not even begun to deal with," said Edmund, the Director of the NEIU Center for Teaching and Learning, "is complete misperceptions of capabilities."

He and I had agreed to meet in the student union to discuss one of his regular campus surveys, and our discussion evolved into a more general conversation about education at NEIU and across the United States. "And personally I feel a lot of that has to do with a pervading ideology about American education where the most important thing—that, I mean, that's been going on since the late sixties/early seventies where you know self-esteem was *the* most important thing that teachers felt they had to instill in students."

After earning graduate degrees in philosophy and linguistics and working in adult education in Germany, Edmund immigrated to the United States where he earned another graduate degree in communications and then a doctorate in educational psychology. He has worked in faculty development for twenty years, and he founded a teaching center and was a psychology professor, as well as published articles and chapters on college teaching and contributed to several award-winning videos on college teaching and learning.

"I mean I'm not against self-esteem," he said, "but when that becomes the sort of holy grail of education—do not threaten a student's self-esteem by letting them know that they are not quite measuring up in a certain way—you are setting students up for total failure, because you are lying to them."

---

4.   Evanston, a suburb five and a half miles northeast of NEIU, is the home of Northwestern University where 96 percent of its students have an ACT score between 24 and 26.

He referred to another of his surveys of 2003 NEIU Summer Transition Program students where more than three in ten considered themselves to be above average in math even though between more than seven in ten were placed in remedial math classes. Similar misperceptions exist, he added, for reading and writing, and the chances of having these confronted and addressed are limited: more than six in ten neither initiate study groups (67 percent) nor use tutorial services (64 percent), and five in ten neither use office hours (52 percent) nor visit academic counselors (50 percent).

"And I think we've been lying to students for decades," Edmund said. "And this is the result, they all feel that they are wonderful because they've been told they are wonderful."

The differences between NEIU students and others across the country, he believes, are differences of degree. Writing is a national problem, he suggests, just more so at NEIU, a condition that is complicated, he added, by the number of nonnative English users. "Even among these," he said, "other differences exist—those who have just begun to learn English as opposed to those who came early enough to be fluent in spoken English but late enough to miss training in written English." Another factor, he suggested, is the number of Chicago Public School graduates, and the best way to help these students and others like them, he explained, is to improve their metacognition, or "the steering mechanisms," in his own words, for assessing their own performance. "They need to become good diagnosticians of their own learning," he said. "That is probably *the* most important skill students should have."

At the outset of her study of Mexican families in the United States, Guadalupe Valdés (1996) explains that educational experts, when asked to account for the educational failure of minority students, offer one of three arguments—a genetic argument, in which the reason is that these students are somehow inferior; a cultural argument, in which they are either unprepared or misprepared; and a class-analysis argument, in which they are, as a result of larger social structures, predetermined to fail (15–25). While the genetic argument, she suggests, has largely fallen from favor, the cultural arguments, which have been used much more often, frequently result in small solutions that focus on instructional alternatives rather than programmatic and institutional changes that, while more complicated, are more effective (27–29). As an illustration, Valdés demonstrates how a parent-education program fails to recognize its impact upon Mexican families, which have very different beliefs about and expectations for education and learning (190–205). Using this and other examples, she critiques the interventions by administrators and teachers who, invoking a medical model, diagnose problems and prescribe cures, and she argues that policymakers and practitioners should recognize, especially given the widespread discussions about diversity, that immigrants bring perspectives to their new communities that both protect them and enrich everyone (199, 203).

Although Valdés seems to overlook the ways that different culture arguments—unprepared or misprepared—produce different subject positions, she nonetheless provides a framework for the explanations of educational experiences at NEIU, including mine before completing this case study of an officially designated Hispanic-Serving Institution and the most ethnically diverse university in the Midwest. Since its origins in the mid-nineteenth century, this institution has been closely connected to Chicago Public Schools and, through them, to larger educational and Americanization efforts across the United States, and over time, it established an institutional independence as it expanded from a teachers college to a state university while maintaining a symbiotic relationship with the metro Chicago community. On the one hand, it has provided access for many—women, working classes, and ethnic minorities—who might otherwise be excluded from higher education. On the other, it has struggled to retain and graduate the students whom it has admitted.

In these struggles with retention and graduation, this institution is not alone, as recent research suggests. For *Crossing the Finish Line,* William G. Bowen, Matthew M. Chingos, and Michael S. McPherson (2009) analyzed data from twenty-five flagship and state universities across the United States as they tracked students who entered in 1999 through transfer, withdrawal, or graduation, in terms of the impact of parental education, income, gender, ethnicity, high-school grades, tests scores, financial aid, and institutional selectivity. Even when controlling for these variables, the authors conclude that ethnic and economic minorities have lower graduation rates and need longer to complete their degrees. While some researchers have criticized the cultural biases of persistence studies and retention theories, others suggest that students and professors, despite their good intentions, misunderstand and fail each other and that conventional institutional culture, including traditional notions of academic literacy, can create obstacles for many students as they attempt to earn college degrees (e.g., Braxton 2000; Cox 2009; Kraemer 1997).

In shifting the focus from the study of literacy instruction to an analysis of sponsored literacies, this project continues the trend to emphasize the intersections of social and cultural conditions that have been highlighted in other studies (e.g., Noguera 2003, 64–65). While these studies often suggest a social stratification within schools, this institutional case study offers a more complicated conclusion about educational equity—most NEIU students struggle, and those who are ethnic minorities and working class struggle even more—that suggests the presence of an institutionalized discrimination and even a "color-blind racism,"[5] which can be seen in the confluence of education and literacy.

Once again, eight in ten of our colleagues across the country believe that high-school graduates are unprepared or underprepared for college, and four in ten of them believe those graduates are not well prepared for college writing (Sanoff 2006). In a similar way, my NEIU colleagues reported, as these PP students and their institutional peers arrived on campus, that many of their students are unprepared for college reading and writing:

NEIU Faculty Perception of Prepared NEIU Students

	Reading (%)	Writing (%)
100-level courses	03	00
200-level courses	13	05
300-level courses	37	28
400-level courses	44	37

Source: NEIU Language Skills Assessment Task Force (2004)

Almost no first-year students, according to NEIU faculty, are prepared for reading and writing, and fewer than half are prepared even at the most advanced undergraduate levels, even though my colleagues and I, to address these conditions, offer additional assistance during office hours (33 percent), respond to drafts (27 percent), refer students to the Writing Lab (25 percent) and tutoring (21 percent), recommend invention strategies (21 percent), and partner poor readers with better ones (15 percent).

And similar to the University of Delaware English professor (Yagoda 2006) and others who see signs of "unfortunate cultural trends," my NEIU colleagues have their own perceptions of these conditions. In terms of reading, one indicated that the preparation is "depressing,"

---

5.   For more, see Bonilla-Silva (2006) or Martinez (2009).

and another suggested that NEIU does not address "this deficit" adequately. Others offered different, yet familiar, accounts:

- Most of my students do not read assigned material—either because they cannot read college-level work, due to their educational deficiencies, or because they lack of any great interest in the subject matter (it is not job-related), or else because they don't have the time due to their working 30 to 40 hours at a job. When all three factors are at work, they become an insurmountable combination.

- Student expectancies, nurtured over many years of taking courses, are to come to class irregularly, not take notes, not read assignments or independently do homework assignments. Of course, they expect to get high grades.

As for writing, one cited the "appalling work" of students at all levels, which many suggested was exacerbated by the significant percentage of English Language Learners, and others linked writing proficiencies to larger social conditions:

- Lack of prep for writing is guaranteed as long as NEIU prides itself on admitting students woefully unprepared for college work. Ideally, they should make up this missing education before they are admitted into a college classroom, where they either fail or are treated to an inflated grade for substandard work. But it is difficult to teach students material they do not value or have no interest in. Most college faculty probably have no interest and no expertise in teaching high-school English. To pretend that an effective reading or writing component can be squeezed into a regular academic course without detracting from college-level work is unrealistic. What is to be done? They can't go back to the high schools they just came from because what they need isn't there, otherwise they would already have it. They are not going to get it in college, for the reasons above, unless college [every college, so they can't escape] builds within itself a compulsory mini high school with specialist teachers. Is there money for this? Who, aside from a few idealists, would be interested in funding it or implementing it? The task would be enormous and time consuming, and would involve nearly every (would-be) college freshman. In the face of these problems, American higher education has evolved an utterly ingenious solution: Grade inflation. NEIU can take pride, either in being a leader in this movement, or in searching for an alternative solution.

- I expect my students to fall into the "prepared" category when they come to my classes, even in my 100-level courses. If they come to me "prepared", I can move them to the "well prepared" category over the course of the semester. If the students come to me "somewhat prepared" (as most do), I find myself unable (unwilling?) to move their writing forward in any significant way.

For many, this inadequate preparation is exacerbated by the number of students who use English as a second language. "Most of our students are of foreign origin," one explained, and would "benefit from a strong ESL sequence."

While my NEIU colleagues might share some sense of perceived preparedness with our colleagues across the country, they do not necessarily share similar understandings of reading and writing, which ranged from proficiencies, habits, and even attitudes. For some, college-level reading is "comprehensive," which consists of no more than "two passes over the same material to gain understanding," or "critical," including the ability to retain relevant information or even synthesize texts. For others, it is requires an expanded vocabulary or timely completion of assignments or even the enjoyment of class reading assignments or the pursuit of other relevant sources. In much the same way, these differences also persisted in terms of the objects of reading. Some suggested that students should be able to read assigned textbooks, while others suggested primary sources—even ones the students had found, and should be motivated to find, on their own—and for one, students should be able to read newspapers and journals to be informed of current events.

In a similar way, NEIU faculty defined writing in ways that ranged from mastery of spelling or conventions to intellectual attitudes. Many referred to the need for "correct grammar and spelling" or language "free of grammar and spelling errors" as well as typos while a few suggested some limited tolerance for nonnative English users. Others identified critical thinking, including rational arguments, or recognizable organizational structures or conventional citation and documentation formats. "I expect students to: a. write in standard, grammatical English," one explained, "b. supply a title, use topic sentences and paragraphs and an introduction, use paragraphs throughout, and finish with a conclusion. c. cite sources if appropriate." Still others included a familiarity with "library research methods" or "[d]ata driven papers: thesis development, analysis of data, results, conclusion which addresses the thesis." While one cited the highest expectations, another explained, "I expect the worst, and usually get it" (Language 2004.)

Although these different perceptions and definitions can only complicate educational challenges, they are not unfamiliar, and neither is the remedy proposed by the institution. Based upon these survey responses and other data, the NEIU Language Skills Assessment Task Force, shortly after these PP students started at NEIU, offered this description of literacy conditions on campus:

> The need is clear. Increasing student diversity, increasing numbers of students for whom English is a second language, decreasing levels of preparation of our entering students, ACT test scores, and extensive data from faculty all point to the need for an approach that does more to prepare for the writing competencies they need to be successful in college and beyond. (NEIU Language 2005, 1–3, 5).

As these PP students completed their third year, another task force of faculty from across the campus, the Writing Implementation Task Force, reconfirmed these initial conclusions:

> Given the linguistic diversity of the Northeastern student body, both in terms of ESL students and native speakers whose first dialect is non-standard, it is essential that the university provide support services that will give students an opportunity to develop the level of academic literacy that they will need in order to pass writing-intensive courses in their majors.

Most important, according to this task force, is the need for the university to "provide opportunities for underprepared students to develop the appropriate level of academic literacy skills" on both its main campus and satellite campuses at the Center for Inner City Studies and El Centro (Writing Implementation 2007).

Later that same year, the remedy was outlined in a grant application for Title V funds—funds available to institutions with official HSI designations—entitled Improving Retention through Academic Literacy that linked ethnolinguistic diversity, through literacy instruction, to the educational mission and social function of the university. This proposal, according to the institution, is "part of the university's strategy for addressing critical barriers and problems that challenge it from fulfilling its mission as an urban university of excellence and access," and it was designed primarily to address "the institutional need to improve retention and graduation rates by addressing key academic literacy skills" through reconfiguring its first-year writing program and requiring writing-intensive (WI) courses in the majors (NEIU 2007, 11–12).

As described in this application, the institution proposed to establish a position of first-year writing coordinator to ensure the uniformity of all sections, as well as their relevance to other WI courses. Also, it promised to train faculty, through weekly seminars over a semester, to design courses that satisfy its WI criteria, as well as to provide templates for those who teach these courses. In addition, it planned to construct a Center for Academic Literacy, as a supplement to the Writing Lab, to assist through tutoring and training both students and faculty with the WI requirements, as well as to provide access to basic writing and plagiarism software, all of which would be assessed through evaluation software and faculty ratings. As a result of these efforts, holistic scores of writing samples from those who complete the first-year program would increase by 5 percent, the first- to second-year retention rate would increase from 69 percent to 74 percent, at least fifty WI courses would be offered and fifty NEIU faculty would be certified to offer them, and writing services for students would increase by 10 percent annually by the end of the grant (NEIU 2007, 19–23).

As these PP students started their fourth year (fall 2007), NEIU learned that it had been awarded $2.8 million to implement this campuswide writing initiative, a process that would continue long after this project ended but before most of these PP students and their institutional peers, at least those who remained, had graduated.

N(CTE)EIU AND SPONSORED LITERACIES

While some might question the logic of adding degree requirements to increase graduation rates, most will likely recognize the proposed campuswide writing program because it is strikingly similar to the one described by Susan McLeod and Elaine Maimon (2000) and to others across the country.

After listening at a WPA conference to "an informed and respected colleague" characterize WAC in ways that neither of them recognized, McLeod and Maimon decided to "expose the myths" in order to "set the record straight" in an article for *College English* (2000, 573). In this attempt to "clear the air," they identify four "myths": that WAC functions as grammar across the curriculum; that WAC is opposed to writing in the disciplines (WID); that writing to learn (WTL) is superior to WID; and that WAC supports institutional agendas and conventional literacy (574). After critiquing each of these misunderstandings, McLeod and Maimon argue that, instead, WAC is a "pedagogical reform movement" and a "programmatic entity" with interrelated components, including faculty development, curricular commitment, student support, assessment aspects, and administrative structures and budgets (579). Finally, they offer suggestions, based upon practice and theory, that promote scholarly research about writing programs (582).

Although McLeod and Maimon attest to the connections of education and literacy, these respected theorists and practitioners, in attempting to clear the air, actually raise more dust. In particular, these *myths* merely mask everyday literacy experiences within institutions, which in my experience as a former WAC Coordinator seem much more complicated. On the one hand, most specialists know that WAC specifically, and composition studies generally, are concerned, at least in theory, with more than surface correctness and that WTL and WID, despite competing theories and histories, are not necessarily incompatible, nor is one inherently better than the other. On the other, our campus colleagues often define good writing as good grammar, and many bring partial, and personal, perspectives on learning and literacy that shape their perceptions of classroom performances. Rather than myths, these conditions, at least the first three, are more paradoxes that, as many WPAs could attest, cannot be resolved simply by explaining educational theories or citing composition research.

While these misrepresentations are minor, their fourth criticism, or the belief that WAC supports institutional agendas and conventional literacy, highlights a larger problem of educational equity at the center of this institutional case study.[6] After criticizing this *myth*, McLeod and Maimon argue that WAC, as "profoundly transformative," actually functions as a critique of U.S. higher education by encouraging "active engagement" with knowledge and ideas while promoting better reading and writing. Again fusing the link between education and literacy, they suggest that this promotion is "more profound" because it reflects "grassroots" efforts to shift from teacher-centered to student-centered

---

6.   In this, McLeod and Maimon (2000) are criticizing Mahala (1991).

classrooms, thereby serving as a "quietly subversive movement" with WPAs as "agents of change" within institutions (574, 577–578).

Once again, everyday realities, at least in my experience, are much more complicated. As "pedagogical reform" efforts, the best practices of WAC can offer alternatives to "the 'delivery of information' model of teaching," and other initiatives can as well. At the same time, these efforts have always been quite conservative, at least in supporting the assimilation of students into academic and U.S. cultures that leaves larger systemic structures and prevailing ideologies unchallenged.[7] According to David Russell (1991), the failure of introductory writing courses in both secondary and postsecondary schools produced WAC and other institution-wide responses, yet the effect, regardless of whether these efforts are the result of English departments or campus-wide initiatives, has largely been to certify students in either generic literacy within introductory writing courses or discipline-specific literacies in campuswide courses. Together, these sponsored literacies require students, as Victor Villanueva (2001) suggests, to first invent the university and then invent disciplines (166).

In fact, this problem — relatively decontextualized literacies — can be seen in what McLeod and Maimon (2000) characterize as "the models for the kinds of work scholars of WAC should aspire to"—John Bean's (1996) *Engaging Ideas,* Christopher Thaiss's (1998) *The Harcourt Brace Guide to Writing across the Curriculum,* and Art Young's (1999) *Teaching Writing across the Curriculum*—that, as they explain near the end of their article, represent "a fair and realistic view of WAC," based upon practice and theory, that enables efforts "to move forward without the promulgation of myths that obscure and distort scholarly exchange" (582). Although these resources offer practical and theoretical direction for engaged professors, as suggested by Bean's (1996) titles, and writing specialists alike, each documents institutional and disciplinary commitment to traditional goals for education and conventional models of literacy.

While Bean offers an accessible justification for writing as thinking, he suggests that intellectual work is, and should be, done through *thesis-driven arguments,* to which he devotes almost the entire chapter on formal writing assignments, and only occasionally other assignments— *thesis-seeking* expository essays, for example, that supplement *thesis-supporting* problem-solving tasks along with a few others (73–95). Although

---

7.   For more, see LeCourt (1996).

Thaiss (1998) presents useful historical contexts for campuswide writing initiatives, he suggests that these initiatives are valuable because "initiating students into academic life means giving them the tools to collect, evaluate, and express information as professionals do" (13). In much the same way, Young (1999) maintains that writing to learn and learning to communicate create "a middle ground of conversational language and learning" from "where students gain knowledge, develop scholarly habits of mind, and acquire rhetorical communication competence in a variety of public and academic contexts" that are nonetheless the result of academic assimilation, not accommodation, and certainly not negotiation of forms or practices or perspectives (57, 58).

In this, McLeod and Maimon (2000) again misrepresent the ways that institutions and disciplines sponsor relatively decontextualized literacies that significantly shape educational experiences.[8] In part, the problem is the way institutions sponsor a tacit English Only policy, which has recently been criticized (e.g., Horner 2001; Horner and Trimbur 2002; Matsuda 2006; Trimbur 2006, 2008). For example, Bruce Horner (2001), in his critique of SRTOL, suggests that it includes a "constellation of assumptions about languages and language users," as "individually homogeneous, static, discrete, politically neutral yet tied indelibly to ethnicity" (742, 743).[9] Together, these policies authorize not only English but also particular institutional identities.

Clearly, such policies, and their assumptions about language and identity, pose particular problems for PP students and others like them. For example, some use English proficiencies to reach conclusions about cognitive ability (e.g., Harklau 2000; Zamel 1995). If any accommodations are made, they are usually transitional, as suggested by the classroom observations of the PP seminar course, while the educational goal, as required by Illinois law, is English Only classrooms where many multilinguals, according to Guadalupe Valdés (2001b), are not well served. Although focusing primarily on K–12, studies suggest that language minority students who receive greater L1 instructional support combined with balanced L2 support have greater academic success, sometimes reaching the norms of the native group after six years, than those who are educated in monolingual L2, or English, classrooms (Collier 1992, 192–193).[10]

---

8.   See also Farr (1993). Such contexts are significant, often with negative consequences, even when education and literacy involve community partnerships or originate outside institutions (e.g., Feldman 2008; Mathieu 2005; Parks and Goldblatt 2000).

9.   For more, see Rodby (1992) and Pennycook (1994).

10. Collier (1992) also suggests that subsequent research might show that the combina-

For this and other reasons, Horner and the others are correct to critique these conditions and contradictions not only in SRTOL but also
in writing programs and U.S. educational institutions, and yet as this
institutional case study suggests, they misrepresent the extent of the
problem by limiting their critique to language policies without considering literacy philosophies. Although, for example, Helen Fox (1994)
acknowledges the need to change both students and universities, she
concedes, in her book on cultural differences in the academy, a relatively universalized notion of academic writing—writing that is clear,
focused, and structured; papers that move beyond description to analysis and criticism; texts that critique authorities without committing plagiarism—almost as if these descriptions can be decontextualized from
disciplinary, institutional, and socio-cultural contexts (108, 114–125).

Such notions of literacy can be found both within and beyond composition studies. As David Bartholomae (1985) describes in his ironic,
and often cited, explanation, students must appropriate, or be appro-
priated by, discourses as if they are full-fledged participants within institutions and disciplines. In a similar way, literacy, according to theorist
James Paul Gee (1996), is the mastery of secondary discourses, or particular combinations of "saying(writing)-doing-being-valuing-believing"
(143, 127). As a result, learning and education are the socialization into
relatively reified discourses—the discourses of historians or lawyers—
through acquisition by everyday exposure or learning by conscious study
(138).[11] These accounts invoke either the relatively absolute terms of
autonomous models of literacy, which as Brian Street (1984, 1993) explains,
are "defined in technical terms" and exist "independent of social context" (1993, 2), or the more specialized terms of *semiautonomous models of
literacy*, which, as I (Schroeder 2006) argue, authorize some differences,
such as disciplinary, while dismissing others, including ethnolinguistic
ones, as educational obstacles to overcome.

As these examples suggest, such institutionalized assumptions about
education and literacy are difficult to overcome even among otherwise
enlightened educators and researchers, as seen for example in the
approach advocated by James Slevin (2001). In outlining his approach,
Slevin uses a linguistics of contact and contact zones to critique language education and English departments and to advocate for new
notions of intellectual work, and while he explicitly acknowledges the

tion of L1 support and other factors produces this increased academic success (207).
11. For more, see Rodby (1992, 19, 33) and Vandenberg (1999).

problems of assimilationist goals, he nonetheless pursues the same problematic ends (2, 6).

At the center of his approach, Slevin suggests, is an attempt to reject *absence* or *lack* in favor of *difference* as he argues for English studies as the study of education and literacy. For instance, colonial literature, such as the story of Pocahontas or the records of Virginia Tidewater, becomes an account of the ways assumptions about education and language, in his own words, "were planted, like the colony itself, in the consciousness of invaders and invaded alike" (4). At the same time, he simultaneously expands and limits composition studies while confronting conventional concerns, such as distinguishing between WAC, with its tendency toward academic socialization, and WID, with its ability, according to Slevin, to position intellectual workers, including students, within "an historical and dialogic intellectual project" (10, 190–191). In addition, he also addresses larger institutional issues, such as assessment and tenure, in which those being evaluated, he argues, should have a much larger role.[12]

One of the strengths of Slevin's perspective is his emphasis upon particularity, often in the form of experience, as the basis for theorizing a unified approach to English studies as the study of education and literacy. In his approach, practice and theory, together as *praxis*, constitute intellectual work regardless of whether he is analyzing his classrooms, explicating *Don Quixote*, or critiquing WPA assessment models. Nonetheless, this perspective often relies upon universalized notions of *discourse*—not just academic discourse but also colonizing discourse—and *identity* as relatively unified and homogeneous entities. As a part of an argument for critical perspectives on academic genres, Slevin suggests, for example, that most will agree upon the importance of joining the academic community and controlling "the genres of academic discourse":

> I think the problem we face rests in the tension between the metaphor of initiation in which we have become ensnared and our desire, finally, to provide for students a critical distance that makes the process of joining the academic discourse community something quite different from an "initiation." (155)

At the same time as he acknowledges this awareness, he elsewhere refers, on multiple occasions, to the symbolic violence of colonizing discourse, the canon, and even education itself, as if these are monolithic phenomena with inevitable effects.[13]

---

12. See also Schroeder (2004).
13. For more, see Stuckey (1991) and T. Fox (1999).

Even as he emphasizes *difference* as the center of education and literacy, Slevin essentializes the effects, particularly in the ways that *difference* overlooks the complexities of enculturation, such as the differences between pursing it and having it imposed, or some complicated combination (e.g., Schecter and Bayley 1997; Valdés 1996). Rather, Slevin authorizes identities for individuals, whether students or immigrants, as (relatively) passive victims of these violations of culture and language even as these experiences are much more contested, as many have attested (e.g., Gilyard 1991; Rose 1989; Roth and Harama 2000; Villanueva 1993) and reported (e.g., Canagarajah 2002; Casanave 2002; LeCourt 2004; Sternglass 1997; Zamel and Spack 2004).

As this study suggest, these PP students and their institutional peers have assumed any number of perspectives and selves even before sitting in college classrooms, not to mention at home and in their neighborhoods, and their presence at NEIU and within other social institutions, such as community literacy programs, suggests a desire for education even if only as a means to another end. At the same time, these students know that the linguistic shifts they make—Spanish to English or Spanglish or any of the more than fifty languages spoken within this institution—or learn to make, or even don't or won't make, are temporary, contingent shifts, ones that are often shifted again as they leave NEIU or work or even their neighborhoods and homes. As many, including Neida, Sophia, and Angela, attest, few expect to survive, let alone thrive, in the world without acquiescing to new selves and different values even as these concessions often fail to fulfill the promises of educational equity and literacy instruction made by institutions and disciplines (e.g., LeCourt 2004).

POLICIES, PHILOSOPHIES, AND POLITICS

While more is needed to understand the educational experiences of ethnolinguistic minorities, these results—the quantitative and qualitative together—offer some insight into education and literacy not only at NEIU but beyond this institution. As suggested already, the histories of NEIU and NCTE share more than the Open Admissions movement (e.g., T. Fox 1999). For example, ethnic diversity and minority identities were a means of legitimacy for educational and social activists not only at NEIU but also in nationwide organizations, including the Student Nonviolent Coordinating Committee (SNCC) and Conference on College Composition and Communication (CCCC), and linguists who shaped support programs and institutional requirements at NEIU were also central to the formation of Students' Rights to Their Own Languages (e.g., MacDonald 2007, 602; Parks 2000, 22).

While education, language, and culture have long received attention at NEIU and throughout NCTE, much more needs to be done to challenge existing linguistic and identity politics, particularly within institutions and throughout disciplines. Too often, institutions and disciplines presuppose the universalizations of a *linguistics of community*, which lead to autonomous and semiautonomous literacies that can only acknowledge some authorized differences, such as a colonizing discourse of the academy, while ignoring others, especially ethnolinguistic ones. As defined by Mary Louise Pratt (1987), a *linguistics of community* seeks the general and the universal within a homogeneous and unified world, as seen, for example, in the notion of *interpretive communities* or *speech communities*, and it reflects larger social beliefs in a stable and unified national community and a universal national identity (50, 57–58).[14]

As an alternative, Pratt (1987) offers a *linguistics of contact*, which focuses on the specific and the particular in a world of heterogeneity and inconsistencies, and it becomes the basis for *contact zones*, or social spaces filled with competing cultures in unequal power relations (Pratt 1987, 61; 1991, 34). Many in composition, including Slevin and myself, have made use of these contact theories (e.g., Wolff 2002) even as they have been criticized for their vagueness and superficiality (e.g., Hall and Rosner 2004; Harris 1997, 117–124). In addition to these criticisms, I want to suggest that while contact theories might enable researchers to recognize linguistic differences in specific situations, these theories have not been used to confront the linguistic and social politics of everyday experiences within institutions.

In this limitation, they resemble situated literacy theories that since their emergence in the 1980s have been challenging assumptions about the absolute differences between orality and literacy, for example, in favor of a continuum of differences (e.g., Cook-Gumperz 1986; Finnegan 1988; Heath 1982, 1983; Street 1984). Although more informed and more complete accounts, situated literacy theories have been criticized for their inability to explain the interrelations of texts, power, and identity in the Western world, as well as the transcontextualized and

---

14. For more, see J. Milroy (1999) and Cooper (2004, 88–89).

transcontextualizing aspects of literacy (e.g., Brandt and Clinton 2002; Collins and Blot 2003, 34–66).

This failure to develop and institutionalize contact theories or situated literacies permits institutions and disciplines to perpetuate a Standard English ideology (SEI), which, according to Terrence G. Wiley and Marguerite Lukes (1996), consists of two assumptions—monolingualism and Standard English—that are fused with other beliefs about language, social mobility, and national unity to form the basis for language policies and literacy pedagogies (512).[15] In particular, the first assumption, according to Wiley and Lukes, is that monolingualism is the typical, and ideal, condition, and the second is that Standard English—the "unaccented" or "literate" variety—is more important and better than other varieties, which together shape perceptions about linguistic diversity (512).

As the basis for language policies and, I would add, literacy philosophies, this SEI is promulgated through "public channels" with literacy as the primary means of promotion. At the same time, it is linked to larger ideologies of individualism, which assign responsibilities for failure to individuals in ways that are particularly problematic for ethnolinguistic minorities in the United States, and it uses language to ascribe status and institutionalize discrimination. Through indexing language and literacy to particular cultural and linguistic norms, this SEI is preserved through the "complaint tradition" of correctness in usage and clarity in communication, and as such, it requires both nonnative and native English users to attend school to acquire social legitimacy (Milroy and Milroy 1999, 30–31).[16]

In part, the problem is that SEI is inconsistent with existing evidence about language and literacy. For example, it is based upon misinformation about linguistic reality. According to an increasing number of researchers and theorists, Standard English, as a set of universal linguistic conventions for speaking or writing, does not exist (N. Baron 2000; Bex and Watts 1999; Corson 2001; Kaplan and Baldauf 2001; Lippi-Green 1997). In practice, linguistic standardization is an ongoing, and partial, process, only realized with dead languages, that suppresses linguistic variability (Milroy and Milroy 1999, 6). For these and other reasons, many maintain that Standard English is an abstract social standard that identities specific varieties of English, often those of white,

---

15. For more, see L. Milroy (1999), Milroy and Milroy (1999), and J. Milroy (2001).
16. For more, see Lippi-Green (1997).

Midwestern, and middle-to-upper-class communities, as unmarked norms (Lippi-Green 1997, 62).[17]

In much the same way, SEI is based upon misunderstandings of literacy. For instance, it is predicated upon overgeneralizations, established in the nineteenth century as a part of the universalization of education in the United States, that are part of a larger social stratification. Throughout that period, which not incidentally coincides with the emergence of NEIU, existing sites of literacy instruction, such as families, communities, and churches, were increasingly replaced by common schools, and existing notions of literacy, as a "multiplicity of practices" with particular uses in work, worship, and civic participation, were synthesized into "a unified system" acquired through sanctioned texts that enabled individuals to be assessed and ranked. Once diverse practices with moral and civic value, literacy became a universal skill disproportionately distributed across populations that became the basis for organizing educational systems (Collins and Blot 2003, 82–87).[18]

These and other presumptions about language and literacy pose educational challenges for students generally, including many PP students and other ethnolinguistic minorities who use more than one language. In particular, SEI dismisses the experience, expertise, and needs of multilinguals. Multilingualism, according to researchers, is a "profound" experience that can range from recognizing code-switching as the unmarked variety to using code-switching as "social symbolism" for ethnic identity and meaning making (e.g., Bialystok 2001; Otheguy and Garcia 1993; Valdés 2001a). At the same time, multilingualism affords intellectual advantages that both reinforce cognitive conditions of monolingualism and offer additional advantages, including greater metalinguistic awareness, better selective attention, earlier maturation of cerebral lateralization, and increased capacity for divergent thinking (Bialystok 2001; Bialystok and Hakuta 1994; Corson 2001). In addition, it can result in different needs that range from a later development of communicative competence to other potential problems of a weakly developed heritage language (Bialystok 2001; Krashen 2000).

Even as SEI ignores the experience, expertise, and needs of multilinguals within educational institutions, it also represents an incomplete account of multilingual reality beyond institutions in a country where monolingualism is neither the norm nor the ideal, an account

17. For more, see Horner and Lu (1999).
18. For more, see Keller-Cohen (1993).

that is considered by some to be antiforeigner and even anti-Hispanic (R. González 2000; Perea 2001; Schmid 2000; Zentella 1997b).[19] In fact, the United States, despite its reputation as a language cemetery, is one of the most multilingual nations in the world, both proud of its multilingual past and accepting of a multilingual present and future where almost two in ten (2006) use a language other than English (Pratt 2003; Schmidt 2000, 69).[20] Given these conditions throughout communities, their denial within schools and other social institutions can result in an internal colonization and even an autocolonization for multilinguals that, as these institutional autobiographies attest, come with significant costs and create substantial losses.[21]

In these and other ways, SEI is based upon presumptions that are inconsistent with everyday experiences of language and literacy (e.g., Wiley 2005). These inconsistencies should be troubling enough to those of us who are concerned about education and literacy. At the same time, the more pressing problem, I maintian, is the role of language policies and literacy philosophies, through SEI, in larger debates over identity politics in the United States that link education and literacy to a U.S. American identity in ways that ignore histories of social injustices. In part, these policies and philosophies preserve the status of English when this status, in fact, is not threatened, insofar as immigrants since the 1960s exhibit the same tendency toward English monolingualism by the third generation as other U.S immigrants after World War II. At the same time, they rely upon a romanticized history of the United States as a land of opportunity, a history that ignores its imperialism and conquest. In addition, these policies and philosophies relegate ethnolinguistic differences to private lives, a position that misunderstands the relation of individual identities to educational institutions that exist within social contexts where ethnolinguistic advantages already exist (Schmidt 2000, 184–198; Wiley 2002).

---

19. For more, see D. Baron (1990), Daniels (1990), Crawford (1991), Greene (1994), Villanueva (2000), Valdés (2001a), Horner (2001), Horner and Trimbur (2002), Judd (2004), Matsuda (2006), and Trimbur (2006, 2008).
20. This ambivalence toward English that characterizes the geohistory of native speakers in the United States has largely been erased, according to John Trimbur (2008), by the post-Dartmouth study of language and literacy in the United States although such a conclusion should be qualified to indicate that it more accurately describes the conditions of research in composition studies and not in other disciplines, such as literacy studies and applied linguistics, where ethnolinguistic differences have been researched for decades.
21. For more, see Villanueva (2000) or R. González (2001).

Along with being a language of opportunity for many, the United States also has a long history of imperialism and racism that still shapes social conditions, including education, and while speaking and writing in particular varieties of English are the proficiencies of power, other languages and literacies, along with their implications for psychological and social identities, cannot be restricted to private lives without reinforcing existing ethnolinguistic inequalities. As such, these policies and philosophies, as conservative forms of identity politics with assimilationist goals, maintian and reinforce an institutionalized discrimination.[22]

EDUCATION AND LITERACY IN MULTICULTURAL INSTITUTIONS

In other words, this SEI, which informs both language policies *and* literacy philosophies at NEIU and throughout NCTE, tends to frame ethnolinguistic differences as educational obstacles to overcome rather than intellectual resources to exploit. For example, these policies and philosophies inhibit efforts to cross borders—to appropriate and/or exploit practices and languages—in order to connect academic and social communities and to establish fluid identities that are particularly important for ethnolinguistic minorities (e.g., Cárdenas 2004; Pennycook 2001). In these and other ways, existing language policies and literacy philosophies at NEIU and within NCTE discriminate against the very ethnic diversity they profess to value and respect.[23]

Since Open Admissions and Mina Shaughnessy, some have been challenging notions of *deficiency*, but many academic institutions and writing programs nonetheless rely upon *autonomous* or *semiautonomous* notions of literacy that position students as *deficiently different* if not *differently deficient*.[24] As a result, those involved in writing programs must do more than resist monolingual assumptions; prepare for a tipping point of more multilingual students; differentiate among monolingual basic, resident ESL, and international ESL students, and inform disciplinary faculty of recent research, as recently suggested (Friedrich 2006, Phillips, Stewart, and Stewart 2006; Preto-Bay and Hansen 2006; Shuck 2006).[25]

For some direction, literacy educators can turn to those in composition studies who have argued that cultural differences are not linguistic errors to eliminate but cultural negotiations to consider. For example,

---

22. For more, see Martinez (2009).
23. For an analysis of these conditions in community literacy programs, see Auerbach (2000).
24. For more, see Schroeder (2006).
25. For more, see Janet Bean et al. (2003).

Min-Zhan Lu (1994) offers a justification of her Malayan student's marked English, and Tom Fox (1999) rereads an African American student from a basic writer to a cultural negotiator (T. Fox 1999, 40–70; Lu 1994, 446–458). From a slightly different perspective, Patricia Bizzell (1999, 2000) identifies greater linguistic variety in academic research and student writing, I (2001) theorize about the possibilities of negotiating literacies, and she and I, along with Helen Fox, edited a collection of essays on alternative discourses as new forms of intellectual work (Schroeder, Fox, and Bizzell 2002).

The problem, however, is that these pluralist approaches, while better than more assimilationist approaches, cannot adequately address existing institutionalized discrimination. In addition to ignoring multilingualism, Tom Fox (1999), near the end of his book advocating local standards, replaces universalized linguistic standards for universalized rhetorical ones that largely ignore linguistic difference altogether (91–109). Both Lu (1994) and Bizzell (1999, 2000) confront issues of ethnolinguistic diversity more directly, but they limit their conclusions to pedagogical suggestions. In much the same way I could not extend my conclusions beyond classrooms, the collection *ALT DIS* (Schroeder, Fox, and Bizzell 2002) was criticized, because it neglected syntactic and grammatical differences, for not being progressive enough (Canagarajah 2006b, 595). In each, the outcome is that larger institutional and social politics remain unchanged.

In all fairness, these limitations—the failures to address the intersections of individuals within institutions—highlight pervasive contradictions between official positions and actual practices of institutions and disciplines. Despite assumptions about ethnolinguistic difference among my NEIU colleagues and even our professional ones (Richardson 2003), pluralist policies have long been the official positions of NCTE, as seen, for example, in the CCCC Students' Right to Their Own Language (1974), and even more recently of the United States government, as seen for instance in the recent U.S. Department of Defense (2005) policy.[26] However, these often invoke misrepresentations of linguistic reality, such as the contrast between Edited American English and other varieties in SRTOL (MacDonald 2007). For instance, the CCCC National Language Policy (1988) cites "oral and literate competence in English, the language of wider communication" as if to suggest that this wider

---

26. See Wible (2009).

communication does not consist of multiple Englishes, and the CCCC Statement on Second Language Writing and Writers (2001) states that writing placement "should be based upon students' writing proficiency rather than their race, native-language background, nationality, or immigration status," as if these variables do not affect writing performance.

In other words, the problem, in part, is the failure to institutionalize pluralist practices, policies, and philosophies.[27] Although Scott Wible (2006), in his return to the work of the Language Curriculum Research Group (LCRG), suggests otherwise, he qualifies his suggestion by acknowledging that the LCRG textbook was never published, which even by his own standards indicates that their efforts have largely perished. In this and other situations, the effect of pluralist policies and philosophies amounts to what Geneva Smitherman (2003), appropriating a linguistics term, calls *subtractive bilingualism* where new languages or literacies replace previous ones rather than add to them (13). As a result, larger institutional and social politics remain relatively unchallengred.

Certainly, these and other pluralist policies and philosophies are improvements that can permit institutions and disciplines to recognize multilingualism and multiliteracies (e.g., Barton, Hamilton, and Ivanič 2000; Cope and Kalantzis 2000) as educational resources and to reconsider language standards and literacy theories as well as social responsibilities (e.g., Canagarajah 2006a, 2006b, 2006c; Wible 2009). At the same time, these policies and philosophies can also acknowledge social injustices and cultural identities, as well as the presence of non-English-using communities with long histories in the United States. However, pluralist policies and philosophies will ultimately fail to provide an adequate challenge because pluralism alone cannot confront institutional and social politics.

This failure can be seen in the experiences of the PP students at NEIU. Throughout their seminar, Neida uses Spanish with her students, yet she assesses their performance, and them, solely in English. Although she can be persuaded to reassess Manuel's educational autobiography as evidence of linguistic negotiations and cultural syncretism, the possibilities that such reconsiderations will occur beyond our conversations or even our classrooms remains uncertain. For example, I asked other NEIU colleagues—professors with specializations in Spanish linguistics and contact languages—to review Manuel's manuscript, and

27. For more, see Smitherman (1999); Schroeder, Fox, and Bizzell (2002, vii–x), or Bruch and Marback (2005).

while they confirmed many of the negotiations that Neida and I identified and found numerous other possibilities, none could offer an adequate answer to the question of what could or should be done with these
negotiations. Clearly, such a question raises other issues, such as intention and awareness (e.g., Bizzell 2000, 8–9) although one could argue
that Manuel is writing or being written by these negotiations. Regardless,
the result is that he remains *deficiently different* if not *differently deficient.*

In part, the bigger problem is that pluralist policies and philosophies too often ignore the linguistic and cultural dilemmas for ethnolinguistic minorities in which the acquisition of spoken and written
English, while perhaps permitting them to overcome their subordinate
social status, often results in the loss of other languages and literacies.
At the same time, these policies and philosophies tend to invoke a lib-
eral individualism that ignores both the instability of multilingual communities and the challenges of cultural differences, both of which cannot be separated from historical and social contexts where choices of
language and literacy are rarely, if ever, choices among equally acceptable alternatives.[28]

This argument is not an argument against standards but rather an
argument about the source of and thinking about standards of institutions and disciplines, particularly those that profess a commitment to
cultural and linguistic diversity. Currently, institutions and programs are
encouraged to establish site-based, context-sensitive, and locally con-
trolled assessments that are not only about ranking and sorting but also
about learning (O'Neill, Moore, and Huot 2009).[29] While these encour-
agements might lead to better educational experiences, they alone
cannot ensure that ethnolinguistic differences are framed not as educational obstacles to overcome but as intellectual resources to exploit.

In part, this effort involves reconsidering the relation between speaking and writing, which shapes our understanding of standards (e.g.,
Milroy and Milroy 1999, 18–23). In relation to human existence, writing
is a relatively recent invention, and while most in the West since Aristotle
believe that writing is transcribed speech, some suggest that writing
actually provides ways for understanding speech and even other aspects
of meaning making, including the human mind (e.g., Olson 1995).
As Naomi Baron (2000) explains in her award-winning history of formal written English, contemporary research theorizes this relationship

---

28. For more, see Schmidt (2000, 198–203); Wiley and Lukes (2002).
29. For more, see Huot (1996, 2002a, 2002b).

through one of five different approaches—historical/cognitive, linguistic, ethnographic, technological, or pedagogical—that produces one of three different perspectives: the opposition perspective, in which spoken and written language are different (i.e., the historical/cognitive and linguistic approaches); the continuum perspective, in which spoken and written language are part of a range of differences (i.e., ethnographic and technical); and the crossover perspective, in which spoken and written language sometimes assume different forms, such as the Chaucer tale that is read aloud or the Shakespeare play that is read silently (21–22).

At least in practice, many institutions and many disciplines invoke the opposition perspective, which in the history of English is the result of particular historical and social forces. As part of increasing the social prestige of English, the standardization process, which began in the fifteenth century, did not separate spoken and written English, as is done in the current correctness tradition, until the end of the nineteenth century. At least in theory, the opposition perspective has largely been discredited since the 1980s as a result of research in situated literacies, which tend to invoke the continuum perspective.[30] According to Naomi Baron, popular perceptions consider written English to be more like informal speech, yet she considers written English to be less than speech, in that it omits pronunciation, intonation, and nonverbal gestures, and more than speech, in that it has its own linguistic, syntactic, and stylistic conventions, as seen, for example, in email that can resemble both (7–24; 262–264).

At the end of Baron's book, she uses her historical overview of formal written English to predict its future. While formal written English, she explains, has historically served seven social functions—bureaucracies, religion, social and financial aspirations, romantic creativity, nationalism, social class, and education—only one—bureaucracies—has any realistic future for this most formal of varieties (262–267).Regardless of what we believe about the future of formal written English, we are limited, in responding to the differences between institutionalized standards and everyday use, to three options: to demand a halt to linguistic time, to accept the gap between standards and use, or to change our standards (96–97). While the first is impossible, the second ensures an increasing social irrelevance for educational institutions and literacy instruction, and it reinforces the persistence of institutionalized discrimination even

---

30. For more, see Collins and Blot (2003, 34–66).

by those who, in accepting the gap between standards and use, recognize the legitimacy of cultural and linguistic pluralism. More is needed if we are to design policies and philosophies of diversity.

THIS PROJECT AND SOME POSSIBILITIES

As indicated in the introduction, the purpose of this institutional case study is to account for the educational experiences of ethnolinguistic minorities within the ostensibly most ethnically diverse university in the midwest and a federally-designated Hispanic-Serving Institution. Based upon the quantitative and qualitative data from the PP students at NEIU and other ethnolinguistic minorities at and beyond the institution, this account suggests that existing language policies and literacy philosophies, which represent a Standard English ideology, discriminate against the very ethnic diversity institutions and disciplines seek and value. In this, NEIU is similar to NCTE, in that neither can confront the institutionalized discrimination within educational institutions or writing programs that ultimately frame ethnolinguistic differences as educational obstacles to overcome and situate ethnolinguistic minorities as *deficiently different* if not *differently deficient.*

To fulfill their official missions and implement their purported positions, both NEIU and NCTE need to move beyond pluralist policies and philosophies, which ultimately fail to confront linguistic and social politics of institutions and disciplines. For instance, such policies permit Spanish as an acceptable option for hallway and classroom conversations even as a standardized English remains the official language and literacy of instruction and, more importantly, assessment. In this and other ways, pluralist policies and philosophies are necessary but insufficient conditions for confronting institutionalized discrimination. For these students and many others, English proficiencies are those of power, *and* ethnolinguistic diversities are significant aspects of everyday experiences and necessary conditions for social unity.[31]

These conditions can clearly be seen in the institutional autobiographies for this project. As a child, Neida longed (in vain) for pencils or stickers embossed with her Spanish name, and as an adult, she associates talking white, in English, with her university colleagues and health professionals. Although she reconsiders these internalized norms as a result of her ropes course experience, she still invokes Richard Rodriguez

---

31. For more, see García (2000, 93, 99) and Schmidt (2000, 172–173, 177).

(1983) as her explanation, even as her experiences seem to complicate Rodriguez's public (English)/private (Spanish) compromise that, as suggested by the poignant picture of his silent father at the end of his book, fails even him. Unlike Neida, Sophia uses Rodriguez as her rallying point for reconsidering her ethnolinguistic identity, yet she must resist messages from her mother and other students, staff, and administrators at significant risk to her survival. Although Angela arrives with clearer expectations for her ethnolinguistic identities, she is rejected by both undergraduate college students and the history graduate program even though she has earned an undergraduate degree from a prestigious Mexican university and a graduate degree from NEIU, which force her to reconsider her own ideas about language, literacy, and identity. Meanwhile, some PP students continue to accumulate credits and grades in pursuit of their degrees, and too many others disappear from our classrooms and campuses, sometimes never to return.

Although the primary purpose of this project is to account for the educational experiences of ethnolinguistic minorities at the most ethnically diverse university in the midwest, I want to suggest, at the end of this institutional case study, one way to address the institutionalized discrimination of prevailing language policies and literacy philosophies. To confront these conditions, institutions and programs must consider the intellectual and social impact of these policies and philosophies upon the cultural minorities who are central to their missions and disciplines. Beyond recognizing cultural and linguistic differences, educational administrators and literacy educators must advocate for institutionalized policies and philosophies of multilingualism and multiliteracies that, while recognizing "transcontextualized" potentials (Brandt and Clinton 2002), are nonetheless linked to the local.

Diverse by design, such policies and philosophies can reframe ethnolinguistic differences as intellectual resources to exploit, which could enable institutions and disciplines to recognize the situated practices of speaking and writing that are central, some have suggested, to Latino/a identities in the United States (e.g., Guerra 2004; Morales 2004). At the same time, these policies and philosophies can supplement incomplete histories of the United States as solely a land of opportunity and resist the socialization of these PP students and others like them into a universalized national identity. In addition, policies and philosophies of linguistic diversity can acknowledge both the prevalence of social injustices and cultural imperialism and the presence of cultural identities throughout institutions and communities in authorized ways that can counterbalance the established privileges of institutionalized Englishes and dominant literacies.

Such ends can be accomplished by policies and philosophies of *pluralist integration*, which highlight both ethnic cohesion and social integration (e.g., Schmidt 2000). In practice, these policies and philosophies would recognize the realities of standardized Englishes and dominant literacies as the proficiencies of power that students want to learn and the realities of multilingual and multiliterate communities as sources of cultural identities to be supported by schools and other social institutions. Within schools and other social institutions, policies and philosophies of pluralist integration would promote multilingual and multiliterate education with a combined commitment to pluralism and integration that can produce social equality and preserve social identities. While Jaime Mejía (1998, 2004a) suggests these results are important to those on the U.S. and Mexico border, I think these conditions are equally, if not more, important for those at HSIs and elsewhere with internalized borders, as Neida, Sophia, Angela, and others suggest—Neida's and Sophia's established in childhood and Angela's after her arrival in the United States. If institutionalized, policies and philosophies of pluralist integration would authorize an additive, and expected, multilingualism and multiliteracies for both ethnolinguistic minorities and mainstream monolinguals that can counterbalance existing linguistic politics of unequal situations (e.g., Ricento 2001, 376–377).

In addition to the increased metalinguistic awareness and other benefits above, these policies and philosophies could result in a more useful cultural diversity and social adaptability, an increased psychological security, and official support for multicultural identities (Corson 2001; E. García 2000). In doing so, these policies and philosophies would sustain identities of multiplicity and indeterminancy, in dialogues or multilogues rather than monologues, in order to reclaim histories and voices (Cooper 2004). At the same time, such policies and philosophies would challenge institutions and programs to recognize the ways that spoken and written Englishes have been, and continue to be, changed by linguistic contact that produces linguistic shifting, mixing, switching, and translating (e.g., N. Baron 2000, 252–259; Bhatt 2005; Canagarajah 2006b; Godenzzi 2006; Lu 1994; Stavans 2003). Given these and other forms of linguistic and cultural syncretism, these politics and philosophies could result in a shift in standards from *linguistic mastery* to *strategic competence*, such as the code-switching and code-mixing of Spanglish that, also rule-governed, is central to some community identities (Connal 2004; Elder and Davies 2006; Zentella 1997a).[32]

In addition to reconsidering standards, such policies and philosophies could have implications for curriculum and learning. For example, they could result in multilingual composition courses, as well as reconsiderations of canonical knowledge and linguistic history, which could require additional changes from requirements to instructors to even assessment (e.g., Artze-Vega, Doud, and Torres 2007; Greene 1994; Lu 2004; Mejía 2004b; Mignolo 2000; Okawa 2000; Trimbur 2006). Already, some have begun to theorize about literacy as negotiation (e.g., Canagarajah 2006a, 2006c; Kells 2004; Schroeder 2001) and learning as situated cognition (e.g., Gee 2003, 184–194).[33] At the same time, such theorization must recognize that cultural binaries, including multilingual and monolingual, can, depending upon the institutional and social context, colonize individuals in unexpected ways (e.g., Modiano 2004; Pennycook 2001): Spanish, in other places and times, has been a colonizing language.

In addition, policies and philosophies of pluralist integration, though necessarily institutionalized, must resist the urge to universalization, particularly at the expense of the local (Canagarajah 2005).[34] As Neida reminds us, researchers and theorists must avoid studying ethnolinguistic minorities like mice in a laboratory and instead must approach them as distinct individuals with potentially different experiences, especially given the range of differences among them (e.g., R. González 2000; Schecter and Bayley 1997).[35] One possibility is a *funds of knowledge* approach, which according to Norma González, Luis C. Moll, and Cathy Amanti (2005), starts in homes, collaborates with families and teachers, uses ethnographic methods to document social practices and social relations, and relies upon study groups for researchers.[36]

At least here in the metro Chicago area, this research has begun (e.g., Farr 2004, 2005a) although much more is needed. For instance, Nicholas De Genova and Ana Y. Ramos-Zayas (2003) report different perspectives among local Mexican Americans and Puerto Ricans on Spanish proficiencies as these reflect assimilation and authenticity, but we also

---

32. For more, see Silva-Corvalan (1993), Roca and Lipski (1993), and Roca and Colombi (2003).
33. For more, see Lave (1996).
34. For more on the problems of essentialization and vernacular writing, see Marzluf (2006).
35. For more, see Zentella (1997a, 2-6), Canagarajah (2005), and Wible (2009, 479).
36. For more, see Moll (2005, 286).

need to know how such perspectives might be altered by other variables, such as multiple generations or educational aspirations that seem significant elsewhere (e.g., Chiang and Schmida 1999; Harklau 2000). The bigger challenge, in my experience, will be linking these accounts of community literacies to literacy work at NEIU and elsewhere throughout the city and across the country.[37] Nevertheless, one option can be seen in the work of Kris Gutiérrez (2008) with what she calls *third space literacies* that link everyday experiences to institutionalized instruction.[38]

In addition to providing links between institutions and individuals, such efforts have the potential to alleviate social and cultural pressures experienced by those in multilingual ethnic groups. While some experience both external pressure to learn English and internal pressure to maintain home languages, others with extensive contact to English often lose primary proficiencies even as those in more isolated ethnic enclaves might both lose primary proficiencies and never acquire English ones (e.g., Scarcella and Chin 1993). For these and others, the sense of self is shaped by linguistic affiliation, personal desire, and social and material resources, yet different configurations can emerge from competing "sociocultural ecologies" even as positive self-identities of mixed-heritage adults might require multiple proficiencies (Norton 1997; Ogulnick 2000; Pao, Wong, and Teuben-Rowe 1997; Schecter and Bayley 1997).

In these and other studies, the clear conclusion is that literacy and identity, which are shaped by cultural variables, are often the result of mixed languages and the product of circumstances and choices (Collins and Blot 2003, 99–120).[39] As a result, policies and philosophies of pluralist integration could give rise to a coalitional identity politics even as the relations among language, literacy, and identity are being challenged in unexpected ways. While some have predicted the Englishization of the world, others have suggested that global-based markets are reducing the ability of nation-states to control language use and language change, such as standardization initiatives, as a means to establish and maintain unification. For example, people can watch television programming or interact with the Internet in any number of different languages (Dor 2004, 111–112). Driven by a global political economy, the linguistic future could be neither global English nor multilingual freedom but a

---

37. For more, see Mathieu (2005) and Feldman (2008).
38. For more, see Kells (2007).
39. For more, see Lanehart (1996).

market-imposed multilingualism based not upon nation-states but upon language zones as participants in this global market adapt to local languages and cultures and produce language-specific commodities.

Whatever the future, institutionalized policies and philosophies of pluralist integration offer an alternative to conventional identity politics, in which individuals align themselves on the basis of a shared cultural variable such as ethnicity or gender, in favor of coalitional identity politics, in which individuals align themselves on the basis of shared interests or goals.[40] Although traditional, or tribal, identity politics can result in valuable forms of self-representation and cultural reclamation (e.g., Cushman 2008), these efforts, with their emphasis on cultural differences, tend to highlight social and cultural divisions. In contrast, a coalitional identity politics could result in alignments regardless of our ethnicities around the right to be educated in languages and literacies valued by the community *and* the right to acquire the language and literacy of power within the community with the understanding that if the first is impossible or impractical then at the very least it could be replaced with the right to enroll in educational institutions that respect, and encourage the use of, the languages or literacies used in their homes or valued by their communities (Corson 2001, 100–102).

In the end, any such efforts cannot be separated from larger narratives about education and literacy in the United States. For example, Catherine Prendergast (2003), in her examination of learning, literacy, and racial justice, links the failures of "national literacy initiatives" to an "ideology of literacy," in which "literacy belongs to Whites," that has been perpetuated, she argues, by "perceived threats to White property interests, White privilege, the maintenance of 'White' identity, or the conception of America as a White nation" (2, 5, 7). Throughout her book, she considers race in relation to court cases and these implications for communities and, with her examination of High School X near the end, educational institutions.

While useful, her analysis seems somewhat incomplete. In particular, she, similar to Tom Fox (1999), uses limited racial categories—white and African-American—that though relevant are far from comprehensive not only here in the metro Chicago area but across the country. For example, Hispanics constitute more than two in 10 of all children under eighteen—an increase from 9 percent to 22 percent since 1980—and of

---

40. For more, see Fish (2008).

these sixteen million Hispanic children, almost nine in ten are either second generation (52 percent), or U.S.-born with at least one foreign-born parent, or third-generation (37 percent), or U.S.-born with two U.S.-born parents (Fry and Passel 2009). For these and countless others, more complicated categories of languages, literacies, and identities are needed to understand their educational and social experiences (e.g., Canagarajah 2006a, 2006b, and 2006c; Chiang and Schmida 1999; O. Garcia and Menken 2006; Kells 2006), especially given the educational implications of institutional representations (e.g., Cox 2009; Harklau 2000).

At the same time, educational equity will depend upon public universities, which must be "the principal engines of progress" in addressing the challenges of retention and graduation in the United States (Bowen, Chingos, and McPherson 2009, 223–225). Central to these efforts will be literacy instruction. After reviewing her results from the study of individuals who have lived throughout the twentieth century, Brandt (2001) concludes that literacy learning must be considered within civil rights contexts in order to establish the relevance of schools for those, especially the poor, people of color, and political refugees, who are often most separate from it. In the end, she argues that as a counterbalance to the increasing use of literacy for private economic benefits, public schools must appropriate evolving literacy standards of new economic relations in ways that strengthen social and political relations, in part by recognizing both the scarcities of certain proficiencies and the excesses of other proficiencies, including the ways that literacies in everyday lives often suffer and disappear as a result of the absence of adequate sponsors of and for them (205–207).

Such efforts can only begin if we will consider education and literacy within larger systemic contexts, particularly the intersections of individuals and institutions within multicultural communities. While schools and literacies can serve as forms of social control, they also provide access to social and cultural capital, which, if expanded, can help us deal with the difficulties of cultural diversity *and* which, we're told, are central to our satisfaction and contentment (Putnam 2007).

As a result of the HSI funds for the campuswide writing program, new full-time instructors were hired, and the first-year composition curriculum was revised. Although my uncertainties had seeped beyond my administrative aptitudes, I nonetheless hoped to acknowledge these uncertainties as I participated as much as I could in this initiative.

When we were invited to help with the hiring of new instructors, I volunteered to review the files, and I intended to participate, or, as one colleague suggested, at least observe, the curriculum-revision workshops. To do so, I had arranged my sabbatical obligations around the workshop schedule, and when, at the initial meeting, I learned that the schedule had been changed, I rearranged my obligations around the new schedule.

Then my office was reassigned to one of the new instructors, who scheduled office hours just before the workshops. I had intended to work in the office while waiting for the late afternoon workshop sessions, but, since it was unavailable, I decided that rather than lug my laptop and lunch to campus on the bus and then find somewhere to work while I waited for the workshops, I would spend the semester away from campus. Circumstances seemed to be conspiring against me, and I was told that no one believed that I would attend the workshops anyway.

The workshops were productive in spite, or perhaps as a result, of my absence. Midway through that semester, the English Department was asked to approve several motions that would standardize the first-year writing program. In particular, it established minimal requirements for the first semester course—at least eighteen pages of graded writing and at least four multidraft projects and one in-class task. It also authorized learning outcomes for this course, including an awareness of rhetorical situations and rhetorical principles; the mastery of the "major modes of organization"; the use of writing "as both a process of composing and an occasion for learning"; the acquisition of "critical thinking, reading, and writing skills" along with the techniques of summary and synthesis; and the "mastery of standard academic writing conventions" such as citation, syntax, grammar, punctuation, and spelling.

Although I was uninvolved in these deliberations and decisions, I can see the benefits of these results. For example, these requirements and outcomes clarify expectations for the first- semester course, which can help those of us who are unsure about the scope and function of this course. At the same time, I have more questions. Haven't we long been asked to reconsider the relevance of the modes or the reality of grammar (Connors 1981; Hartwell 1985)? Can we conclude that this course should be limited to autonomous academic writing (Downs and Wardle 2007; Miles et al. 2008)? And have we begun to consider the interaction of ethnolinguistic diversity and writing, not to mention the role these courses play, and should play, in the pursuit of educational equity in multicultural institutions and communities?

At least I'm not responsible for a writing program.

On the walk to my kids' school, other parents are cordial yet aloof, perhaps, I'm told, because we are a diverse couple. Oak Park is, explained Ernest Hemingway, a community of wide yards and narrow minds.

I have tried to talk with their teachers and school administrators about educational equity and cultural diversity, yet I have been unable to obtain answers to even more basic questions about educational efficacy. After too many conflicts over their elementary school years, I have learned to limit my efforts to advocating for my kids, yet I have failed to achieve even these much more modest goals.

Sometimes I wonder if I am biased by a parental perspective that clouds clarity, and then I am confronted by seemingly obvious objections once again. My kids, for example, were recommended for the gifted program through Northwestern University, and as a part of their admission application, they completed the EXPLORE assessment, a college readiness test designed by ACT to place eighth and ninth graders into high-school classes and to help them plan for college.

According to the results, my fourth-grade daughter could read as well as eight in ten eighth graders across the country, yet for most of her fourth-grade year, she only met, and did not exceed, fourth-grade reading standards. In a similar way, my third-grade son could succeed in science as well as six in ten eighth graders across the country, yet for his entire third grade school year, he met only third-grade science standards.

In the principal's office, I explained that I'm not concerned about these grades as evidence of intelligence but as indicators of engagement. However, I was told, before I was ushered to the door, that my desire for perfect grades is understandable, and I was urged to review statewide grade-level standards on the Internet and to await their ISAT results in the fall.

While I acknowledge other explanations for these and other seeming inconsistencies, I cannot help but wonder about the implications of my failures for others who have fewer educational and economic resources. Public schools in the United States, I realize, have more pressing problems, but if purportedly good schools cannot get multicultural education right, then how can public education be more than empty promises?

At least my kids are no longer being recommended for speech therapy.

Before I can finish this project, I am invited to participate in a five-year, multimillion-dollar federal grant that is a collaboration among twenty Chicago Public Schools and four local universities to redesign teacher-preparation programs, and my role is to work with other literacy researchers across the city to establish learning outcomes and design required courses to ensure that all teacher candidates, especially those who are heading to urban schools, have an adequate language-arts background.

Although honored and humbled, I wonder whether I'll have anything useful to add when I cannot even find certainty in my own classrooms. I taught Sophia's ENGL 101 course, and as she movingly explains, I couldn't reconcile what she had done in her thoughtful and complex portfolio, which reminded me of the experiments by Gloria Anzaldúa, with what the university wanted me to certify. At the same time, I was unaware of what she was experiencing in my class and throughout her time at NEIU.

As Sophia suggests, these students face challenges I can never know. One Puerto Rican student describes his efforts to avoid Chicago gangs in order to protect his newborn marriage and tiny daughter.

Another Mexican student apologizes after class for her missing homework, which she explains by telling me that she was sitting next to the woman—her cousin—whose shooting had recently been reported on the local news. A Jordanian American credits his English proficiency for convincing an Israeli judge that he is a U.S. American, which secures his release from jail for curfew violations while on vacation in the West Bank and transforms him into a Palestinian activist after he returns to the United States.

These students and many others live lives I can never know, and they possess proficiencies I will never understand. I know I am expected to explain the secrets of *autonomous literacies*—some express a desire for these proficiencies—in introductory writing classes, as the programwide rubric requires:

Thesis or focus

Thesis or focus refers to the main idea that unifies a text. In excellent writing, the thesis/focus is appropriate for the text's purpose and audience, is supported throughout the text, and possesses originality and complexity. In good writing, the thesis/focus is clear throughout the text, although it may be somewhat less original or complex. In adequate writing, there is still a thesis or focus, but parts of the text may stray from this main idea. In inadequate writing (graded below a C), there is no clear thesis or focus that guides the whole text.

Development of ideas

Development refers to how thoroughly and thoughtfully you have discussed the ideas in your text (the complexity of your evidence, support, and analysis). In excellent writing, the development is insightful and extensive throughout the text. In good writing, the development is appropriate and consistently sufficient, though perhaps less insightful. In adequate writing, the text may be unevenly developed, with parts of the essay requiring further development. In inadequate writing (graded below a C), the text offers little or no support, may simply restate the thesis, and/or fails to meet the minimum length requirement.

Organization	Organization refers to the structure of a text (introduction, body, and conclusion) and the connections between and within paragraphs. In excellent writing, the organization is logical and flows smoothly. In good writing, the organization is clear but less smooth. In adequate writing, the organization is occasionally disjointed or simplistic. In inadequate writing (graded below a C), the introduction and/or conclusion may be missing, the connections between paragraphs may be missing or blurred, and/or the body may not contain suitable paragraph breaks.
Written conventions	Written conventions refer to the text's grammar, syntax, punctuation and spelling. The most important conventions involve recognizing when a sentence ends (avoiding run-ons, comma splices, and fragments). Using verbs correctly (S-V agreement; verb tense; verb forms) is also a major concern. Correct use of other punctuation and spelling is somewhat less important, but errors here shouldn't be numerous. Conventions are evaluated based on the seriousness, quantity, and variety of errors. Writing is inadequate (graded below a C) if the errors are so extensive that they interfere with an ordinary reader's ability to understand the text.
Style	Style refers to the sentence structure and word choice in your writing. In excellent writing, the style is both creative and clear. In good writing, the style is consistently clear but perhaps less creative. In adequate writing, the style is usually clear but at times may be unclear or redundant. In inadequate writing (graded below a C), the style is often unclear and/or overly simple.

Source: NEIU First Year Writing Program

Most students decline my invitation to write in Spanish or Tagalog or another language—we can find volunteers, I say, who can translate—and too many complain on student evaluations that I am unclear or, worse, unfair. What can I tell them about believing and doubting games, translating and reviewing goals, normal and abnormal discourses, and even prior and passing theories that might be useful?

Even as I acknowledge the legitimacy of their ethnolinguistic experiences, I also recognize the limits of local theories of language and literacy. According to Deborah Brandt and Katie Clinton (2002), situated theories, in responding to the determinism of Great Divide notions of literacy, overemphasize local contexts and undertheorize literacy technology as a thing and a tool, thereby missing the "trans-contextualized and transcontextualizing potentials of literacy—particularly its ability to travel, integrate, and endure" (377). As a part of their critique, they reread an account by Niko Besnier (1995) of older women in a Polynesian community who were wearing t-shirts with sexualized slogans in English (71). While Besnier suggests that these slogans are meaningless because they are unconnected to local literacies, Brandt and Clinton (2002) suggest that these slogans instead indicate the presence of Western commercialism among Nukulaelae society (344).

Although I obviously wasn't there, I suspect that these slogans also attest to the significance of social relations—emigrants to an English-dominant country perhaps and their continued connections with family and friends who remain behind—that as I've witnessed are undeniable aspects of these experiences. As best as I can tell, anything can be added to those big *balikbayan* boxes—clothes and toys and candy and even things, I'm told, that can be bought inexpensively in the Philippines. Once overflowing, these boxes are tied with taut rope by straining men, somehow familiar strangers, who come when called to carry these boxes to trucks that drive them to ships—cheaper than planes yet fittingly lack specific delivery dates and often take weeks to arrive—as part of a long chain of keeping *balikbayan* connected, perhaps as *pasalubong*, or those gifts given by travelers to those who remain behind.

These and other experiences suggest we have only just begun to consider the complicated conditions of language and literacy, which in turn can only complicate conversations about educational equity in multicultural communities. Certainly, we must consider the impact of linguistic contact on language standards and the relation of speaking to writing and a number of other important issues. At the same time, we must situate these issues within larger sociolinguistic politics, which my students and kids experience and which I have seen only on a small scale.

Spanish allows me to identify with others at the immigration march. Tagalog permits me to connect with my kids' relatives. English is the means of judging them and me. My broken efforts—slippery Spanglish and tenuous Taglish—are amusing yet admit me even as my English—the only language of my childhood—is still, and is no longer, the most comfortable and comforting. Language connects us and binds us and keeps us apart.

7
AN AFTERWORD. AND A REMINDER

Victor Villanueva

Let me begin with a confession. Everything that follows draws on an essay I cowrote with C. Jan Swearingen and Susan McDowall. And, really, Susan McDowall gets the real credit for what's here. The original essay appears in *Research on Composition: Multiple Perspectives on Two Decades of Change*, edited by Peter Smagorinsky.

What I want to do is just to remind readers about contrastive rhetoric, a branch of applied linguistics, the pedagogical branch of linguistics-writ-large. I bring it up for two reasons. First, I'm nervous about the gaze of Chris Schroeder's critical eye. He's sharp at pointing to the contradictions and shortcomings of all of us who have ventured into the language debate, trying to work through our multiple cultural and especially linguistic identities and the degree to which the academy keeps trying to enforce one linguistic identity. And the degree to which we must give into the hegemonic argument: I can't work against the students' own desires for access into a linguistically uncompromising world. And, second, given the lack of reference to contrastive rhetoric, I figure it should be a part of the conversation. This is, after all, where Chris leaves us: with a need for more conversation, with a lack that even the most diverse (with a parenthetical "ethnic" always thrown in—always a troubling word for me) university of the U.S. midwest must come to recognize and to engage with.

I don't believe that contrastive rhetoric is the answer to Chris's search. But it adds to the Spanglish/Taglish thing. When the discourse itself is Spanglish (like this writing at this point), even though the language is so clearly English, these days even a bit archaic English (since I simply can't split an infinitive and be okay with it, no matter what the new rules say).

Contrastive rhetoric was first coined by Robert Kaplan in 1966. It's an attempt to conceptualize language and language practices in ways that are embedded in culture. Ulla Connor (1996) writes that it's "an area of research in second language acquisition that identifies problems in composition encountered by second language writers and, by referring to the rhetorical strategies of the first language, attempts to explain them" (5). She retells the narratives of students who have difficulty composing in English because they are attempting to translate words, phrases, and organization from their home languages into English, telling, for instance of what happens when students try to translate common jokes and tales from the home culture to English. They fail, mainly because they (and us) can't distinguish the different discursive tropes at play. We read the words, understand the words, but fail to gather the meaning, the import. Yet rather than see the problems as rhetorical, readers read these failed translations as steeped in "error," if understood at all. Contrastive rhetoric tries to account for rhetorical differences between languages by seeking to understand language and writing as culturally bound phenomena, not as universal constructs. As such, contrastive rhetoric endeavors to understand language as differently identified within particular contexts.

Kaplan was drawing on the Sapir-Whorf hypothesis that logic is culturally bound (Sapir 1949), Kaplan arguing that because of language's ability to communicate and shape culture, native speakers of different languages compose and make meaning using different rhetorical structures. For example, Kaplan argued that English is particularly linear in its construction—that the paragraph in English begins with a topic sentence and then "by a series of subdivisions of that topic statement, each supported by example and illustrations, proceeds to develop that central idea in its proper relationship with the other ideas in the whole essay" (297). In contrast, he writes, Asian rhetoric is constructed as a spiral, circling the main idea, "showing it in a variety of tangential views, but the subject is never looked at directly" (302). The upshot of his argument is that rhetorics should be seen as viable and recognizable parts of given languages, as different among languages as grammatical structures.

Now, contrastive rhetoric got a bad rap when it first came on the scene. Its claims were too grand—that we can know how a person thinks—its methodology was questioned by fellow linguists, it risked linguistic and rhetorical stereotyping. Yet in 1982, the *Annual Review of Applied Linguistics* devoted the entire issue to contrastive rhetoric and matters of text-based study. Articles included rather detailed analyses of several languages and their relation to English and particularly featured articles on English and American Indian Languages (Leap 1982), English and German (Clyne 1982), English and Hindi (Kachru 1982), English and Japanese (Hinds 1983), English and Korean (Chang 1982), English and Mandarin (Tsao 1982) and English and Marathi (Pandharipande 1982). This issue, along with deBeaugrande (1980), rekindled interest in whole-text analysis and issues of contrastive rhetoric. Connor and Kaplan (1987) further augmented the study of contrastive rhetoric, investigating the different rhetorical patterns of other languages that previously had not been studied using the framework of contrastive rhetoric. Purves (1988) continued the theoretical and linguistic considerations of contrastive rhetoric, again contrasting different rhetorical styles to English. Purves also engaged theoretical considerations of curricula, the selection of writing tasks, and assessment issues.

Then in the 1990s, contrastive rhetoric moved away from a strict linguistic perspective. Connor turned to composition studies (in ways that have not proven reciprocal), pointing to our earlier cognitive models of writing and the increasingly large body of work that views writing as inherently social. The problem remained, however, that the literature was Anglocentric. Land and Whitely (1989) worried that "in teaching Standard Written English rhetorical conventions, we are teaching students to reproduce in a mechanical fashion our preferred vehicle for understanding" (285). Twenty years ago, Land and Whitely were stating the same concerns Schroeder brings up here in reference to his most (ethnically) diverse school. Land and Whitely argued that those who work with students whose principal language is not English should "recognize, value, and foster the alternative rhetorics that the ESL student brings to our language" (286). The focus, according to Land and Whitely, should not be on assimilation of U.S. English rhetorical patterns; the focus should be complementary, investigating the textual rhetorical patterns of students, but also negotiating those rhetorical patterns.

Although contrastive rhetoric and applications of contrastive rhetoric should always be viewed with some skepticism, given its history and some of its practitioners' propensity to reify culturally accepted notions of racist essentialism, it remains, I believe, a promising field of pedagogical theory because it does not view language as universal, but as inherently social—and as rhetorical. As Clayann Panetta (2000) has argued, even though teachers may not be specifically trained in the home language and culture of each student, contrastive rhetoric allows teachers to frame students' knowledge and knowledge making in a way that is less prescriptive and error centered.

Contrastive rhetoric can also assist us teachers in acknowledging our own culturally formed notions of knowledge making—allowing us to complicate notions of power as they are related to language —and allowing us to make conventions—as conventions—explicit to students. As discourses and rhetorical conventions are made explicit, students might begin to understand what are sometimes ephemeral rules for what they are: socially derived conventions. Panetta argues that as students are taught how to identify rhetorical conventions for what they are, they are more readily able to understand the nuances of a particular language. They gather greater metalinguistic awareness (Hartwell 1985).

As contrastive rhetoric moves out of the scientific, taxonomizing culture of linguistics and becomes more informed by postcolonial and poststructuralist notions of discourse, it broadens and becomes more applicable not only to students in ESL classes, but to all students of writing.

Chris Schroeder is so obviously correct in recognizing that our hearts and our pedagogies are not as one. The case he provides is compelling. Maybe—just maybe— contrastive rhetoric might be a way in, as Panetta (2000) argues as she moves to theorizing contrastive rhetoric from within contexts other than an ESL classroom, engaging the possible uses of contrastive rhetoric for students of color more generally, for women, and for gay men. And maybe not. But we can't know until we move away from the kinds of ethnocentric and fatalistic discourse that currently continues to dominate our discussions, as Chris has so well explained.

REFERENCES

ACT. 2010. College readiness standards: English. http://www.act.org/standard/planact/english/index.html.

Allen, Kerri. 2006. The Hispanic-Serving designation: Asset or deficit? *Diverse: Issues in Higher Education* 23: 34–35.

Allensworth, Elaine. 2006. Update to: From high school to the future: A first look at Chicago public school graduates' college enrollment, college preparation, and graduation from four-year colleges. Chicago: Consortium on Chicago School Research at the University of School.

America's Best Colleges 2008. 2008. *U. S. News and World Report.* http://colleges.usnews.rankingsandreviews.com/usnews/edu/college/rankings/rankumregion_brief.php.

American Council on Education. 2005. ACE releases its annual status report on minorities in higher education. http://www.acenet.edu/AM/Template.cfm Section=Home&CONTENTID=3701&TEMPLATE=/CM/ContentDisplay.

Aronowitz, Stanley. 2008. *Against schooling: For an education that matters.* Boulder, CO: Paradigm Publishers.

Artze-Vega, Isis, Elizabeth I. Doud, and Belkys Torres. 2007. Más allá del inglés: A bilingual approach to college composition. In Kirklighter, Cárdenas, and Murphy, 99–117.

Auerbach, Elisa Roberts. 2000. When pedagogy meets politics: Challenging English Only in adult education. In González with Melis, 177–204.

Banks, James A., and Cherry A. McGee Banks, eds. 1995. *Handbook of research on multicultural education.* New York: Macmillan.

Baron, Dennis. 1990. *The English Only question: An official language for Americans?* New Haven, CT: Yale University Press.

Baron, Naomi S. 2000. *Alphabet to email: How written English evolved and where it's heading.* London: Routledge.

Bartholomae, David. 1985. Inventing the university. In *When a writer can't write: Studies in writer's block and other composing-process problems,* ed. Mike Rose, 134–165. New York: Guilford.

Barton, David, Mary Hamilton, and Roz Ivanič, eds. 2000. *Situated literacies: Reading and writing in context.* London: Routledge.

Bauer, Dale M. 2003. Embedded pedagogy: How to teach teaching. Review of *Writing/teaching: Essays toward a rhetoric of pedagogy,* by Paul Kameen, and *ReInventing the university: Literacies and legitimacy in the postmodern academy,* by Christopher Schroeder. *College English* 65: 427–438.

Bean, James et al. 2003. Should we invite students to write in home languages? Complicating the yes/no debate. *Composition Studies* 31: 25–42.

Bean, John. 1996. *Engaging ideas: The professor's guide to integrating writing, critical thinking, and active learning in the classroom.* San Francisco: Jossey-Bass.

Besnier, Niko. 1995. *Literacy, emotion, and authority: Reading and writing on a Polynesian atoll.* Cambridge: Cambridge University Press.

Bex, Tony, and Richard J. Watts, eds. 1999. *Standard English: The widening debate.* London: Routledge.

Bhatt, Rakesh M. 2005. Expert discourses, local practices, and hybridity: The case of Indian Englishes. In Canagarajah, 25–54.

Bialystok, Ellen. 2001. *Bilingualism in development: Language, literacy, and cognition.* Cambridge: Cambridge University Press.

————, and Kenji Hakuta. 1994. *In other words: The science and psychology of second-language acquisition.* New York: Basic Books.

Bizzell, Patricia. 1999. Hybrid academic discourse: What, why, how. *Composition Studies* 27: 7–21.

————. 2000. Basic writing and the issue of correctness, or what to do with "mixed" forms of academic discourse. *Journal of Basic Writing* 19: 4–12.

Bonilla-Silva, Eduardo. 2006. *Racism without racists: Color-blind racism and the perspective of racial inequality in the United States.* 2nd ed. Lanham, MD: Rowman & Littlefield Publishers.

Bowen, William G., Matthew M. Chingos, and Michael S. McPherson. 2009. *Crossing the finish line: Completing college at America's public universities.* Princeton: Princeton University Press.

Brandt, Deborah. 2001. *Literacy in American lives.* New York: Cambridge University Press.

————, and Katie Clinton. 2002. Limits of the local: Expanding perspectives on literacy as a social practice. *Journal of Literacy Research* 34: 337–356.

Braxton, John M., ed. 2000. *Reworking the student departure puzzle.* Nashville: Vanderbilt University Press.

Brooks, David. 2005. The education gap. *New York Times,* September 25.

Bruch, Patrick, and Richard Marback, eds. 2005. *The hope and the legacy: The past, present, and future of "Students' Right to Their Own Language."* Cresskill, NJ: Hampton Press.

Canagarajah, A. Suresh. 2002. *Critical academic writing and multilingual students.* Michigan: University of Michigan Press.

————, ed. 2005. *Reclaiming the local in language policy and practice.* Mahwah, NJ: Lawrence Erlbaum.

————. 2006a. Negotiating the local in English as a lingua franca. *Annual Review of Applied Linguistics* 26: 197–218.

————. 2006b. The place of world Englishes in composition: Pluralization continued. *College Composition and Communication* 57: 586–619.

————. 2006c. Toward a writing pedagogy of shuttling between languages: Learning from multilingual writers. *College English* 68: 589–604.

Cárdenas, Diana. 2004. Creating an identity: Personal, academic, and civic literacies. In Kells, Balester, and Villanueva, 114–125.

Carroll, Lee Ann. 1997. Pomo blues: Stories from first-year composition. *College English* 59: 916–933.

Casanave, Christine Pearson. 2002. *Writing games: Multicultural case studies of academic literacy practices in higher education.* Mahwah, NJ: Lawrence Erlbaum Associates.

Center for Teaching and Learning. 2004. NEIU student profile. New faculty orientation, fall, at Northeastern Illinois University, Chicago, IL.

————. 2006. Results from last semester's faculty survey. *CTL Bulletin,* September 15.

————. 2007a. Coming to NEIU: Faculty share their experiences. *CTL Bulletin,* October 15.

————. 2007b. Diversity issues and the curriculum. *CTL Bulletin,* April 01.

————. 2007c. Faculty portrait: Dr. Harold Hild, communication. *CTL Bulletin,* April 15.

Chang, Suk-Jin. 1982. English and Korean. *Annual Review of Applied Linguistics* 3: 85–98.

Chiang, Yuet-Sim D., and Mary Schmida. 1999. Language identity and language ownership: Linguistic conflicts of first-year university writing students. In *Generation 1.5 meets college composition: Issues in the teaching of writing to U.S.-educated learners of ESL,* ed. Linda Harklau, Kay M. Losey, and Meryl Siegal, 81–96. Mahwah, NJ: Lawrence Erlbaum Associates.

Chiseri-Strater, Elizabeth. 1991. *The public and private discourse of university students.* Portsmouth, NH: Boynton/Cook.

Clyne, Michael G. 1982. English and German. *Annual review of applied linguistics* 3: 38–49.

Cintron, Ralph. 1997. *Angels's town: Chero ways, gang life, and rhetorics of the everyday.* Boston: Beacon.

Clifford, James, and George E. Marcus, eds. 1986. *Writing culture: The poetics and politics of ethnography.* Berkeley: University of California Press.

Collier, Virginia. 1992. A synthesis of studies examining long-term language minority student data on academic achievement. *Bilingual Research Journal* 16: 187-212.

Collins, James, and Richard K. Blot. 2003. *Literacy and literacies: Texts, power, and identity.* Cambridge: Cambridge University Press.

Conference on College Composition and Communication. 1974. Students' Right to Their Own Language. *College Composition and Communication* 25: 1-32.

———. 1988. CCCC National Language Policy. http://www.ncte.org/cccc/resources/positions/nationallangpolicy.

———. 2001. CCCC Statement on Second Language Writing and Writers. http://www.ncte.org/cccc/resources/positions/secondlangwriting.

Connal, Louise Rodríguez. 2004. Hybridity: A lens for understanding mestizo/a writers. In Lunsford and Ouzgane, 199–217.

Connor, Ulla. 1996. *Contrastive rhetoric: Cross-Cultural aspects of second-language writing.* New York: Cambridge University Press.

Connor, Ulla, and Robert Kaplan, eds. 1987. *Writing across languages.* Reading, MA: Addison-Wesley.

Connors, Robert J. 1981. The rise and fall of the modes of discourse. *College Composition and Communication* 32: 444–455.

Cook-Gumperz, Jenny, ed. 1986. *The social construction of literacy.* New York: Cambridge University Press.

Cooper, Marilyn M. 2004. Nonessentialist identity and national discourse. In *Rhetoric and ethnicity*, ed. Keith Gilyard and Vorris Nunley, 87–102. Portsmouth, NH: Boynton/Cook .

Cope, Bill, and Mary Kalantzis, eds. 2000. *Multiliteracies: Literacy learning and the design of social futures.* London: Routledge.

Corson, David. 2001. Social justice, language policy, and English Only. In González with Melis, 95-120.

Cox, Rebecca D. 2009. *The college fear factor: How students and professors misunderstand one another.* Cambridge: Harvard University Press.

Crawford, James. 1991. *Bilingual education: History, politics, theory, and practice.* 2nd ed. Los Angeles: Bilingual Educational Services.

Cruz, Wilfredo. 2007. *City of dreams: Latino immigration to Chicago.* Lanham, MD: University Press of America.

Cushman, Ellen. 2009. Toward a rhetoric of self-representation: Identity politics in Indian country and rhetoric and composition. *College Composition and Communication* 60: 321–365.

Daniels, Harvey A., ed. 1990. *Not Only English: Affirming America's multilingual history.* Urbana, IL: National Council of Teachers of English.

De Genova, Nicholas, and Ana Y. Ramos-Zayas. 2003. *Latino crossings: Mexicans, Puerto Ricans, and the politics of race and citizenship.* New York: Routledge.

Del Valle, Tony. 2002. *Written literacy features of three Puerto Rican family networks in Chicago.* New York: Mellen.

———. 2005. "Successful" and "unsuccessful" literacies of two Puerto Rican families in Chicago. In *Latino language and literacy in ethnolinguistic Chicago,* Farr, 97-131.

Delbanco, Andrew. 2007. Scandals of higher education. *The New York Review of Books,* March 29.

Delpit, Lisa, and Joanne Kilgour Dowdy. 2002. *The skin that we speak: Thoughts on language and culture in the classroom.* New York: The New Press.

DiPardo, Anne. 1993. *A kind of passport: A basic writing adjunct program and the challenge of student diversity.* Urbana, IL: National Council of Teachers of English.

Donoghue, Frank. 2008. *The last professors: The corporate university and the fate of the humanities.* New York: Fordham University Press.

Dor, Daniel. 2004. From Englishization to imposed multilingualism: Globalization, the internet, and the political economy of the linguistic code. *Public Culture* 16: 97–118.

Downs, Douglas, and Elizabeth Wardle. 2007. Teaching about writing, righting misconceptions: (Re)envisioning "first-year composition" as "introduction to writing studies." *College Composition and Communication* 58: 552–584.

Elder, Catherine, and Alan Davies. 2006. Assessing English as a lingua franca. *Annual Review of Applied Linguistics* 26: 282–301.

Elliot, Norbert. 2005. *On a scale: A social history of writing assessment in America.* New York: Peter Lang.

English Language Program. 2004. ELP course matrix. http://www.neiu.edu/~elp/elp-coursematrix.htm.

Farr, Marcia. 1993. Essayist literacy and other verbal performances. *Written Communication* 10: 4–38.

———, ed. 2004. *Ethnolinguistic Chicago: Language and literacy in the city's neighborhoods.* Mahwah, NJ: Lawrence Erlbaum Associates.

———, ed. 2005a. *Latino language and literacy in ethnolinguistic Chicago.* Mahwah, NJ: Lawrence Erlbaum Associates.

———. 2005b. Literacy and religion: Reading, writing, and gender among Mexican women in Chicago. In *Latino language and literacy in ethnolinguistic Chicago,* Farr, 305–321.

Feldman, Ann M. 2008. *Making writing matter: Composition in the engaged university.* Albany, NY: State University of New York Press.

Finder, Alan. 2006. Debate grows as colleges slip in graduations. *The New York Times,* September 15.

Finnegan, Ruth. 1988. *Literacy and orality.* Oxford: Oxford University Press.

Fish, Stanley. 2008. When "identity politics" is rational. *The New York Times,* February 17. http://fish.blogs.nytimes.com/2008/02/17/when-identity-politics-is-rational/.

Fox, Helen. 1994. *Listening to the world: Cultural issues in academic writing.* Urbana, IL: National Council of Teachers of English.

Fox, Tom. 1999. *Defending access: A critique of standards in higher education.* Portsmouth, NH: Boynton/Cook.

Frederick, Duke. 1978. *Early times at Northeastern.* Chicago: Northeastern Illinois University.

Friedrich, Patricia. 2006. Assessing the needs of linguistically diverse first-year students: Bringing together and telling apart international ESL, resident ESL, and monolingual basic writers. *Journal of the Council of Writing Program Administrators* 30: 15–36.

Fry, Richard, and Jeffrey S. Passel. 2009. Latino children: A majority are U.S.-born offspring of immigrants. Pew Hispanic Center. http://pewhispanic.org/files/reports/110.pdf.

Fuentes, Pedro. 2005. Proyecto Pa'Lante student enrollment, retention rate & profile, April 20.

García, Eugene E. 2000. Treating linguistic and cultural diversity as a resource: The research response to the challenges inherent in the Improving America's Schools Act and California's Proposition 227. In González with Melis, 90–113.

García, Ofelia, and Kate Menken. 2006. The English of Latinos from a plurilingual transcultural angle: Implications for assessment and schools. In *Dialects, Englishes, creoles, and education,* ed. Shondel J. Nero, 167–183. Mahwah, NJ: Lawrence Erlbaum Associates.

Garrod, Andrew, Robert Kilkenny, and Christina Gómez, eds. 2007. *Mi voz, mi vida: Latino college students tell their life stories*. Ithaca, NY: Cornell University Press.

Gee, James Paul. 1996. *Social linguistics and literacies: Ideology in discourses*. 2nd ed. Bristol, PA: Falmer Press.

———. 2003. *What video games have to teach us about learning and literacy*. New York: Palgrave Macmillan.

Gilyard, Keith. 1991. *Voices of the self: A study of language competence*. Detroit: Wayne State University Press.

Godenzzi, Juan C. 2006. Spanish as a lingua franca. *Annual Review of Applied Linguistics* 26: 100–122.

González, Juan. 2000. *Harvest of empire: A history of Latinos in America*. New York: Penguin.

González, Norma, Luis C. Moll, and Cathy Amanti, eds. 2005. *Funds of knowledge: Theorizing practices in households, communities, and classrooms*. Mahwah, NJ: Lawrence Erlbaum Associates.

González, Roseann Dueñas. 2000. Introduction. In *Language ideologies: Critical perspectives on the official English movement: Volume 1: Education and the social implications of official language*, ed. Roseann Dueñas González with Ildikó Melis. Urbana, IL: National Council of Teachers of English, xxvii–xlvii.

———. 2001. Introduction. In *Language ideologies: Critical perspectives on the official English movement: Volume 2: History, theory, and policy*, ed. Roseann Dueñas González with Ildikó Melis. Urbana, IL: National Council of Teachers of English, xxv–liii.

Gordon, Avery, and Christopher Newfield, eds. 1997. *Mapping multiculturalism*. Minneapolis: University of Minnesota Press.

Gorski, Paul. 2008. 20 (Self-)critical things I will do to be a better multicultural educator. EdChange Multicultural Pavilion. http://www.edchange.org/multicultural/resources/self_critique.html.

Grabill, Jeffery T. 2001. *Community literacy programs and the politics of change*. Albany, NY: State University of New York Press.

Graff, Harvey J. 1987. *The legacies of literacy: Continuities and contradictions in western culture and society*. Bloomington: Indiana University Press.

Greene, Jamie Candelaria. 1994. Misperspectives on literacy: A critique of an Anglocentric bias in histories of American literacy. *Written Communication* 11: 251–69.

Guerra, Juan C. 1998. *Close to home: Oral and literate practices in a transnational Mexicano community*. New York: Teachers College Press.

———. 2004. Emerging representations, situated literacies, and the practice of transcultural repositioning. In Kells, Balester, and Villanueva, 7–23.

Gutiérrez, Kris D. 2008. Developing a sociocritical literacy in the third space. *Reading Research Quarterly* 43: 148–64.

Guzmán, Betsy. 2001. The Hispanic population. *U.S. Census Brief*. May. http://www.census.gov/prod/2001pubs/c2kbr01-3.pdf.

Hahs, Sharon K. 2007a. NEIU: A mosaic work in progress. *Insights* 9: 1.

———. 2007b. NEIU: The university of the future. Inaugural address at Northeastern Illinois University, Chicago.

Hall, R. Mark, and Mary Rosner. 2004. Pratt and pratfalls: Revisioning contact zones. In Lunsford and Ouzgane, 95–109.

Harklau, Linda. 2000. From the "good kids" to the "worst": Representations of English language learners across educational settings. *TESOL Quarterly* 34: 35–67.

———, Kay M. Losey, and Meryl Siegal, eds. 1999. *Generation 1.5 meets college composition: Issues in the teaching of writing to U.S.-educated learners of ESL*. Mahwah, NJ: Lawrence Erlbaum Associates.

Harris, Joseph. 1997. *A teaching subject: Composition since 1966*. Upper Saddle Creek, NJ: Prentice Hall.

Hartwell, Patrick. 1985. Grammar, grammar, and the teaching of grammar. *College English* 47: 105–127.

Heath, Shirley Brice. 1982. Protean shapes in literacy events: Ever-shifting oral and literate traditions. In *Spoken and written language: Exploring orality and literacy*, ed. Deborah Tannen, 91–117. Norwood, NJ: Ablex.

———. 1983. *Ways with words: Language, life, and work in communities and classrooms*. Cambridge: Cambridge University Press.

Hispanic Association of Colleges and Universities. HACU 101. http://www.hacu.net/hacu/HACU_101_EN.asp?SnID=853890761.

Horner, Bruce. 2001. "Students' Right," English Only, and re-imagining the politics of language. *College English* 63: 741–758.

———, and Min-Zhan Lu. 1999. *Representing the "other": Basic writers and the teaching of basic writing*. Urbana, IL: National Council of Teachers of English.

———, and John Trimbur. 2002. English Only and U.S. composition. *College composition and communication* 53: 594–630.

Hoy. 2008. Educación para toda la familia. December 2.

Huot, Brian. 1996. Toward a new theory of writing assessment. *College Composition and Communication* 47: 549–566.

———. 2002a. *(Re)articulating writing assessment for teaching and learning*. Logan, UT: Utah State University Press.

———. 2002b. Toward a new discourse of assessment for the college writing classroom. *College English* 65: 163–180.

Illinois Legislative Latino Caucus. 2006. Hearing on graduation rates of Latinos and status of Latinos at NEIU. Northeastern Illinois University, Chicago, September 12.

Judd, Elliot L. 2004. Language policy in Illinois: Past and present. In Farr, 33–49.

Kachru, Braj. 1987. The bilingual's creativity: Discoursal and stylistic strategies in contact literatures. In *Discourse across cultures: Strategies in World Englishes*, ed. Larry E. Smith, 125–140. New York: Prentice Hall.

Kachru, Yamuna. 1982. English and Hindi. *Annual Review of Applied Linguistics* 3: 50–77.

Kaplan, Robert, and Richard Baldauf, Jr. 2001. Not Only English: English Only and the world. In González with Melis, 293–315.

Kaplan, Robert B. 1966. Cultural thought patterns in inter-cultural education. *Language Learning* 16: 1–20.

Kasai, Masahiro. 2004a. Using ACT English scores for writing placement. NEIU Assessment & Testing Center research report. http://www.neiu.edu/~assess/EnglishPTandACT.pdf.

———. 2004b. Using ACT reading scores for reading placement. NEIU Assessment & Testing Center research report. http://www.neiu.edu/~assess/ReadingPTandACT.pdf.

Keller-Cohen, Deborah. 1993. Rethinking literacy: Comparing colonial and contemporary America. *Anthropology & Education Quarterly* 24: 288–307.

Kells, Michelle Hall. 2002. Linguistic contact zones in the college writing classroom: An examination of ethnolinguistic identity and language attitudes. *Written Communication* 19: 5–43.

———. 2004. Understanding the rhetorical value of *Tejano* codeswitching. In Kells, Balester, and Villanueva, 24–39.

———. 2006. Tex Mex, metalingual discourse, and teaching college writing. In *Dialects, Englishes, creoles, and education*, ed. Shondel J. Nero, 185–201. Mahwah, NJ: Lawrence Erlbaum Associates.

———. 2007. Writing across communities: Diversity, deliberation, and the discursive possibilities of WAC. *Reflections* 6: 87–108.

———, Valerie Balester, and Victor Villanueva, eds. 2004. *Latino/a discourses: On language, identity, and literacy education*. Portsmouth, NH: Boynton/Cook.

Kirklighter, Cristina, Diana Cárdenas, and Susan Wolff Murphy, eds. 2007. *Teaching writing with Latino/a students: Lessons learned at Hispanic-Serving Institutions.* Albany, NY: State University of New York Press.

Kozol, Jonathan. 1991. *Savage inequalities: Children in America's schools.* New York: Crown.

Kraemer, Barbara A. 1997. The academic and social integration of Hispanic students into college. *The Review of Higher Education* 20: 163–179.

Krashen, Stephen D. 2000. Bilingual education: The debate continues. In González with Melis, 137–160.

Lanehart, Sonja L. 1996. The language of identity. *Journal of English Linguistics* 24: 322–331.

Lauter, Paul. 1991. *Canons and contexts.* New York: Oxford University Press.

Lave, Jean. 1996. Teaching, as learning, in practice. *Mind, Culture, and Activity* 3: 149–164.

Leap, William L. 1982. English and American Indian languages. *Annual Review of Applied Linguistics* 3: 24–37.

LeCourt, Donna. 1996. WAC as critical pedagogy: The third stage? *JAC* 16: 389–405.

———. 2004. *Identity matters: Schooling the student body in academic discourse.* Albany, NY: State University of New York Press.

Leki, Ilona. 2006. The legacy of first-year composition. In *The politics of second language writing,* ed. Paul Kei Matsuda, Christina Ortmeier-Hooper, and Xiaoye You, 59–74. West Lafayette, IN: Parlor Press.

Li, Xiao-Ming. 1996. *"Good writing" in cross-cultural context.* Albany, NY: State University of New York Press.

Lippi-Green, Rosina. 1997. *English with an accent: Language, ideology, and discrimination in the United States.* London: Routledge.

Little, Darnell. 2007. Census measures ethnic shifts. *Chicago Tribune,* August 9.

Lockett, Reginald. 2006. How I started writing poetry. *Asili: The Journal of Multicultural Heartspeak* 6, no. 3 (August/September/October), http://asilithejournal.com/ASILI/VOLUMES/Vol%20VI-3/Reginald%20Lockett.htm.

López, Sophia. 2007a. English as a first language: The standards debate. *The NEIU Independent,* January 23.

———. 2007b. The perils of being Hispanic at NEIU. *The NEIU Independent,* October 9.

Lu, Min-Zhan. 1994. Professing multiculturalism: The politics of style in the contact zone. *College Composition and Communication* 45: 442–58.

———. 2004. Composing postcolonial studies. In Lunsford and Ouzgane, 9–32.

Lucas, Brad. 2001. Review of *Reinventing the university: Literacies and legitimacy in the post-modern academy,* by Christopher Schroeder. *Academic.Writing* 6, (August 21), http://wac.colostate.edu/aw/reviews/schroeder_reinventing_2001.htm.

Lunsford, Andrea, and Lahoucine Ouzgane, eds. 2004. *Crossing borderlands: Composition and poscolonial studies.* Pittsburgh: University of Pittsburgh Press

Lyman, Rick. 2006. Census shows growth of immigrants. *The New York Times,* August 15.

MacDonald, Susan Peck. 2007. The erasure of language. *College Composition and Communication* 58: 585–625.

Mahala, Daniel. 1991. Writing utopias: Writing across the curriculum and the promise of reform. *College English* 53: 773–789.

Martindale, Mike. 2007. Letter to the editor. *NEIU Independent,* February 6.

Martinez, Aja Y. 2009. "The American way": Resisting the empire of force and color-blind racism. *College English* 71: 584–595.

Marzluf, Phillip P. 2006. Diversity writing: Natural languages, authentic voices. *College Composition and Communication* 57: 503–522.

Mathieu, Paula. 2005. *Tactics of hope: The public turn in English composition.* Portsmouth, NH: Boynton/Cook.

Matsuda, Paul Kei. 1999. Composition studies and ESL writing: A disciplinary division of labor. *College Composition and Communication* 50: 699–721.

————. 2006. The myth of linguistic homogeneity in U.S. college composition. *College English* 68: 637–51.

McLeod, Susan, and Elaine Maimon. 2000. Clearing the air: WAC myths and realities. *College English* 62: 573–583.

Mejía, Jaime. 1998. Tejano arts of the U.S.-Mexico contact zone. *JAC* 18: 123–136.

————. 2004a. Arts of the U.S.-Mexico contact zone. In Lunsford and Ouzgane, 171–198.

————. 2004b. Bridging rhetoric and composition studies with Chicano and Chicana studies: A turn to critical pedagogy. In Kells, Balester, and Villanueva, 40–56.

Methodology: Campus ethnic diversity. 2008. *U.S. News and World Report*, August 21. http://www.usnews. com/articles/education/best-colleges/2008/08/21/methodology-campus-ethnic-diversity.html.

Michaels, Walter Benn. 2006. *The trouble with diversity: How we learned to love identity and ignore inequality.* New York: Metropolitan Books.

Mignolo, Walter D. 2000. *Local histories/global designs: Coloniality, subaltern knowledges, and border thinking.* Princeton, NJ: Princeton University Press.

Miles, Libby, Michael Pennell, Kim Hensley Owens, Jeremiah Dyehouse, Helen O'Grady, Nedra Reynolds, Robert Schwegler, and Linda Shamoon. 2008. Commenting on Douglas Downs and Elizabeth Wardle's "Teaching about writing, righting misconceptions": Thinking vertically. *College Composition and Communication* 59: 503–511.

Miller, Richard. 2005. *Writing at the end of the world.* Pittsburgh: University of Pittsburgh Press.

Milroy, James. 1999. The consequences of standardisation in descriptive linguistics. In Bex and Watts, 16–39.

————. 2001. Language ideologies and the consequences of standardization. *Journal of Sociolinguistics* 5(4): 530–555.

————, and Lesley Milroy. 1999. *Authority in language: Investigating language prescription and standardisation.* 3rd ed. London: Routledge.

Milroy, Lesley. 1999. Standard English and language ideology in Britain and the United States. In Bex and Watts, 173–206.

Modiano, Marko. 2004. Monoculturalization and language dissemination. *Journal of Language, Identity, and Education* 3: 215–227.

Moll, Luis C. 2005. Reflections and possibilities. In González, Moll, and Amanti, 275–87.

Morales, Ed. 2002. *Living in Spanglish: The search for Latino identity in America.* New York: St. Martin's Press.

National Commission on Writing in America's Schools and Colleges. 2003. The neglected "r": The need for a writing revolution. http://www.writingcommission.org/prod_downloads/writingcom/neglectedr.pdf.

National Endowment for the Arts. 2004. Literary reading in dramatic decline, according to National Endowment for the Arts survey. http://www.nea.gov/news/news04/ReadingAtRisk.html.

NEIU. 2004. Northeastern Illinois University academic catalog 2004–2005.

————. 2007. Improving retention through academic literacy. Title V Grant.

————. 2008. Northeastern Illinois University's strategic plan initiative.

NEIU Committee on General Education. 2005. General education assessment: Results 2004–2005.

NEIU Language Skills Assessment Task Force. 2004. Are students prepared for college-level reading and writing? Results of a faculty survey sponsored by the FCAA Language Assessment Task Force.

————. 2005. Strengthening student writing at NEIU: History and a plan for action.

Nettle, Daniel, and Suzanne Romaine. 2000. *Vanishing voices: The extinction of the world's languages.* New York: Oxford University Press.

Noguera, Pedro. 2003. *City schools and the American Dream: Reclaiming the promise of public education.* New York: Teachers College Press.

Norton, Bonny. 1997. Language, identity, and ownership of English. *TESOL Quarterly* 31: 409–429.

Ogulnick, Karen, ed. 2000. *Language crossings: Negotiating the self in a multicultural world.* New York: Teachers College Press.

Ohlemacher, Stephen. 2007. Whites now minority in 1 in 10 counties. *Chicago Tribune,* August 9.

Okawa, Gail Y. 2000. From "bad attitudes" to linguistic pluralism: Developing reflective language policy among preservice teachers. In González with Melis, 276–296.

Olson, David R. 1995. Writing and the mind. In *Sociocultural studies of the mind,* ed. James V. Wertsch, Pablo Del Rio, and Amelia Alvarez, 95–123. New York: Cambridge University Press.

O'Neill, Peggy, Cindy Moore, and Brian Huot. 2009. *A guide to college writing assessment.* Logan, UT: Utah State University Press.

Ortmeier-Hooper, Christina. 2008. "English may be my second language, but I'm not ESL." *College Composition and Communication* 59: 389–419.

Otheguy, Ricardo, and Ofelia García. 1993. Convergent conceptualizations as predictors of degree of contact in U.S. Spanish. In Roca and Lipski, 135–154.

Palumbo-Liu, David. 1995. *The ethnic canon.* Minneapolis: University of Minnesota Press.

Pandharipande, Rajeshwari. 1982. English and Marathi. *Annual Review of Applied Linguistics* 3: 118–36.

Panetta, Clayann Gilliam, ed. 2000. *Contrastive rhetoric revisited and redefined.* Mahwah, NJ: Mahwah.

Pao, Dana L., Shelley D. Wong, and Sharon Teuben-Rowe. 1997. Identity formation for mixed- heritage adults and implications of educators. *TESOL Quarterly* 31: 622–631.

Paral, Rob, and Michael Norkewicz. 2003. The metro Chicago immigration fact book. Institute for Metropolitan Affairs, Roosevelt University. http://www.roosevelt.edu/ima/pdfs/immigration-factbook.pdf.

———, Timothy Ready, Sung Chun, and Wei Sun. 2004. Latino demographic growth in metropolitan Chicago. Institute for Latino studies research report 2004.2, University of Notre Dame. http://latinostudies.nd.edu/pubs/pubs/paral.pdf.

Parks, Steven. 2000. *Class politics: The movement for the students' right to their own language.* Urbana, IL: National Council of Teachers of English.

———, and Eli Goldblatt. 2000. Writing beyond the curriculum: Fostering new collaborations in literacy. *College English* 62: 584–606.

Pennycook, Alastair. 1994. *The cultural politics of English as an international language.* London: Longman.

———. 2001. Lessons from colonial language policies. In González with Melis, 195–220.

———. 2003. Global Englishes, Rip Slyme, and performativity. *Journal of sociolinguistics* 7: 513–533.

Perea, Juan F. 2001. The new American Spanish war: How the courts and the legislatures are aiding the suppression of languages other than English. In González with Melis, 121–139.

Phillips, Talinn, Candace Stewart, and Robert D. Stewart. 2006. Geography lessons, bridge- building, and second language writers. *Journal of the Council of Writing Program Administrators* 30: 83–100.

Pratt, Mary Louise. 1987. Linguistic utopias. In *The linguistics of writing: Arguments between language and literature,* ed. Nigel Fabb, Derek Attridge, Alan Durant, and Colin MacCabe, 44–66. New York: Methuen.

———. 1991. Arts of the contact zone. *Profession 91*: 33–40.

———. 2003. Building a new public idea about language. *Profession 2003*: 110–119.

Prendergast, Catherine. 2003. *Literacy and racial justice: The politics of learning after Brown v. Board of Education.* Carbondale, IL: Southern Illinois University Press.

Preto-Bay, Ana Maria, and Kristine Hansen. 2006. Preparing for the tipping point: Designing writing programs to meet the needs of the changing population. *Journal of the Council of Writing Program Administrators* 30: 37–58.

Putnam, Robert D. 2007. *E pluribus unum*: Diversity and community in the twenty-first century: The 2006 Johan Skytte Prize Lecture. *Scandinavian Political Studies* 30: 137–74.

Ricento, Thomas. 2001. Afterword: Lessons, caveats, and a way forward. In González with Melis, 369–382.

Richardson, Elaine. 2003. Race, class(es), gender, and age: The making of knowledge about language diversity. In Smitherman and Villanueva, 40–66.

Rivera, Janeida. 2007. Teresita Díaz: Director of Proyecto Pa'Lante. *Que Ondee Sola* 35: 6–7.

Roca, Ana, and M. Cecilia Colombi, eds. 2003. *Mi lengua: Spanish as a heritage language in the United States.* Washington, DC: Georgetown University Press.

Roca, Ana, and John M. Lipski, eds. 1993. *Spanish in the United States.* Berlin: Mouton de Gruyter.

Rodby, Judith. 1992. *Appropriating literacy: Writing and reading in English as a second language.* Portsmouth, NH: Boynton/Cook.

Roderick, Melissa, Jenny Nagaoka, and Elaine Allensworth with Vanessa Coca, Macarena Correa, and Ginger Stoker. 2006. *From high school to the future: A first look at Chicago Public School graduates' college enrollment, college preparation, and graduation from four-year colleges.* Chicago: Consortium on Chicago School Research at the University of Chicago.

Rodriguez, Richard. 1983. *Hunger of memory: The education of Richard Rodriguez.* New York: Bantam Books.

Rose, Mike. 1989. *Lives on the boundary: A moving account of the struggles and achievements of America's educationally underprepared.* New York: Penguin.

———. 1995. *Possible lives: The promise of public education in America.* New York: Penguin.

Roth, Wolff-Michael, and Hitomi Harama. 2000. (Standard) English as a second language: Tribulations of self. *Journal of Curriculum Studies* 32: 757–775.

Rury, John L. 2005a. Schools and education. The electronic encyclopedia of Chicago. Chicago Historical Society. http://www.encyclopedia.chicagohistory.org/pages/1124.html.

———. 2005b. School desegregation. The electronic encyclopedia of Chicago. Chicago Historical Society. http://www.encyclopedia.chicagohistory.org/pages/1121.html.

Russell, David R. 1991. *Writing in the academic disciplines, 1870–1990: A curricular history.* Carbondale: Southern Illinois University Press.

Sachs, Jerome M. 1987. *Reminiscences about Northeastern Illinois University or there must be a pony here somewhere.* Chicago: Northeastern Illinois University.

Sánchez, Rebecca. 2008. Con educación, sí se puede lograr el éxito, Comunidad. *Hoy*, December 8.

Sanchez, Reymundo. 2000. *My bloody life: The making of a Latin King.* Chicago: Chicago Review Press.

Sanoff, Alvin P. 2006. A perception gap over students' preparation. *The Chronicle of Higher Education*, March 10, B9.

Santiago, Deborah. 2008. Hispanic-Serving Institutions: 2005–06. *¡Excelencia! in Education*, http://edexcelencia.org/pdf/HSIList-2005-06.pdf.

Sanz, Cristina. 2000. What form to focus on? Linguistics, language awareness, and the education of L2 teachers. In *Form and meaning: Multiple perspectives*, ed. James F. Lee and Albert Valdman, 3–24. Boston: Heinle & Heinle.

Sapir. Edwin. 1949. *Language: An introduction to the study of speech.* New York: Harcourt Brace Jovanovich.

Sayles, John. 1996. *Lone star*. Culver City, CA: Columbia Pictures.

Scarcella, Robin, and Kusup Chin. 1993. *Literacy practices in two Korean-American communities. Research report 8*. National Center for Research on Cultural Diversity and Second Language Language. http://repositories.cdlib.org/crede/ncrcdsllresearch/rr08.

Schecter, Sandra R., and Robert Bayley. 1997. Language socialization practices and cultural identity: Case studies of Mexican-descent families in California and Texas. *TESOL Quarterly* 31: 513–541.

Schmid, Carol. 2000. The politics of English-Only in the United States. In González with Melis, 62–86.

Schmidt, Ronald. 2000. *Language policy and identity politics in the United States*. Philadelphia: Temple University Press.

Schroeder, Christopher. 2001. *ReInventing the university: Literacies and legitimacy in the postmodern academy*. Logan, UT: Utah State University Press.

———. 2004. Review of *Introducing English: Essays in the intellectual work of composition*, by James Slevin. *Composition Studies* 32: 143–146.

———. 2006. The limits of institutionalized literacies: Minority bilinguals at one U.S. university. *Community Literacy* 1: 67–82.

———. 2007. Educating Northeastern. *The NEIU Independent*, September 11.

———, Helen Fox, and Patricia Bizzell, eds. 2002. *ALT DIS: Alternative discourses and the academy*. Portsmouth, NH: Boynton/Cook.

Severino, Carol. 2009. "We are not all the same": Latino students, Hispanic-Serving Institutions, and the need to reform rhetoric and composition. Review of *Teaching writing with Latino/a students: Lessons learned at Hispanic-Serving Institutions*, by Cristina Kirklighter, Diana Cárdenas, and Susan Wolff Murphy, eds. *College Composition and Communication* 60: 137–145.

Shen, Fan. 1989. The classroom and the wider culture: Identity as a key to learning English. *College Composition and Communication* 40: 459–466.

Shuck, Gail. 2006. Combating monolingualism: A novice administrator's challenge. *Journal of the Council of Writing Program Administrators* 30: 59–82.

Silva, Tony, and Ilona Leki. 2004. Family matters: The influence of applied linguistics and composition studies on second language writing studies—past, present, and future. *Modern Language Journal* 88: 1–13.

Silva-Corvalán, Carmen. 1994. *Language contact and change: Spanish in Los Angeles*. Oxford: Oxford University Press.

Slevin, James F. 2001. *Introducing English: Essays in the intellectual work of composition*. Pittsburgh: University of Pittsburgh Press.

Smitherman, Geneva. 1999. CCCC's role in the struggle for language rights. *College Composition and Communication* 50: 349–376.

———. 2003. The historical struggle for language rights in CCCC. In Smitherman and Villanueva, 7–39.

———, and Victor Villanueva, eds. 2003. *Language diversity in the classroom: From intention to practice*. Carbondale, IL: Southern Illinois University Press

Sochen, June. 2005. Northeastern Illinois University. The electronic encyclopedia of Chicago. Chicago Historical Society. http://www.encyclopedia.chicagohistory.org/pages/1447.html.

Soltow, Lee, and Edward Stevens. 1981. *The rise of literacy and the common school in the United States: A socioeconomic analysis to 1870*. Chicago: The University of Chicago Press.

Starfield, Sue. 2002. "I'm a second-language English speaker": Negotiating writer identity and authority in sociology one. *Journal of Language, Identity, and Education* 1: 121–140.

Stavans, Ilan. 2003. *Spanglish: The making of a new American language*. New York: Rayo.

Sternglass, Marilyn S. 1997. *Time to know them: A longitudinal study of writing and learning at the college level.* Mahwah, NJ: Lawrence Erlbaum Associates.

Street, Brian. 1984. *Literacy in theory and practice.* New York: Cambridge University Press.

———. 1993. The new literacy studies. In *Cross-cultural approaches to literacy,* ed. Brian Street, 1–21. London: Cambridge University Press.

Stuckey, J. Elspeth. 1991. *The violence of literacy.* Portsmouth, NH: Boynton/Cook.

Swearingen, C.J., Victor Villanueva, and Susan McDowall. 2006. Research and rhetoric. *Research on composition: Multiple perspectives on two decades of change,* ed. Peter Smagorinsky, 170–186. New York: Teachers College Press.

Tan, Amy. 2003. Mother tongue. In *The opposite of fate: A book of musings,* 271–279. New York: Putnam.

Thaiss, Christopher. 1998. *The Harcourt Brace guide to writing across the curriculum.* Fort Worth: Harcourt Brace.

Thompson, Roger M. 2003. *Filipino English and Tagalog.* Amsterdam: John Benjamins Publishing.

Trimbur, John. 2006. Linguistic memory and the politics of U.S. English. *College English* 68: 575–88.

———. 2008. The Dartmouth conference and the geohistory of the native speaker. *College English* 71: 142–169.

Tsao, Fen-Fu. 1982. English and Mandarin. *Annual Review of Applied Linguistics* 3: 99–136.

U.S. Census Bureau. 2006. American Community Survey 2005. http://www.census.gov/acs/www/index.html.

U.S. Department of Defense. 2005. A call to action for national foreign language capabilities. http://www.eric.ed.gov/ERICDocs/data/ericdocs2sql/content_storage_01/0000019b/80/1b/b7/f3.pdf.

Valdés, Guadalupe. 1992. Bilingual minorities and language issues in writing: Toward professionwide responses to a new challenge. *Written Communication* 9: 85–136.

———. 1996. *Con respeto: Bridging the distances between culturally diverse families and schools: An ethnographic portrait.* New York: Teachers College Press.

———. 2001a. Bilingual individuals and language-based discrimination: Advancing the state of law on language rights. In González with Melis, 140–170.

———. 2001b. *Learning and not learning English: Latino students in American schools.* New York: Teachers College Press.

Vandenberg, Peter. 1999. Taming multiculturalism: The will to literacy in composition studies. *JAC* 19: 547–568.

Village of Oak Park. 2001. Village background. http://www.oak-park.us/Village_Background/Village_History.html.

———. 2003. Diversity statement. http://www.oak-park.us/Village_Background/Village_History. html.

Villanueva, Victor. 1993. *Bootstraps: From an American academic of color.* Urbana, IL: National Council of Teachers of English.

———. 2000. Afterword: On English Only. In González with Melis, 333–342.

———. 2001. The politics of literacy across the curriculum. In *WAC for the new millennium: Strategies for continuing writing-across-the-curriculum programs,* ed. Susan H. McLeod, Eric Miraglia, Margot Soven, and Christopher Thaiss, 166–78. Urbana, IL: National Council of Teachers of English.

White, Harry. 2007a. Letter to the editor. *NEIU Independent,* February 20.

———. 2007b. Blowing the whistle on the English department. *NEIU Independent,* October 9.

Wible, Scott. 2006. Pedagogies of the "Students' Right" era: The Language Curriculum Research Group's project for linguistic diversity. *College Composition and Communication* 57: 442–478.

————. 2009. Composing alternatives to a national security language policy. *College English* 71: 460–485.

Wiley, Terrence G. 2002. Accessing language rights in education: A brief history of the U.S. context. In *Language policies in education: Critical issues,* ed. James W. Tollefson, 39–64. Mahwah, NJ: Lawrence Erlbaum Associates.

————. 2005. *Literacy and language diversity in the United States.* 2nd ed. Washington, DC: Center for Applied Linguistics.

Wiley, Terrence G., and Marguerite Lukes. 1996. English-only and standard English ideologies in the U.S. *TESOL Quarterly* 30: 511–535.

Williams, Joseph M. 2003. *Style: Ten lessons in clarity and grace.* 7th ed. New York: Longman.

Wolff, Janice M., ed. 2002. *Professing in the contact zone: Bringing theory and practice together.* Urbana, IL: National Council of Teachers of English.

Wood, Peter. 2003. *Diversity: The invention of a concept.* San Francisco: Encounter Books.

Writing Implementation Task Force. 2007. Report from writing implementation task force sent to Harold Hild, chair of faculty council on academic affairs. Northeastern Illinois University.

Writing Lab. 2008. Preparing for the English competency exam (ECE). Northeastern Illinois University. http://www.neiu.edu/~ewlab/word/ECEgeneralmaster.doc.

Yagoda, Ben. 2006. The seven deadly sins of student writers. *The Chronicle of Higher Education,* September 08, B13.

Yezierska, Anzia. 1994. America and I. In *The Heath anthology of American literature.* Vol. 2. 2nd ed., edited by Paul Lauter et al., 1865–1872. Lexington, MA: D.C. Heath and Company.

Young, Art. 1999. *Teaching writing across the curriculum.* 3rd ed. Upper Saddle River, NJ: Prentice Hall.

Zamel, Vivian. 1995. Strangers in academia: The experiences of faculty and ESL students. *College Composition and Communication* 46: 506–521.

————, and Ruth Spack, eds. 2004. *Crossing the curriculum: Multilingual learners in college classrooms.* Mahwah, NJ: Lawrence Erlbaum.

Zentella, Ana Celia. 1997a. *Growing up bilingual: Puerto Rican children in New York.* Malden, MA: Blackwell.

————. 1997b. The hispanophobia of the official English movement in the U.S. *International Journal of the Sociology of Language* 127: 71–86.

INDEX

ABOUT THE AUTHOR

Christopher Schroeder is associate professor of English at Northeastern Illinois University, where he teaches undergraduate and graduate courses in composition, ethnolinguistics, and U.S. literatures. He is author of the book *ReInventing the University: Literacies and Legitimacy in the Postmodern Academy* (Utah State University Press 2001) and co-editor of *ALT DIS: Alternative Discourses in the Academy* (Boynton-Cook/ Heinemann 2002).